Opting Out of the European Union

European integration continues to deepen despite major crises and attempts to take back sovereignty. A growing number of member states are reacting to a more constraining European Union by negotiating opt-outs. This book provides the first in-depth account of how opt-outs work in practice. It examines the most controversial cases of differentiated integration: the British and Danish opt-outs from Economic and Monetary Union and European policies on borders, asylum, migration, internal security and justice. Drawing on over 100 interviews with national representatives and EU officials, the author demonstrates how representatives manage the stigma of opting out, allowing them to influence even politically sensitive areas covered by their opt-outs. Developing a political sociological approach to European integration, the book shows how everyday negotiations transform national interests into European ideals. It is usually assumed that states opt out to preserve sovereignty, but Adler-Nissen argues that national opt-outs may actually reinforce the integration process.

REBECCA ADLER-NISSEN is Associate Professor in the Department of Political Science at the University of Copenhagen. Her research focuses on international relations theory, diplomacy, sovereignty, security and European integration. She is editor of *Bourdieu in International Relations: Rethinking Key Concepts in IR* (Routledge, 2012) and co-editor of *European Integration and Postcolonial Sovereignty Games: The EU Overseas Countries and Territories* (Routledge, 2012) and *Sovereignty Games: Instrumentalizing State Sovereignty in Europe and Beyond* (Palgrave, 2008).

D1347596

Opting Out of the European Union

Diplomacy, Sovereignty and European Integration

REBECCA ADLER-NISSEN
University of Copenhagen

CAMBRIDGE
UNIVERSITY PRESS

CAMBRIDGE
UNIVERSITY PRESS

University Printing House, Cambridge CB2 8BS, United Kingdom

Cambridge University Press is part of the University of Cambridge.

It furthers the University's mission by disseminating knowledge in the pursuit of education, learning and research at the highest international levels of excellence.

www.cambridge.org
Information on this title: www.cambridge.org/9781107618343

© Rebecca Adler-Nissen 2014

First published 2014
First paperback edition 2015

A catalogue record for this publication is available from the British Library

Library of Congress Cataloguing in Publication data
Adler-Nissen, Rebecca, 1979–
Opting out of the European Union : diplomacy, sovereignty and European integration / Rebecca Adler-Nissen.
pages cm
ISBN 978-1-107-04321-3 (hardback)
1. Europe – Economic integration – Political aspects. 2. Europe – Economic integration – Social aspects. 3. Europe – Politics and government. 4. European Union countries – Politics and government. 5. European Union countries – Foreign relations. 6. Nationalism – Europe. 7. Group identity – Political aspects – Europe. 8. Political sociology. I. Title.
JN15.A5955 2014
341.24202–dc23
2014002509

ISBN 978-1-107-04321-3 Hardback
ISBN 978-1-107-61834-3 Paperback

Contents

Figures and Tables

Figures

Tables

Acknowledgements

National opt-outs from the EU are a matter of both high politics and everyday routine. They place British and Danish officials in positions of inferiority in situations that truly test their diplomatic skills. National representatives and European Commission officials are the people at the centre of this book, and I am indebted to them for taking time out of their inhumanly busy schedules to speak to me, and for trusting me with their personal experiences. If they can recognise their own world in the following pages, an important aim of this book will have been met: to unravel one of the most fascinating and perplexing aspects of the current process of European integration – the diplomacy of opting out.

In contrast with their daily struggles, writing this book has been a great pleasure. I believe this is due to the tremendous support that I have enjoyed from the people who have taken the time to discuss my work.

The Department of Political Science at the University of Copenhagen has been my academic home. It was here that I defended my PhD dissertation, the starting point for this book. I wish to thank my former supervisor, Marlene Wind, for her unwavering support and warm encouragement. I also wish to extend my deep gratitude to the members of my committee who have now also become my friends: Martin Marcussen, who helped me pitch the argument; Iver B. Neumann, an intellectual lighthouse, whose influence in the following pages will be obvious to anyone who is familiar with his work; and Antje Wiener, whose work on European and global law and politics has inspired me tremendously.

I wish to thank my good friends and current and (former) colleagues at the Department of Political Science, University of Copenhagen: Louise Andersen, Jens Bartelson, Ulrik Pram Gad, Caroline Grøn, Hendrik Huelss, Peter Viggo Jakobsen, Lotte Jensen, Mads Dagnis Jensen, Morten Kelstrup, Alan Klæbel, Tim Knudsen, Kristian Søby Kristensen, Dorte Sindbjerg Martinsen, Matilde Høybye-Mortensen, Liv Mogensen, Peter Nedergaard, Birgitta Gomez Nielsen, Lene Holm Pedersen, Karen

Lund Petersen, Kajsa Ji Noe Pettersson, Anne Rasmussen, Ben Rosamond, Frederik Rosén, Olivier Rubin, André Sonnichsen, Camilla T.N. Sørensen, Catharina Sørensen, Maja Møller Sousa, Peter Dahl Thruelsen, Anders Wivel, Ole Wæver and my wonderful comrade Ulrik Pram Gad and my outstanding friend and mentor Lene Hansen. My thanks to the department would not be complete without mentioning the administration, especially Dicte Madsen, Jette Spøer and Barbara Jespersen.

The book owes a lot to my research stay at the European University Institute. I wish to thank Adrienne Héritier, whose critical questions helped me to understand what I wanted to do, and those I also had the privilege of discussing my research ideas with: Virginie Guiraudon, Bruno De Witte, Christian Joerges, Christoph Herrmann, Alexander Trechsel and Neil Walker. I wish to extend thanks to my fellow researchers and friends at the Magic Mountain: Stine Andersen, Clara Brandi, Poul Fritz Kjær, Andrew Glencross, Anne Nielsen, Max Spinner, Michael Kuur Sørensen, Michael Tatham and Thomas Teichler; as well as four fabulous girls and cronies: Emelyne Cheney, Sarah De Lange, Mia Sussman and Natalia Timus.

I wish to thank Ian Manners and colleagues for a couple of intensive and rewarding months spent at the Danish Institute for International Studies, writing a report for the Danish Parliament on the Danish opt-outs. It has benefited this book hugely. It was there that I had the great privilege of working with Thomas Gammeltoft-Hansen, an experience that showed me how research can be an intense, intellectual voyage that creates deep and lasting friendships.

For their inspirational comments on my preliminary thoughts, I wish to thank particularly Tanja E. Aalberts, Emanuel Adler, Derek Beach, Christopher Bickerton, André Broome, Sevasti Chatzopoulou, Jeffrey T. Checkel, Brendan Donnelly, Kevin Featherstone, Sieglinde Gstöhl, Knud Erik Jørgensen, Niilo Kauppi, Anna Leander, Cormac MacArmleigh, Paul Magnette, Richard W. Mansbach, Lee Miles, Rens Van Munster, Daniel Naurin, Rasmus Leander Nielsen, Rasmus Brun Pedersen, Nikolaj Petersen, David Phinnemore, Uwe Puetter, Fritz W. Scharpf, Leonard Seabrooke, Alexander Stubb and Ben Tonra. I also owe great thanks to Stefano Guzzini, whose intellectual generosity and support for junior scholars is truly outstanding.

I wish to thank my former colleagues at the Danish Ministry of Foreign Affairs in Copenhagen, where my one-year placement gave me invaluable insights into European integration. I am grateful to the officials at the Cabinet Office, the Home Office, and the Foreign and Commonwealth Office and the Treasury for their time and I wish to thank the European clerks at the House of Lords and the House of Commons for their comments and support. In Brussels I owe great thanks to the busy officials at the different Permanent Representations in Brussels.

I am grateful to Cambridge University Press, particularly John Haslam and the two anonymous reviewers, for making the book possible. Many thanks are owed to Jon Jay Neufeld, Amy Edmunds and Bonnie Craig for proofreading.

This research was made possible thanks to generous grants from the GARNET Network of Excellence and the Centre for European Politics at the University of Copenhagen. I want to thank Løgumkloster Refugium for the study grant to finish the book in tranquil surroundings. I am also grateful to T.V. Paul, Vincent Pouliot and Frédéric Mérand for hosting me as visiting scholar at the Center for International Peace and Security Studies at McGill University and Université de Montréal.

My deepest thanks go to my wonderful family for all of their support and love.

Abbreviations

AFSJ	Area of Freedom, Security and Justice
ASEAN	Association of South-East Asian Nations
BEPGs	Broad Economic Policy Guidelines
COREPER	Committee of Permanent Representatives (Comité des représentants permanents)
DG ECFIN	Directorate General for Economic and Financial Affairs, European Commission
DG JLS	Directorate General for Justice, Freedom and Security, European Commission
DIIS	Danish Institute for International Studies
DKRep	Danish Permanent Representation to the European Union
DUPI	Danish Foreign Policy Institute
EBRD	European Bank for Reconstruction and Development
EC	European Communities
ECB	European Central Bank
ECJ	European Court of Justice
ECOFIN	Economic and Financial Affairs Council
EEA	European Economic Area
EFC	Economic and Financial Committee
EFTA	European Free Trade Association
EGW	Eurogroup Working Group
EMS	European Monetary System
EMU	Economic and Monetary Union
EP	European Parliament
EPC	Economic Policy Committee
ERM II	Exchange Rate Mechanism II
ESCB	European System of Central Banks
EU	European Union
FCO	Foreign and Commonwealth Office
FOCJ	functional, overlapping, competing jurisdictions
IGC	Intergovernmental Conference

IR	International Relations
JHA	Justice and Home Affairs
MEP	Member of the European Parliament
Mercosur	from the Spanish *Mercado Cumún del Sur*
NATO	North Atlantic Treaty Organization
QMV	qualified majority voting
SGP	Stability and Growth Pact
TEC	Treaty Establishing the European Community
TEU	Treaty on European Union
UK	United Kingdom
UKRep	UK Permanent Representation to the European Union
US/USA	United States/United States of America
VAT	value-added taxation
WTO	World Trade Organization

1 | *Introduction*

The euro crisis has led scholars, policy-makers, practitioners and the general public to conclude that the process of European integration has gone off course. Europe's crisis appears to be at a Titanic moment, which threatens to bring down not only the EU's major economies but also its political *raison d'être*. 'The future of the euro is inseparable from European unity,' said German Chancellor Angela Merkel in her address to the German Parliament in December 2011. At this point, Merkel received support to amend EU treaties to tackle the debt crisis that had shaken Europe and threatened the future of the common currency. Two years later, the EU suffered a damaging split when British Prime Minister David Cameron promised British voters a choice – to exit the EU or to negotiate a looser relationship with it. The question echoing across Europe was: what if the attempts to take back sovereignty represent the end of one of the most significant Western political projects since the Second World War?

As the EU has moved into areas that were exclusive to the nation-state, such as government budget-making, criminal law and border control, the image of a quasi-automatic integration process has appeared more frequently in public debates across Europe. During the past two decades, doubts over the benefits of EU membership have led to some member states opting out from EU treaties, indicating a preference for 'outsiderness' over full membership of the EU. During the Lisbon Treaty negotiations, the UK, Poland and the Czech Republic secured exemptions from the Charter of Fundamental Rights.[1] Their exemptions are recent examples of a general trend of states formally securing national

---

[1] Poland was particularly keen to ensure that the Charter of Fundamental Rights did not affect national legislation in the sphere of public morality and family law; the UK was particularly concerned that social and economic rights were included in the same document as civil and political rights; the Czech Republic wanted guarantees that the charter did not expand the competence of the EU (Barnard 2010).

sovereignty through instruments of differentiation. Differentiation is the collective term for rejecting common rules and moving towards a form of co-operation where various member states have different rights and obligations within specific policy areas (Kölliker 2006: 2). National opt-outs and other instruments of differentiation are likely to be used much more as the EU expands geographically, continues to introduce new policies and struggles with eurosceptic populations.

Former Belgium Prime Minister and MEP Guy Verhofstadt did not mince his words when he said: 'In actual fact, opt-outs constitute a de facto negation of the idea of European cooperation' (Verhofstadt 2006: 214). Is he correct, are opt-outs a 'negation of the idea of European cooperation'? Or are they a pragmatic way of integrating states – a testimony to the *sui generis* nature of the EU?

Opt-outs are highly politicised and surrounded by myths. Eurosceptic politicians and media claim that opt-outs protect national sovereignty and can be used as an example to other member states (Giddings 2004: 158; Baker 2001). In contrast, pro-European ministers argue that they lose political influence when they 'are shown the door' at Council of Ministers meetings because of the opt-outs (Burkitt and Mullen 2003). As a result, national opt-outs are generally perceived to be controversial, leading to a dangerous fragmentation of the EU. At the same time, opt-outs represent the conviction that it is possible to (re)constitute the boundary of the state in the face of European integration. They draw a symbolic, legal and political line in the sand to establish an area where the state should remain sovereign.

When the Maastricht Treaty (1992) granted the UK and Denmark opt-outs from the Economic and Monetary Union (EMU) and the Area of Freedom, Security and Justice (AFSJ), EU lawyers argued that it would lead to a 'Europe in bits and pieces' (Curtin 1993; Weiler 1999), and political scientists predicted a destructive fragmentation of the EU (see Andersen and Sitter 2006). Existing research largely interprets opt-outs from EU treaties as a way to preserve member state sovereignty (Wallace 1997; Moravcsik 1998; Risse 2002). However, the consequences of opting out for the individual member states and the European integration process have yet to be fully explored.

This book has two aims. Empirically, it provides a deeper understanding of the EU as a political project. Using national opt-outs as a lens, it analyses European integration as a member state-driven process, which at the same time transforms the member states. It challenges the claim that opt-outs lead to the marginalisation of certain member states and contribute to European disintegration. The book looks at the most controversial form of differentiated integration: the British and Danish opt-outs from the EMU and borders, asylum, migration and justice policies. Thus the analysis covers two of the most important and dynamic policy areas in the EU. More specifically, it analyses how opt-outs contribute to labelling British and Danish officials as certain types of 'players' in the EU's Council of Ministers, the primary diplomatic forum for interstate bargaining in Europe where ministers and officials from the 28 member states negotiate.

Based on this in-depth analysis, I propose a different interpretation: opt-outs may actually reinforce the integration process. The reason for this counterintuitive dynamic is to be found in the diplomatic handling of the controversial sovereignty claims. In fact, the everyday management of opt-outs signals a retreat from national sovereignty rather than an expression of it. As this book shows, sovereignty claims, such as those made as part of the British and Danish opt-outs, become a 'stigma' – a discrediting mark on national representatives. Overall, the comparative analysis illustrates that direct sovereignty claims are considered inappropriate in Brussels. In areas where the UK and Denmark have opted out, their countries are perceived as unorthodox or even as threats to the EU's cohesion. The coping strategies used by British and Danish officials reveal that the EU is partially created through the stigmatisation of transgressive states.

Theoretically, this book develops a political sociology of European integration. As such it seeks to contribute to the so-called practice or sociological turn in EU and IR studies by offering a new interpretation of European integration as an everyday social process. This process is largely driven by a group of unelected national officials who meet to negotiate in Brussels in relative isolation from domestic populations. The book develops an approach to analysing the practices, group pressures and identity constructions inside the EU's Council of Ministers. This leads to a new understanding of how power relations play out between the member states.

More generally, the book demonstrates how insights from the sociology and anthropology of Pierre Bourdieu and Erving Goffman can be combined. Their work in combination creates a dynamic understanding of the disciplining and exclusionary practices that uphold the EU as a political order – and ways in which this order can be successfully challenged. This makes it possible to address an important (yet neglected) aspect of the ongoing struggle to produce an authoritative interpretation of European integration and what it takes to be a (good) member state.

European integration is a radical process. Over the years the EU has changed what it means to be a European state. As this book illustrates, a political sociological approach to integration provides a different and more detailed account of the consequences of European integration for national sovereignty than the dominant theories of 'liberal intergovernmentalism' (Moravcsik 1998), 'multi-level governance' (Marks 1998), 'accumulated executive order' (Curtin and Egebjerg 2008), 'European Administrative Space' (Hoffman 2011; Olsen 2009) or 'post-sovereignty' (Keating 2004), which all prioritise formal institutions over social processes. This book challenges these conventional explanations and argues that European integration is driven by a body of national representatives struggling to position their nations in diplomatic settings. European integration is neither the result of promoting domestically defined preferences (Moravscik 2004; Pollack 2010) nor merely the outcome of multilevel governance. By examining how sovereignty claims are managed in practice, the book draws attention to the finer points of day-to-day European integration, such as diplomatic negotiations. This is where we encounter what is otherwise an entirely abstract phenomenon, reified with the label 'the state'.

The book shows that a 'late sovereign diplomacy' grows out of day-to-day negotiations in the Council of Ministers and its hundreds of working groups. Leading political forces in the European states now see their nations as so deeply rooted within the supranational institutions of the EU that they blur their national interests with those of the EU. Political and legal authorities overlap, territorial exclusivity is replaced by functional boundaries and states begin to speak with one voice. As a result of over 50 years of painstaking work by officials from the European states, a social field has developed – an autonomous social system comprising a pattern of practices and shared meanings, where certain rules and roles result in competent action. An analysis of this field, its logic and the way in which states are punished for breaching its tacit rules provides a deeper insight into the diplomatic handling of the political, economic and social crises – as well as the stability of the European integration project. The EU is a fragile organisation maintained by *une certaine idée* about Europe, which requires constant care and attention from member states. This is why national diplomacy is so crucial to European integration.

Opting out to safeguard sovereignty

This book focuses on how the British and Danish opt-outs from the euro, common borders and Area of Freedom, Security and Justice (AFSJ) are managed. The proliferation of British opt-outs has contributed to the image of the UK as the 'awkward partner' (George 1994; Rosamond 2004; Geddes 2013) and a 'stranger in Europe' (Wall 2008). Because of the UK's opt-outs, observers underline the 'paradoxes' and 'tensions' in Danish EU policy (Kelstrup 2006; Miles 2005b). This book examines what lies behind these labels.

With the Maastricht Treaty (1992), the EU pressed forward with its ambitious plans to create a common currency, eliminate national border controls, introduce common asylum and immigration policies, and establish EU citizenship and a common foreign policy. Two states – the UK and Denmark – were particularly reluctant to surrender authority in these areas and this almost destroyed the treaty. The domestic political debates in both the UK and Denmark revolved around national identity being undermined, and control over daily lives and money being surrendered to faceless foreign bureaucrats. In the UK, 'Maastricht' became synonymous with the creation of a federal superstate and generated 'the longest lasting and arguably the deepest' division over the UK's relationship with Europe since the Second World War (Baker and Seawright 1998: 2). In Denmark, a range of specific issues were grouped under the banner of sovereignty, including the fear of an army of federal armed forces; the presence of foreign police officers on Danish soil; the application of EU law to sensitive questions of criminal justice; a common currency; the perception of a self-amending treaty; and the enhanced role of the European Parliament and EU citizenship (Hansen 2002).

To prevent the UK from blocking the Maastricht Treaty, it was granted opt-out clauses, which meant that it did not have to participate in the third stage of the EMU and the Social Chapter. These two Maastricht innovations had been the most controversial for the UK. Even then, parliamentary ratification was challenged by the opposition Labour and Liberal Democrat MPs, and crucially by the 'Maastricht Rebels' within the governing Conservative Party (Ludlam 1998: 33ff). The long and agitated debates about the Maastricht Treaty in Westminster revealed a bitterly divided political landscape. Parliamentarians were arguing over a treaty that they thought would impact not just on the British position in the global political economy but also on 'the very sovereignty of the British nation' (Baker et al. 1995: 53). As part of the Amsterdam Treaty (1997), the UK was given an opt-out from the Schengen agreement (abolishing controls and checks at national borders between EU member states) and the possibility of opting in to Title IV TEC (Treaty establishing the European Community) dealing with 'visas, asylum, immigration and other policies related to free movement of persons. Apart from these treaty opt-outs, the UK has been granted exemptions from secondary legislation, most famously perhaps by opting out of the working time directive (Barnard et al. 2003). As Gifford concludes, 'Clearly, the principle of opt outs and "red lines" in European negotiations has become enshrined as the British way of dealing with the EU' (Gifford 2010: 326).

Denmark was also a reluctant negotiator in Maastricht. However, when it was granted a protocol on the EMU, the Danish government accepted the treaty. At the political level, a broad consensus was established between the government parties (Conservatives, Liberals and Social Liberals) and the Social Democratic Party over the Maastricht process. Against this backdrop the Danish Parliament voted overwhelmingly for the Maastricht Treaty in the spring of 1992. However, this was followed by the unexpected rejection by the Danish population in a referendum in June 1992. The Danish *nej* (and the narrow French *oui*)[2] came as a shock to EU leaders and led to a dramatic ratification crisis. It was clear that the European populations no longer just accepted or ignored integration. As Lord notes, 'More than any other single event, it was the crisis in 1992–3, provoked by the ratification of the Maastricht Treaty on European Union (TEU), which shattered any illusion that the legitimising of EU power was a "non-problem"' (Lord 2000: 4). In Weiler's words, the Maastricht crisis was 'the beginning or end of a deeper process of mutation in public ethos or societal self-understanding' (Weiler 1999: 3). Whether or not one accepts the rejection and ratification crisis of the Maastricht Treaty as a 'constitutional moment' (Weiler

---

[2] Despite expectations of a landslide, the French public barely approved the Maastricht Treaty in 1992; voters were largely concerned about the sovereignty of France (Lewis-Beck 2007).

1999: 3), the so-called permissive consensus appeared to be a thing of the past.

Following the Danish referendum in June 1992, the Social Democrats, together with a majority in the Parliament, demanded significant revisions in the form of exemptions, which would make the treaty acceptable to the public in another referendum. These elements constituted the so-called 'National Compromise', which the government had to accept in October 1992.[3] In December 1992 the four demands of the National Compromise were accepted by the European Council in the 'Edinburgh Decision'. The decision focused on the main topic in the Danish referendum debate: the transfer of national sovereignty to the EU. Four key opt-outs were attached to the treaty: Denmark would not adopt the euro; European citizenship would not replace national citizenship; Denmark would not participate in the development of a common European defence; and Denmark would not participate in supranational AFSJ co-operation.

On 18 May 1993, 56.7 per cent of Danes voted 'yes' to the four opt-outs, which meant that Denmark could ratify the Maastricht Treaty. However, opposition groups argued that the opt-outs were an illusion and that, even with the Edinburgh Decision, Denmark was on a slippery slope towards a European federal state. The 'yes' vote triggered riots in Copenhagen, which were considered to be among the worst in Denmark's peacetime history. On the night of the second Danish referendum, Danish police shot into a crowd of demonstrators who had created an 'EU-Free Zone' in Nørrebro, a district in the centre of Copenhagen. At least 11 people were injured in the shooting and the 'Nørrebro night' is still a very sensitive issue in Denmark. Memories of the event have left Danish police suffering from a traumatic 'Vietnam syndrome' (Scharling 2003).[4]

---

[3] The National Compromise could 'unite the population on Denmark's continued participation in the EC'. In the document, the 'no' is carefully interpreted as a rejection of the 'United States of Europe', but not as a rejection of European Communities (EC) membership or European co-operation. With this interpretation the agreement created a united Danish people, to be politically represented in the opt-outs and to legitimise continued EU membership (<www.euo.dk/dokumenter/traktat/eu/nationalkompromis/> Adopted by all parties in Parliament with the exception of the Progress Party, 27 October 1992, author's translation).

[4] See the official report published on 18 May 1993 entitled *Beretning i henhold til lov nr. 389 af 22. maj 1996 om undersøgelse af Nørrebrosagen* ('Report pursuant

The sharp contrast between outraged anti-EU demonstrators in the streets of Copenhagen and more pragmatic governments negotiating in the glass-and-steel buildings in the Quartier Européen of Brussels show how sensitive opt-outs can be. These two images reveal a mental and physical gulf between large segments of the European populations who are attached to various concepts of national sovereignty and a Europeanised body of politico-administrative elites in Brussels who are focused on securing a strategically advantageous position for their country in Brussels.

While British and Danish governments may point out the detrimental effects of opt-outs on their country's position in the EU, they still have to guarantee to their citizens that they respect the protocols. In the UK and Denmark, the opt-outs are interpreted as bulwarks against European integration and symbolise the preservation of national sovereignty – emphasising an image of the state with full political and legal authority over people, territory and currency – which makes them seem almost sacrosanct. As a result, during the Constitutional Treaty negotiations, the British government said that the opt-outs would not be touched by what former Secretary of State Jack Straw called a 'simple tidying-up exercise' (Church and Phinnemore 2006: 8). Likewise, Danish Prime Minister Anders Fogh Rasmussen promised that the opt-outs would be safeguarded and that the Danish people would remain in full control:

> There will be no trickery. There will be no cherry picking. The opt-outs will stand clear and clean in the new treaty. And the Danish people shall decide on this treaty including the opt-outs. (Rasmussen 2003)

Domestically, opt-outs produce a fiction of national unity and fabricate a united domestic public despite apparent political disagreements over the EU issue. As such, the opt-outs do not just define a relationship between the state and the EU but also mediate between different domestic sub-audiences. Elsewhere I have looked at how opt-outs as a claim to sovereignty are constantly reconfigured by government representatives who present different 'truths' about the opt-outs to the domestic and the European audience, respectively, leading to 'organized duplicity' (Adler-Nissen 2008a). In this book I will focus primarily on the Brussels scene and less on the domestic scene. While domestic politics is crucial to why the UK and Denmark opted out, it – surprisingly perhaps – plays a lesser

to act no. 389 of 22 May 1996 on the investigation of the Nørrebro case') and the special issue of the magazine *Dansk Politi* ('Danish Police') (2003, no. 5).

role in the everyday management of the opt-outs in the Council of Ministers.

Opt-outs raise controversial questions about the degree of solidarity between member states and the political, legal, social and philosophical limits to European integration. In seemingly tedious treaty protocols, politicians (and ordinary citizens) have invested a lot of energy in discussing sovereignty, identity and democracy. So the image of an autonomous state is sought and preserved at home via the opt-out, despite the state's continuous entanglement in the European integration process. On the European scene, the opt-outs change from being a principled stance against more integration to a more flexible position, which allows ministers and diplomats to choose from the buffet of new EU initiatives. As such, opt-outs, and the diplomatic strategies surrounding them, serve as a prism for understanding the transformation of sovereignty in the EU.

A crucial case of differentiation

The British and Danish opt-outs are seen as the most controversial and high-profile protocols in the EU. A continuum of opt-outs exists, ranging from heavily debated policy areas, such as the EMU, Schengen and the common security and defence policy, to relatively uncontroversial protocols on reindeer husbandry in Finland and Sweden, the acquisition of second homes in Malta (and Denmark) and Swedish chewing tobacco (*snus*). Specific derogations at primary law level in favour of some member states are not a new phenomenon (Hanf 2001: 7), but most of these protocols have a limited effect and do not threaten the cohesion of the EU.[5]

Contrary to protocols with minor opt-outs or transition periods, on, for example, the free movement of people when a new state joins the EU, a number of member states have been granted permanent opt-outs in the last two decades, which have had extensive consequences. Apart from the UK and Denmark, Ireland is the only member state with major exemptions from 'Freedom, Security and Justice'; however, so far Ireland mainly follows the UK and will not be considered further in

---

[5] Germany's 'Banana Protocol', attached to the Rome Treaty (1957), which allowed duty-free access for Central and Latin American bananas into Germany, was also controversial (see Alter and Meunier 2006).

this book.[6] Sweden has a de facto opt-out in the EMU (it has thus far evaded the obligation to join the EMU by failing to satisfy certain criteria), but only the UK and Denmark have formal opt-outs in this area. In other words, the UK and Denmark are the current opt-out champions. Being granted an opt-out is very difficult to achieve, as newer member states (e.g. Poland and the Czech Republic) and prospective members (e.g. Norway) have experienced. During the latest enlargement negotiations, the European Commission (on behalf of the EU) 'saw it fit to rule out any opt-out possibilities for the candidate countries. The *acquis* is one of the most sacred of EU concepts and is expressly designed to prevent any prospective member of "shopping around" for its own mix of obligations' (Tatham 2009: 331–332).[7]

Opt-outs are an established part of the EU, while 'enhanced co-operation' (where a minimum of nine EU member states can establish advanced integration or co-operation in an area within EU structures but without the other members being involved) has only been applied twice – in the fields of divorce rules and patents, and it is approved for the field of a financial transaction tax. There are also many examples of breakaway groups of member states that have co-operated more closely outside the treaties. Usually, however, this co-operation ends up being codified in the treaties after some years, as the Schengen and EMU co-operation illustrate.

In summary, the British and Danish opt-outs appear to fly in the face of the very idea of an ever closer union. They present us with a most-likely case: if opt-outs do help to safeguard national sovereignty and threaten integration as we know it, this is most likely to show in the British and Danish cases. However, if British and Danish national exemptions are dissolved, as this book demonstrates, we have reason

---

[6] For an interesting account of how Ireland has been forced to follow the UK in the AFSJ to save the Common Travel Area, see Meehan (2000a; 2000b) and Laffan and O'Mahony (2008). Ireland has attached a declaration to the Lisbon Treaty ensuring that Ireland only participates in EU military operations if there is a UN mandate and the majority of the Irish Parliament backs the decision (see Hummer 2006). However, compared with the Danish defence opt-out, which ensures that Denmark does not participate in the military dimensions of the European Defence and Security Policy, the Irish declaration is much less restrictive.

[7] 'It would therefore appear that only current Member States can successfully argue for opt-outs from new policy developments; such point appears to be confirmed as much by the current British, Danish and Swedish opt-outs from the latest stages of the EMU' (Tatham 2009: 331–332).

to question the dominant assumption that such claims to sovereignty endanger the integration process.

This book makes two basic comparisons of two distinct policy areas: the EMU and the co-operation on border, asylum, migration and justice; and of the diplomacy of two countries: the UK and Denmark. Comparisons are made at both the micro- and macrolevels. My interests lie in how individuals and groups of national officials position themselves, and how their moves relate to the overall power structures in the EU: how do the two policy areas differ in terms of, for example, negotiation styles, tacit understandings and distribution of status between the member states, and what, if anything, does that do to European integration and sovereignty?

The EMU and the co-operation on AFSJ are particularly interesting to compare because they are some of the fastest-growing areas in the EU and are politically sensitive for all member states.[8] Covering two distinctive areas of European co-operation, these opt-outs also have obvious differences. For example, the UK has floating exchange rates whereas Denmark participates in the Exchange Rate Mechanism II (ERM II) along with newer member states that have yet to adopt the euro. There is also a huge difference between the Danish opt-out and the British opt-in possibility on asylum, immigration and judicial co-operation in civil matters. The UK is not part of the Schengen border agreement whereas Denmark is.

This book demonstrates how the particular design of the opt-out and specific policy areas make a difference to the effects of opting out. Some policy areas appear to be a better 'fit' with differentiated integration than others; the exclusionary effects and the loss of influence differ from policy area to policy area. In the case of the euro, British and Danish ministers and officials are physically excluded from meetings but they can be present and participate actively in the negotiations about co-operation in AFSJ. The differences between the two policy areas are not automatic – they are diplomatically negotiated. A combination of everyday practical concerns and political, and even symbolic, rationales help to explain the varying effects of opt-outs.

---

[8] The Danish defence opt-out is also arguably controversial. But as the UK participates fully in the European Security and Defence Policy, it is not possible to draw comparisons between the two countries.

The comparisons between the UK and Denmark consider their representatives' diplomatic practices and strategies. This involves exploring the differences and similarities in their perception of their roles in the European integration project, which takes us beyond the superficial idea of the UK and Denmark as 'sceptical' nations in the EU. In the debate about member states' roles in the integration process, which will be developed in chapters 2 and 3, I suggest a move away from seeing the state as a unitary actor in the EU (and in international politics more generally) and look to those who act in the name of the state.[9] Therefore, when comparing the UK and Denmark, I do not try to understand the 'peculiarities of some national character – or 'soul' (see Bourdieu 2002: 268) – but the particularities and patterns of different strategies in concrete negotiations. They are, for instance, able to influence the policy-making process if acting for 'the best of Europe', despite having lost the formal voting right. In practice, the ability of the opt-out to ensure legal immunity is challenged. However, there are also major differences between the countries. British participation in Schengen, the common border zone, for instance, is unimaginable for most British representatives (and their European partners), while Danish officials signal that Denmark is only waiting for the right moment to hold a referendum to surrender the opt-outs.

The UK and Denmark have at least one important similarity: they became members in 1973 (together with Ireland) and are both struggling with a predominantly eurosceptic public. However, their size and position in the EU are very different. The UK sees itself as (and is generally regarded as being) one of the most important powers in Europe, together with France and Germany, whereas Denmark sees itself as a 'small state'. Another difference is the origins of their opt-outs, which differ fundamentally. The UK's opt-outs are the result of a long-term governmental position shared (to a large extent) by both the Conservative and Labour parties. In contrast, the Danish exemptions stem from a referendum 'against' the pro-European government and the equally pro-European social democratic opposition.

This book shows that history, size and self-perception make a difference – not only to how the two countries manage their respective opt-outs but also to how the two countries are perceived in Brussels.

---

[9] For useful discussions about statehood, see Jackson (2004), Neumann (2004) and Weldes (1999).

Overall the comparative analysis shows that a particular European diplomatic field has developed in and around the Council of Ministers, where outright claims to sovereignty are seen as inappropriate. However, there are different ways of coping with this. Some of the British and Danish strategies consolidate the stigma and, in doing so, increase marginalisation. Other strategies successfully reduce the stigma of opting out. In the EMU, for instance, British and Danish officials try to reduce the exclusionary effects of the euro opt-outs and gain influence in the European decision-making process. While the UK adopts a missionary strategy to move the EU in an alternative direction, Denmark acts as a shadow euro-member state trying to be a credible partner.

Is Europe in 'bits and pieces'?

Despite the considerable political attention given to the phenomenon of opting out, political scientists have largely ignored national exemptions (see Leuffen et al. 2012; Kölliker 2006; Stubb 2002; Warleigh 2002; Naurin and Lindahl 2010 for valuable exceptions). Even liberal inter-governmentalism with its focus on national interests struggles to explain opt-outs (Moravcsik and Nicolaïdis 1999: 83). As such 'the picture of a both more integrated and more differentiated EU . . . poses a challenge for theories of European integration' (Leuffen et al. 2012: 27). As I will discuss in more detail in Chapter 2, research on opt-outs and differentiated integration is instead dominated by legal scholars. Lawyers generally regard opt-outs as deeply problematic (Shaw 2003; De Witte 2002; Curtin 1993). Their main argument is that opt-outs challenge the fundamental principles of solidarity and equality that underpin the EU's legal system. Curtin describes the British and Danish opt-outs from the Maastricht Treaty as a 'hijacking' of the *acquis communautaire* (Curtin 1993: 88). From this perspective, opt-outs represent a threat to the uniform application of EU law (Búrca and Scott 2000; Curtin 1993). However, there are also some legal scholars who believe that we should not buy into the usual assumptions regarding the problems of opting out vis-à-vis the unity of the EU's legal order. In this light, opt-outs represent an integral aspect of the 'post-sovereign' perspective in which sovereignty is shared, dispersed and disaggregated (MacCormick 2002).

On a more abstract level, political theorists and politicians frequently refer to differentiation in the so-called 'finality debate' on possible or legitimate endpoints of the European integration process (e.g. Fischer 2000; Bankowski and Christodoulidis 1998; Bellamy and Castiglione 1997; Scharpf 2006; Olsen 2005). A more flexible Europe has been a cornerstone in British European policy from Margaret Thatcher to David Cameron. French politicians have also promoted differentiated integration, from Jean Monnet and Jacques Delors to Édouard Balladur, but in a very different way, with France as the avant-garde of a two-tier Europe. Meanwhile, political representatives from some newer member states have been more sceptical. As Czech President Vaclav Claus wrote, the 'fashionable idea of "flexibility" [. . .] indicates some sort of freedom of choice for individual countries but it is not true. It was explicitly stated by the Commission that the idea of flexibility "was conceived for those who wanted to advance forward", not for those "who want to advance backwards and reduce integration or remove themselves from certain policies"' (Claus 2000).

A diverse but growing group of social scientists are enthusiastic about the perspective of differentiated integration, albeit for different reasons (e.g. Delanty and Rumford 2006; Habermas 2003; Schmitter 2001; Warleigh 2002; Hix 1998). A normative stance emerges from these ideas: opt-outs do not pose a threat but are an inevitable (and perhaps even promising) avenue for the future of the EU. Therefore, while the anti-differentiation group of scholars see opt-outs as expressions of national sovereignty, the pro-differentiation camp sees opt-outs as part of a process where authority relationships become more complex and sovereign power more dispersed within the EU (Bellamy and Castiglione 2003: 19).

I share an abiding scepticism with this latter camp concerning the power of traditional integration theory to enlighten our understanding of European integration. Moreover, I agree that the conditions for making sovereignty claims in Europe have fundamentally changed. Yet I do not believe that abstract notions regarding 'neo-medieval' (Zielonka 2006: 9) or 'post-modern' (Plattner 2003: 54) measures of differentiation bring us close enough. Instead we must zoom in on those driving the integration process to understand how they negotiate in the Council of Ministers – a highly structured space of interaction. The challenge is to analyse what happens to state sovereignty (and, more precisely, the British and Danish opt-outs) when diplomats negotiate.

The few researchers who have inquired into the consequences of opt-outs for individual member states suggest that the UK and Denmark are experiencing a real and tangible loss of influence because of their opt-outs (Larsen 2000; Tonra 2000; Wallace 2000; Petersen 1998). An opt-out may guarantee 'immunity from disliked European legislation', as Helen Wallace claims (Wallace 1997: 682), but the price of autonomy is loss of influence because the member state cannot participate in the policy-making process and is not an attractive coalition partner (Mouritzen and Wivel 2005: 36). Indeed, the majority of efforts made by scholars to understand co-operation in the EU reflect top-down applications of analytic frameworks to existing case material. Their analyses suggest that an opt-out is a relatively stable legal arrangement or collective identity position in the EU.

In Latin, *optare* means 'to choose' or 'to wish' (*Oxford English Dictionary* 2013). The concept of choice, however, presupposes much of what needs to be uncovered. At first glance a national opt-out is simply a legal protocol attached to a treaty, which usually implies that a member state will not formally participate in the decision-making process and will not adopt or implement EU legislation in the area covered by the opt-out. In practice, however, Danish and British officials participate in meetings where new legislation covered by their protocols is dis-cussed, only without always casting their formal vote. Instead of assuming that protocols have automatic effects, the book analyses the social setting in which the opt-outs are managed.

The book explores the practice dimension of sovereignty. It examines the crucial question of how opt-outs are perceived and handled by national representatives in the EU, by considering the relationship between opt-out protocols and whether officials can be accepted as 'good and constructive Europeans'. Hence it analyses not only the causal but also the constitutive effects that opt-outs may have on diplomacy. Sovereignty claims cannot be solely understood on the basis of formal rules or the various legal interpretations of these rules – identities and social con-texts will always modify the implications of rules. The book therefore introduces an alternative theoretical approach to the diplomacy of opting out by incorporating the perceptions and norms that govern the European integration process.

A political sociology of European integration

The discussion about the relationship between state sovereignty and European integration has been intense – mostly between those who consider the state to be the main player and those who believe that the state is weakened by processes of globalisation and Europeanisation. Perhaps the most crucial debate has taken place between liberal intergovernmentalists and various (multilevel) governance and neofunctionalist scholars (Hooghe and Marks 2001; Jachtenfuchs 2001; Kohler-Koch and Eising 1999; Marks et al. 1996; Scharpf 1997). Currently, however, EU scholars are more divided over specific ways of operationalising concepts such as 'Europeanisation' than broader theoretical questions relating to the nature of the EU and how to make sense of it (see Bickerton 2012 for an important exception).[10] Today, little thought is given to the ontology and epistemology of EU research (Eilstrup-Sangiovanni 2006: 466). This is unfortunate because it prevents us from asking some key questions about the nature of European integration.

To fully understand how national diplomacy works in the context of European integration, we need to take a closer look at how national interests are represented in Brussels. Of course, the management of the opt-outs does not take place in a vacuum; national parliaments, public opinion and media coverage influence the way in which officials handle the exemptions (Kelstrup 2006: 385). But the number of people directly involved in the diplomatic handling of opt-outs is limited. National representatives become the centre of attention because they are the ones managing the opt-outs, be it in meetings in Brussels, the lobby or during coffee breaks. The focus is on their interpretations, and legal and political strategies when managing British and Danish protocols.

When talking about diplomacy, I focus on the negotiations between the member states. The people in charge of these negotiations are diplomats – officials (employed in the diplomatic services or members of the national home civil services) who represent their member states in EU decision-making. I thus use the concepts of 'diplomacy' and 'diplomats' to cover not only officials from the foreign services with diplomatic status, but also officials from other ministries such as treasury officials. Although not all of the national representatives whom I focus on are diplomats in a strict formal sense, they perform functions that are usually labelled as diplomatic: representing their nations and negotiating with foreign powers on behalf of their state (for definitions of diplomacy

---

[10] For arguments supporting this view, see Checkel (2004: 243) and Rosamond (2006). For an earlier discussion of the state of the art in EU studies, see also Jupille et al. (2003).

along these lines, see Watson 1982; Sending et al. forthcoming). As I discuss at length in Chapter 6, the entanglement of the diplomatic and governance functions is key to understanding European integration.

This books steps into the 'engine room' of European integration, the Council of Ministers and its many working groups. Most scholars and observers of the EU assume that (despite supranational institutions and qualified majority voting) national representatives still work only to promote their country's national interests in the EU. Despite recognising the increasing power of the Council of Ministers Secretariat and the bureaucratisation of the Council of Ministers, the Council is still seen as a classic forum for intergovernmental bargaining (Curtin and Egeberg 2008: 653). Numerous studies have focused on negotiations in the Council of Ministers system, but most are distanced from the experiences of those who actually negotiate (for excellent exceptions, see Lewis 2005; Puetter 2006; Naurin and Wallace 2009). They often focus on voting behaviour, and they tend to ignore social structures, and informal norms and dynamics that are crucial to the negotiations (see also Heisenberg 2009).

This is where political sociology becomes useful. It provides us with analytical concepts that link everyday diplomacy with macroprocesses of inclusion and exclusion – that is, the overall integration process. It shows that learning processes only work when they are embedded in a greater understanding of what makes them meaningful. It also prompts us to ask questions that are not usually asked in EU studies. For example, how do national officials prepare for Council of Ministers working group meetings? Why are some states seen as being more powerful than others? What is seen as a constructive proposal and what is seen as obstructive? How do officials manoeuvre between loyalty to their nation and affiliation to the European project? And how do the everyday workings of European integration relate to structural changes in co-operation, such as the introduction of the euro?

One of the great sources of inspiration in the recent turn to political sociology in EU studies is Pierre Bourdieu.[11] He wrote extensively about

---

[11] A new classic is Favell and Guiraudon (eds) (2009), but see also Adler-Nissen (2008b), Ekengren (2002), Kauppi (2003), Johler (2008), Guiraudon (2003), Mudge and Vauchez (2012), Madsen (2007), Cohen and Vauchez (2007) and Favell (2011). Within IR 'the practice turn' has been promoted by scholars such as Emanuel Adler, Iver B. Neumann and Vincent Pouliot (Adler and Pouliot 2011; Pouliot 2007; Neumann 2002).

the civil service and was a critical observer of the EU (Bourdieu 1989; Bourdieu 2003; see also Manners 2007: 83). However, it is as a social theorist that I believe Bourdieu to be most enlightening for an analysis of European integration. This book explores how a Bourdieu-inspired political sociology can be applied in European integration and IR studies more broadly.

To counter Bourdieu's tendency towards structuralism, I use insights from the work of the pioneer of symbolic interactionism, Erving Goffman, on role-playing, stigma management and face-work, which allow the agent more room for improvisation and strategic action. The coupling of Goffman and Bourdieu is not as odd as it may sound. Neil Fligstein (2001) has successfully combined the two in his arguments about social skills and fields. Goffman and Bourdieu shared a fascination with the exotic minutiae of everyday life and social exclusion, but their respective contributions to the study of stigmatisation – as a form of negative capital – have not yet been developed into a distinct theoretical framework. Combining these two perspectives means that we can capture the practitioner's point of view without losing the structural picture and reducing power to observable relations.

The framework developed in this book conceptualises power relations between member states as being structured by a particular social field in which certain positions and actions are rewarded. This framework helps to uncover under-researched social hierarchies in the Council of Ministers, which are of great relevance to the diplomacy of opting out and the European integration process more broadly. Indeed, from this perspective, European integration can be conceptualised as a social process driven by politico-administrative elites, who work within a relatively narrow understanding of possible political positions and ideas. This is an empirically informed approach to European integration, which begins by looking at the face-to-face interactions between individuals and groups who negotiate on behalf of their states or the EU institutions. From this perspective, sovereignty (and the way in which it has been translated into legal and political agreements with other states) is continuously constructed and reconstructed in diplomatic practice.

Analysing the understandings shared by the national officials negotiating in Brussels provides a key to understanding the complex relationship between sovereignty and European integration. A tacit understanding treated as if it were an objective 'truth' constitutes what Bourdieu would call 'doxa' – the undisputed and taken-for-granted premise for social interaction in a particular field (Bourdieu 1977: 164). The subsequent chapters show how the idea that Europe must continue to move forward is a shared assumption (or doxa) that is very rarely questioned by any national or EU official during negotiations. The doxa of European integration is captured in the preamble of the Treaty of Rome (1957), which states that the gathering nations of Europe are 'determined to lay the foundations of an ever closer union among the peoples of Europe'. Indeed, the *acquis communautaire* has been interpreted as more than the legal provisions, procedures and rules of the TEU; it has been perceived as 'an embedded acquis' or 'an institution which forms part of an ongoing process of constructing meaning and applying knowledge' (Wiener 1998: 302).[12] The doxa of 'an ever closer union' legitimises the EU's actions to its own civil servants in the European Commission and to the national representatives when they negotiate in Brussels.

However, as I will discuss in more detail in chapters 6 and 7, rising euroscepticism and new generations of political leaders in Europe make this doxa fragile. In 2013 UK Prime Minister David Cameron made the 'heretical proposition' (to use his own words) that Britain's goal is not the European Treaty's 'ever closer union among the peoples of Europe'. If the idea of an ever closer Union is openly and consistently challenged, opt-outs beyond the UK are likely to become less controversial. Yet so far the European Commission and core member states have successfully managed to put pressure on states that may opt out and defend the integration doxa.

Methods and sources

It is striking that many of the scholars who argue that opt-outs lead to a loss of influence and marginalisation have not conducted interviews with those involved in the management of opt-outs. This book seeks to reconstruct the practical experience that is tied up with managing opt-outs. To do this I pursued a methodological strategy of combining different types of qualitative data source. As guidelines for how to apply international political sociology or practice approaches systematically

---

[12] One of the most important ways in which the EU moves forward is through law. When the states became EU members, 'they also implicitly signed up for more integration, because – in EC rhetoric – law (and obedience to law) has traditionally meant integration' (Shaw 1996: 237).

in empirical cases are generally lacking, the book includes an appendix explaining the methods and sources in more detail.

There is little written material on opt-outs in the archives of British and Danish ministries, as the management of the exemptions is based on tacit knowledge. Due to the secretive and sensitive nature of Council of Ministers negotiations, the informal norms and strategies are not directly accessible to the outsider. Consequently the best way of understanding this aspect of European integration is to interview the people in charge of tackling national positions on a day-to-day basis.

The data-gathering process was divided into three stages: the pilot study (exploration); the actual in-depth interviews and gathering of archival material and other  analysis); and the follow-up conversations and supplementary reading of documents and participant observation (double-checking and nuances).

A relatively exclusive group of people regularly deals with the opt-outs. As a senior official in the British House of Commons explained, even the best-informed national parliaments in the EU (i.e. the British House of Commons and the Danish Folketing) 'do not have a clue about the implications of the opt-outs'.[13] it is true that parliaments are not the key managers of opt-outs. While it is often claimed that domestic politics is increasingly important for the EU's development, one should not be led to believe that the everyday integration process (below the level of ministers) is necessarily impacted on by a rise in euroscepticism. As this book demonstrates, diplomats often find a way to get round domestic concerns.

Moreover, the European Parliament is not particularly important to the diplomacy of opting out. There are a number of reasons why this is the case. First, the two policy areas of AFSJ and EMU have been only partly under the competence of the European Parliament. Second, the legal and political interpretations of the opt-outs – especially those pertaining to the field of AFSJ – are often quite technical and demand considerable expertise in EU law (Papagianni 2001: 123). In the EMU, the degree of technical knowledge is also important. For these reasons, institutions such as the national parliaments and the European Parliament are largely excluded from participating in the interpretation and management of the euro opt-outs. Third, and more importantly, the opt-outs are seen as an issue to be dealt with by the states that have opted

---

[13] Interview, House of Commons, April 2007.

out. In day-to-day work, the British and Danish opt-outs are therefore mainly interpreted and managed by officials from the UK and Denmark.

In total I completed 123 in-depth interviews with diplomats and officials from the UK, Denmark and 11 other member states, as well as EU officials. They are complemented by official material (e.g. Council of Ministers regulations and directives, and European Court of Justice (ECJ) cases) and archival sources (e.g. documents from the negotiation process, draft regulations and internal notes). The in-depth interviews aimed to achieve detailed and analytical understanding of the opt-outs and the representatives' attitudes, beliefs and practices. I used a semi-structured interview guide (see also Fielding 1993: 136). Discussion of the interview guide and the interpretation of the interviews in my presentation of the analytical strategy can be found in Appendix A.

My main source of information, which provided insights into how the opt-outs are experienced and managed, was from interviews with 30 British and 37 Danish middle- and high-ranking officials between December 2005 and October 2010. The British interviewees were located in the:

- UK Permanent Representation in Brussels
- Cabinet Office
- Foreign and Commonwealth Office
- Treasury
- Home Office
- Department of Constitutional Affairs
- House of Lords
- House of Commons.

The Danish officials worked in the:

- Danish Permanent Representation
- Ministry of Foreign Affairs
- Ministry of Finance
- Ministry of Justice
- Ministry of Refugees, Immigrants and Integration Affairs
- Danish Parliament.

I also interviewed:

- eight officials working in the Directorate-General for Justice, Freedom and Security (DG JLS);

- three officials from the DG for Economic and Financial Affairs, the European Commission (DG ECFIN);
- three officials from the Legal Service of the European Commission;
- seven officials from the Council Secretariat and its Legal Service, and the Eurogroup secretariat.

In addition, I interviewed 15 officials from the Permanent Representations in Brussels of other member states:

- Belgium
- France
- Germany
- Greece
- Ireland
- Luxembourg
- Netherlands
- Norway[14]
- Poland
- Sweden
- Spain.

This gave me an understanding of how officials from other member states viewed and dealt with the British and Danish officials, and the opt-outs.

A follow-up phase made it possible to return to the field after a period of writing to reconsider my interpretations of the data. This activity aimed to refine my theoretical framework and my working hypothesis about stigma and stigma management. It reflects Bourdieu's reflexive move, according to which there is a return to the field after the rupture or the objectivation of the object (Jenkins 2005: 19). This provided situations that allowed me to distance myself from the information provided by the informants.

Finally, the analysis also builds, to a lesser degree, on my own experiences as Head of Section in the Department of European Policy at the Danish Ministry of Foreign Affairs in 2010–2011. For a year I was part of the team responsible for preparing the Danish Prime Minister for the European Council meetings (the so-called EU summits between the heads of state and government). This included writing the

---

[14] As an active EEA member, Norway has a mission to the EU.

Danish Prime Minister's speech notes, preparing his negotiations, and drafting non-papers and strategic interventions. In addition I worked on Denmark's general European policy, including the country's position on treaty changes, the political and institutional consequences of the euro crisis and the EU's reactions to the Arab Spring in 2011. I was closely involved in the preparations for the Danish EU presidency in 2012, drafting the Danish presidency programme and national priorities. The language, tone and atmosphere within the buildings of the European Council, European Commission and Permanent Representations in Brussels and the ministries and departments in London and Copenhagen are an essential part of the social web in which the opt-outs are handled. Of course, reports from the negotiations remain classified and I have taken great care not to cross the line of confidentiality. However, these experiences contribute to the story that I am trying to tell.

Structure of the book

Chapter 2 discusses the recent trend towards differentiation and the failure of existing theoretical approaches to account for this development. Moreover, it deconstructs the crude image of an EU under threat of disintegration due to increased differentiation. It specifically criticises the assumption that opt-outs have inevitable consequences.

Building on this critical review, Chapter 3 sets out a political sociology of European integration and presents the analytical framework. It introduces a number of analytical concepts, such as field, habitus, doxa and stigma. These help to paint a different picture of diplomatic practices and the way in which national interests are promoted in the EU. The framework conceptualises the Council of Ministers as a social field where a body of national representatives come to share a particular sense of their place. It then suggests a number of mechanisms related to the diplomatic management of sovereignty claims in the EU: the imposition of stigma by the insiders and the reactions against these processes by British and Danish representatives through stigma management.

Chapter 4 uses the framework in a detailed study of the co-operation on the EMU. It analyses the diplomatic struggles over the stakes defining the field of economic EMU, unexplored until now. It begins with an analysis of the overall development of the policy area and the way in which co-operation has changed over time. The thrust of the chapter shows how euro-outsiders are increasingly stigmatised and excluded from the most important decisions in the EU.

Chapter 5 is an in-depth analysis of the co-operation on asylum, immigration, civil law, border control, and police and criminal matters. It reveals that the division between 'insiders' and 'outsiders' is far more blurred in AFSJ. It illustrates how British and Danish ministers and officials have developed sophisticated means of circumventing the opt-outs to reduce their exclusionary effects.

Chapter 6 discusses the empirical findings and explains the book's contribution to overall theory development in EU studies and IR theory. More specifically, it conceptualises member state interaction as 'late sovereign diplomacy'. This argument implies that the intense negotiations between state elites in the EU have led to a quiet revolution of national diplomacy. The chapter suggests – with important qualifications – that we can identify similar dynamics to those seen in European integration in other multilateral settings around the world. It puts forward a number of alternative ways to form a European Union that is more responsive to popular demands and concerns.

Chapter 7 is the conclusion. It shows how the identified stigma management and the analysis of the transformative nature of national diplomacy in Europe challenge existing theories of European integration, and it points to the need to rethink the notions of national sovereignty, identity and legitimacy. It highlights that although opt-outs might help to preserve the symbolic figure of an autonomous state, they can be seen as part of the state's fundamental transformation. Until now, attempts to close the EU's 'legitimacy deficit' have failed because they have not addressed everyday diplomatic interaction in Brussels (i.e. a treaty change is not enough). As long as the tacit norms guiding diplomacy in the EU are not challenged, integration will continue to deepen despite major crises and attempts to take back sovereignty.

2 | *Disintegrating Europe?*

Introduction

In 1994 the French Prime Minister, Eduard Balladur, presented his vision of a Europe of three concentric circles: a strong central core of France, Germany and the Benelux countries; a middle tier made up of the other member states, unable or unwilling to join the EMU; and an outer circle consisting of the other European states, not part of the EU but with close economic and security links nonetheless (Pilkington 1995: 249). But it is not only those leaders with a pro-European slant who have issued calls for a differentiated Europe. On occasion, sceptics have also expressed a wish for a differentiated approach to integration in order to avoid having to implement policies that they find unpalatable.

While France's leaders are often heard to speak of the necessity of a 'two-speed Europe' allowing for enhanced or closer co-operation in the eurozone, those political leaders with a more sceptical outlook talk of opt-outs. UK Prime Minister John Major, for example, argued in favour of a 'multi-faceted, multi-speed, multi-layered' Europe (Major 1994; see also Denman 2004; Diez 1999: 608). However, he perceived any talk of permanent divisions as a threat on the grounds that the UK would become the outsider:

I see real danger in talk of a 'hard core' of inner and outer circles, a two-tier Europe. I recoil from ideas for a Union in which some would be more equal than others. There is not, and should never be, an exclusive hard core of countries or of policies. (Major 1994)

The debate about the EU becoming more divided has rumbled on and on. This discussion, dramatised at summits between heads of state and the government in Brussels, concerns the very nature of the EU as a political project. At its most fundamental level it raises the question of European unity. In theoretical terms it concerns the ability of international organisations, such as the EU, to effectively bind their member states.

In the first part of this chapter I will consider why opt-outs are seen as so controversial in discussions about the nature of the legal and political order of the EU. Opt-outs, I will argue, raise questions about the legitimacy of the EU and the solidarity between its member states. On the one side, social scientists have traditionally been committed to notions of European unity and a common legal order. From this perspective, claims to sovereignty – for example, in the form of national opt-outs – threaten the symbolic authority of the EU's legal and political order and ultimately the very idea of European integration. Though it is largely unaware of its own normative bias, the EU's vision of unity has proved to be attractive to a host of audiences, ranging from pro-European politicians to lawyers, economists, political scientists and political theorists. Conversely, those in the pro-differentiation camp – in sharp contrast with the more standard EU scholarship – hail national opt-outs as a means of enhancing the legitimacy of the European political order. We should, they argue, encourage legal and political differentiation in order to accommodate national differences. Notwithstanding disagreements as to whether opt-outs are harmful or helpful, most scholars agree that differentiated integration challenges the symbolic capacity of EU law and the political order that it seeks to represent. Yet the claim that opt-outs threaten the symbolic authority of the EU's legal and political order and its sovereignist self-understanding has yet to be demonstrated in more detailed analysis.

I will then discuss the limitations of IR and integration theory when seeking to explain the effects of an increasingly differentiated EU. Despite valuable insights from the Europeanisation and socialisation literature, practitioners and scholars (of all convictions) have neglected to examine the real-life dynamics of European integration. Aside from the negotiation of opt-out protocols in connection with intergovernmental conferences, little is known about how opt-outs are managed and how they relate to European integration. When evaluated against the few existing empirical analyses of the effects of opt-outs, the various approaches – be they agency- or structure-oriented, rationalist or reflectivist – have proved to be inadequate to explain the complex effects of opt-outs on the positions and influence of member states, not least because they fail to explore the actual social and political practices surrounding the opt-outs, and because their conceptualisation of power is excessively narrow. In the chapter's concluding section I will argue that diplomacy in the EU ought to be explored by analysing not only the formal institutional setup but equally the social context, norms and ideas within which processes of negotiation take place.

Hijacking the European legal and political order

Why do so many lawyers, political scientists and pro-European politicians recoil at the very notion of the opt-out? No fewer than three types of objection can be identified, which are – sometimes cumulatively – used to protest against major opt-outs being granted to member states. Each of these objections derives from a particular understanding of what the EU is and, accordingly, what the role of the (member) state should be. First, major national opt-outs may be rejected on the grounds that they invalidate the unified EU legal order; second, they are denounced as threatening the democracy and transparency of the EU policy-making process; and third, they are seen as undermining the solidarity between member states. Each of these objections is briefly examined below. As I will argue in greater detail, they are either rooted in a particular normative vision of European integration or build on questionable assumptions about the European integration process. Nevertheless, given that opt-outs are seen as problematic not only by scholars but also by those in charge of the integration process, a critical discussion of the various ways in which they are interpreted serves to uncover the negative associations that the UK and Denmark may encounter in Brussels as a result of opting out.

The unity vision

Deirdre Curtin famously described the introduction of the British and Danish opt-outs from the Maastricht Treaty as a 'hijacking' of the *acquis communautaire*, which is the body of common rights and obligations binding the member states together (Curtin 1993: 88). This critical diagnosis also suggests its own cure: those questioning the uniform order ought to be punished. The prevailing conviction among legal scholars is that opt-outs represent a threat to the uniform application of EU law (Búrca and Scott 2000; Curtin 2003; Hine 2001). Major national opt-outs undermine the unified EU legal order, which is believed to differ fundamentally from standard international law. EU law has a unique character in accordance with the doctrine of the ECJ. The most enduring manifestation of this view has been the idea of the 'constitutionalised treaty' – that is, the notion that the EU treaties form a constitutional order.[1] In light of this, national opt-outs and other forms of differentiated integration represent a threat to the unified legal order – the treaties and the *acquis communautaire*.[2] This constitutional reading of EU law indicates why opt-outs will invariably always be seen as controversial. The established constitutional perspective is linked to a pivotal idea concerning the integration process, namely that it should lead to what the founding Treaty of Rome (1957) referred to in its preamble as an 'ever closer union between the peoples of Europe'. This can be seen as European integration's legally institutionalised vision of unity (Weiler 1999; Wiener 2003: 175–176).[3]

To understand why EU opt-outs are seen as so deeply problematic, it is necessary to consider the 'self-understanding' of many EU lawyers. As Walker notes,

> there is a significant strain of EU scholarship which for reasons of intellectual training, professional socialisation and associated normative commitments is minded to embrace the official constitutional perspective and object-language of the EU as its own, and to develop the best sense and best defence of those of the ECJ's various doctrines of constitutional self-assertion – not just supremacy but also direct effect, implied powers etc. – which seem to embrace and confirm a *sovereignist self-understanding*. (Walker 2003: 12–13)

This 'sovereignist self-understanding' implies that the EU's legal order is supreme and independent of national constitutions. Accordingly, opt-outs represent not so much a national claim to sovereignty as a threat to the EU's own claims to authority – that is, 'its own claim to sovereign authority within a limited sphere' (Walker 1999: 18). Curtin argues, therefore, that member states must pay a price for infracting on the EU legal order:

---

[1] Indeed, the twin concepts of direct effectiveness and supremacy are the legal instruments by which the ECJ is said to have constitutionalised the EC Treaty (Búrca 2003).

[2] It should also be noted that opt-outs are not the sole enemy of a unified legal order; 'pillarisation' and limits to the jurisdiction of the ECJ also contribute to the uncertain nature of the EU's legal system, at least in the eyes of the European Commission (Búrca 1996: 262–266).

[3] It could also be argued more pragmatically that all law requires unity; otherwise a legal order cannot deliver what it promises, namely to reduce – if not to eliminate – conflict by means of authoritative decision-making (Prechal and Roermund 2008).

Those who nevertheless 'opt-out' should be obliged to accept the majority's droit de regard including in the final analysis the right of the partners to define their behaviour as 'destabilising or unacceptable'. (Curtin 1995: 251)

Curtin's position characterises the bulk of legal scholarship on opt-outs. Indeed, it seems as though those scholars defending the EU's legal order against opt-outs are guided not merely by analytical considerations and positivist legal methods but also by this particular (self-)understanding or normative concern for the *telos* of the integrative process and the EU's own claims to supreme authority.

Transparency and democracy misconstrued

A second objection to differentiated integration comes from scholars who argue that national exemptions undermine transparency, democracy and the rights of individual citizens. It can be argued that opt-outs compound the already complicated relationship between the national and European legal orders (Kostakopoulou 1998: 166). The need to distinguish, for instance, between legal acts applying to all EU member states, to the Schengen members or to Schengen without Denmark does not aid the establishment of a clear and comprehensive *acquis* in the area of immigration. Consequently, immigrants and immigration officials are faced with a bewildering range of different sets of legislation due to the Schengen opt-outs (Monar 1999: 24–26). From the perspective of the individual citizen, differentiation leads to uncertainties regarding their judicial status and rights. Moreover, the pragmatic terminology of differentiation renders it even more difficult for the individual European citizen to identify with the EU (Walker 1998: 381–382).

Furthermore, opt-outs appear to threaten democratic principles (e.g. Curtin 1993; Hine 2001; Shaw 2002; Slot 1994; Walker 2000; Weatherill 2000). Arguably, 'democracy may be relegated to a side-issue in a larger struggle between different institutional orders, and may even become its causality' (Walker 1998: 381). In a discussion of the Danish Schengen protocol, Jo Shaw remarks that opt-outs have a 'perverse effect' on democracy. Her sharp criticism deserves mention:

Although a member of Schengen, Denmark has resisted the creation of an intra-EU solution to the problems which its extra-EU status has created. Oddly, therefore, Denmark seems to be resisting – in a manner which seems contrary to its strong adherence to Parliamentary democracy and its traditions of transparency and open government – those aspects of the integration of the Schengen acquis which are highly positive from precisely those points of view. In opting out of the integration of the Schengen acquis [...] Denmark seems to be sacrificing democracy and openness on the altar of resistance to encroachment upon its state sovereignty. This does seem a little perverse. (Shaw 1998: 77)

Denmark's Schengen position is 'perverse' in Shaw's view because there is no democratic control of the Danish position in Schengen. Indeed, as I will demonstrate in Chapter 6, the Danish government is essentially forced to adopt legal provisions agreed upon by other member states, only in the form of intergovernmental treaty law. This would indeed appear to be a high price for the safeguard of what can only be a limited conception of state sovereignty.

A threat to solidarity

A third objection to opt-outs is that they challenge the principles of solidarity and equality between member states. According to Joseph Weiler, 'Fundamentally, a "flexible" Europe represents an abandonment of the principle of solidarity' (Weiler 1997: 311). The argument that opt-outs challenge member state solidarity is also prevalent in the literature on monetary policy and immigration, and police co-operation (Wincott 1996: 411).

Opt-outs are believed to endanger the entire integration process on the grounds that they inspire similar demands from other member states or candidate countries. This is partly why economists such as George Soros argue against Greece leaving the eurozone. Soros believes that 'economic deterioration and political and social reintegration will mutually reinforce each other' (Soros 2012). Consequently 'we need to find a European solution for the euro crisis because national solutions would lead to the dissolution of the EU, and that would be catastrophic' (Soros 2012).

The debate on the European common foreign policy is characterised by a similar argument:

While constructive abstention and opt-out provisions can be politically expedient, and can even increase decision-making efficiency, they also could weaken the perception of European-wide action in foreign policy. One could argue that constructive abstention or the exercise of an opt-out would violate a member state's duty of loyalty and mutual solidarity. The success of the EU's foreign policy might hinge on this issue. (Duquette 2003: 78)

Duquette's claim seems convincing at first glance. Denmark, for instance, maintains an opt-out from the EU's common defence policy and pulled its troops out of Bosnia when the EU took over from NATO in 2004. It sent them instead to Iraq to support the US-led war – against the wishes of France and Germany, among others. The problem with Duquette's solidarity claim is that Denmark was not the only country to support the US invasion. In fact, the EU was split in two over Iraq, suggesting that differentiation was not decisive for the crisis. Rather it was the diversity of national positions that prevented the EU from speaking with one voice on Iraq (Howorth 2003). It does not seem likely that one or two member states opting out would undermine the EU's foreign policy. Generally speaking, one should be very careful when arguing that national opt-outs are crucial to the success or failure of EU foreign policy, or any other EU policy for that matter.

In summary, for most legal scholars and observers, opt-outs represent an unwanted disintegration and breach of solidarity between member states. These strong objections may help to explain why the EU is so reluctant to grant member states exemptions from treaties. However, they do not explain why the integration project has survived despite the increasing number of national reservations and opt-outs. Moreover, self-critical reflection about their own normative position is often absent. This is where other scholars begin their attack.

Differentiation as a political vision for Europe

On the other side of the fence are those who caution against buying into traditional assumptions about the problems of opting out vis-à-vis the unity of the EU legal order. Some scholars even find that differentiation increases the likelihood of co-operation. Downs, Rocke and Barsoom (1998) have argued that deeper integration is generally possible if the states preferring more co-operation integrate first, allowing other states to join them later. Other scholars hail differentiated integration and opt-outs as means of developing new modes of governance that might even strengthen EU democracy. These scholars assume that neither the state nor the EU possesses ultimate supreme authority. In this light, opt-outs are an integral aspect of the 'post-sovereign' (MacCormick 2002) perspective in which sovereignty is shared, dispersed and disaggregated. From the pro-differentiation perspective, sovereignty is not a question of either-or but rather a question of both-and.

While the anti-differentiation camp sees opt-outs as expressions of national sovereignty, the pro-differentiation camp perceives them as part of a process whereby authority relationships become increasingly complex, as sovereign power is dispersed within the EU (Bellamy and Castiglione 2003: 19). Those in this second camp call for a pragmatic approach to EU law that takes into account the dynamics of integration and disintegration within the EU legal order (Dehousse 2003; Shaw 1996).[4] This camp of legal scholarship is joined by a diverse group of political and social scientists who are enthusiastic about the potential of differentiated integration, albeit for different reasons (e.g. Delanty and Rumford 2006; Habermas 2003; Schmitter 2001). As I will go on to show, the complexity of authority relationships is indeed an important element of European integration. However, this does not mean that decisions to opt out are seen as an example of best practice. On the contrary, the unity vision described above most often leads to such decisions earning the member state in question a reputation as a free rider.

Neomedievalism

Some have conceptualised the notion of a differentiated Europe as a form of neomedievalism. John Ruggie, for example, has influentially argued that the way in which EU members conduct their politics is reminiscent of medieval rule with its 'overlapping forms of authority' and 'non-exclusive forms of territoriality' (Ruggie 1993: 148–174).[5] Due to the de facto lack of a single legal order, the EU can be characterised as a 'polycentric' entity; a set of interlocking legal orders within which no one is privileged.[6] As Marlene Wind has argued, polycentrism

---

[4] Interestingly, this does not mean that the idea of a constitutionalised treaty must be abandoned. Rather, differentiation is taken as an indication of the evolving and subtle project of the constitutionalisation of the EU (Shaw 2000). Moreover, it supposes a break with the notion that a constitutional framework can only apply to states and not to contexts beyond the state (Wiener 2007a: 2–5).

[5] This debate can be linked back to Wolfers (1962) and Bull (1977: 254–255). For a detailed account of neomedievalism and its relevance to contemporary international relations, see Friedrich (2001).

[6] Neil MacCormick was an important representative of this approach. He believed that the 'suigenericity' of the EU ought to be upheld – that is, that the EU is neither an ordinary international organisation nor a state (MacCormick 2004: 14–15). For a powerful critique of polycentrism as a normative project, especially its potential neoliberal tendencies and hostility towards collective action, see Houtzager (2005).

is originally a legal concept according to which the law cannot be seen as a hierarchically unified system originating from an authoritative centre; instead the law increasingly derives from multiple sources due to decentralisation and internationalisation (Wind 2003).[7]

To understand what this neomedieval perspective implies, Neil Walker's notion of 'late sovereignty' is helpful to capture the immense legal and political transformations in Europe, particularly since the end of the Second World War.[8] In the age of late sovereignty, European states continue to claim territorial authority, but non-state polities also make claims to authority, often an authority that is bounded by function. Likewise, this is why opt-outs are not so much problematic as simply part of a wider tendency in European governance. Boundaries are no longer merely territorial; they have also become functional (Walker 2003: 3). Consequently the EU effectively claims authority over policy sectors such as international trade, agricultural and monetary policy. The development of such claims to functional competence does not mean that the territorial integrity of the state is threatened, but it allows for a new conception of authority relations with numerous boundary disputes in a pluralist constitutional order.

Zielonka (2006) suggests a similar perspective with his empire metaphor, which captures the EU's non-hierarchical structure, in which differentiation is a central element. He distinguishes between two possible models of future development of the EU: the Westphalian and neomedieval models (Zielonka 2001). The latter points towards overlapping authorities, divided sovereignty, diversified institutional arrangements and multiple identities, together with the acceptance of the right and opportunity to opt out. The former model points

---

[7] Polycentrism entails an order of numerous overlapping centres of legal authority and political control. It implies that there are 'no fixed hierarchical relations, and the relations of internal deviation that can be proved in a conflict do not exist in a stable form' (Wind 2003: 122). Polycentrism leads to a demand for new rights and new forms of political control and influence (Skelcher 2005).

[8] The crude distinction between two different phases of sovereignty in Europe involves ideal-type characterisations rather than all-embracing categories. Accepting this, however, one can describe the Westphalian phase as characterised by territorially separated states in a one-dimensional configuration of political and legal authority, whereas the late sovereign order has rival representational practices of state and non-state polities with overlapping legal and political authority and competences. Late sovereignty displays considerable continuity with the old order yet has distinctive features. Indeed, this combination of continuity and change is what renders 'late' sovereign diplomacy 'late' rather than 'post'.

towards the concentration of power, hierarchy, sovereignty and clear-cut identity.

A critique of Zielonka would begin by arguing that it remains unclear exactly how flexible integration is going to help democracy. Questions of accountability and the stability of the system remain unanswered. Also, in operational terms, it is difficult to see how the member states would agree to a mini-EU of 'open choice' policies. Finally, how is it that differentiated integration 'disperses power and brings governance structures closer to the citizens' (Zielonka 2007: 204)? Is it really easier for citizens to influence or identify with a political system that is deconcentrated, divided and fragmented? Yes, Zielonka argues: since there is no clearly identified hierarchical centre in the EU, 'the abuse of power is also less likely' (Zielonka 2007: 204). As we have seen, however, critics adhering to the unity vision would argue that the lack of clear hierarchies renders it more difficult to hold political leaders to account. Consequently, when viewed against the backdrop of transparency, Zielonka's neomedieval empire may quickly lose its appeal.

However, Zielonka is far from alone in promoting the idea that differentiated integration, including national opt-outs, will help to solve the EU's legitimacy deficit. Kalypso Nicolaïdis (2001), for instance, also argues that the EU gains legitimacy by becoming more differentiated, in the sense that it becomes more responsive to the plural interests and identities of its citizens. On a more radical note, Frey and Eichenberger (1999; 2000) propose a whole new EU based on voluntary and partial co-operation that cuts across territorial borders, focuses on specific policies and is legitimated by direct democracy. Opting in and out is a central feature of this utopian model. Their alternative consists of a new European construction characterised by selective and 'partial entry' in functional, overlapping, competing jurisdictions (FOCJ). Each citizen decides for themselves which FOCJ they want to be a member of. The functions (be they education, environment, military etc.) must be self-financed and with a minimum of costs. The jurisdictions or units are created on the basis of functional needs and can overlap geographically or functionally. Frey and Eichenberger's proposal is fascinating but raises difficulties. They basically ignore the historical stability of the state system, the symbolic importance and popular attachment to the notion of sovereignty, as well as the enormous challenges of creating transparency and legal certainty in a system with overlapping and competing units.

In summary, the pro-differentiation camp is united by an enthusiasm for conceiving governance beyond the state. As such, it provides an important counter-argument to the dominant and sceptical interpretation of opt-outs. By questioning accepted understandings of the European legal and political order, this camp suggests the possibility of opt-outs as prototypical arrangements for the future of European governance. Aside from the refreshing intellectual creativity of these alternative approaches, they have yet to demonstrate their value to a more detailed understanding of the actual dynamics of integration.

The limitations of IR and integration theory

Turning to IR and specifically European integration theories (which a priori should be interested in differentiated integration) to find an answer is hardly encouraging. De Neve writes that 'all theories of European integration – both rationalist and constructivist – [should] be revisited to come up with a satisfactory analysis of the processes of differentiated integration' (de Neve 2007: 515). Despite the considerable political attention directed towards the opt-out phenomenon, few students of European integration have analysed how national exemptions relate to European integration. As I will show here, most of these analyses suffer from an undertheorised understanding of the state and national interests.

One possible reason for integration theory's inability to account for the emergence of differentiation is that it traditionally focuses on 'homogenous integration', where integration is understood to be more or less uniform across states (Andersen and Sitter 2006). While there are a range of theories addressing the 'normal' mode of integration under the headings of 'federalism', 'neofunctionalism' and 'intergovernmentalism', there seems to be no place for the opt-out in existing theories of European integration. Substantive EU opt-outs are theoretically perplexing because they represent an exemption to the general mode of European integration. In the most systematic and detailed mapping of differentiated integration to date, Leuffen, Rittberger and Schimmelfennig (2012) apply intergovernmentalism (both its realist and its liberalist versions), supranationalism (neofunctionalism and historical institutionalism) and constructivism to different cases of differentiation: the single market; the EMU; security and defence; and AFSJ. Their impressive study concludes that 'no single theory offers an exclusively valid, complete, or completely convincing

explanation of integration and differentiation in all four policy areas'
(Leuffen et al. 2012: 259).

The real problem, however, goes even deeper. Despite theorists'
various assumptions about what drives integration, the notion that
opt-outs reflect one unitary national interest is never questioned in
integration theory. Even Leuffen and his colleagues (2012), who adopt
a nuanced view on integration, argue that 'the propensity of a country
to steer clear of or opt-out from integration is a function of the distance
of its material or ideational preferences from the mainstream: preference outliers are most likely to stay out or opt-out' (Leuffen et al. 2012:
261). However, not only can a government and/or population be deeply
split over whether to introduce or keep the opt-outs (as has been the case
in both the UK and Denmark) but also the national representatives
managing these opt-outs may not fully identify with them. As I will
show, this assumption about one unitary national interest blinds us not
only to important dynamics of differentiation, inclusion and exclusion
within the EU but also to how European integration and international
co-operation work more generally.

The blind alley of liberal intergovernmentalism

Liberal intergovernmentalists argue that regional integration is based
upon situations in which the government aggregates the preferences of
domestic groups into a consistent preference before carrying out international negotiations (Moravcsik 1993). Liberal intergovernmentalism
reproduces an image of member state relations in which the inside and
outside of the state are clearly demarcated by diplomacy (Moravcsik
1993: 23). In this context, diplomacy is the art of bridge-building, which
constitutes the state as a state; a separate entity, which acts and has
national interests that are distinct and separate from those of other
states. Consequently, an opt-out protocol does nothing more than
express the outcome of intergovernmental bargains reflecting the preferences of a participating state.

From this perspective the handling of sovereignty claims should be
straightforward as they represent a national preference like any other.
As Moravcsik writes, 'member governments are no longer as willing
as they once were to accept all obligations [...] Deeper cooperation is
increasingly achieved through exemptions and special arrangements as
well as opt-outs by recalcitrant countries' (Moravcsik 1998: 5). Liberal

intergovernmentalists expect the interests of the increasing number of
member states to continue to differ, and that conflicts over financial
redistribution will intensify – 'Varying numbers of participants and a
proliferation of opt-outs constitute a lawyer's nightmare but may be
the most effective means of maintaining efficient EU policymaking'
(Moravcsik 1998: 48). Certainly, as we have seen, lawyers tend to be
critical of differentiated integration, but Moravcsik leaves no clues to
help us to understand the actual effects of sovereignty safeguards on EU
policy-making. As I will aim to demonstrate, liberal intergovernmentalism fails to address differentiated integration because it relies on a
preconceived view of how sovereignty is managed. Indeed, rationalist-
oriented perspectives, when accounting for the effects of opt-outs on
member states' positions, have a tendency to resort to ad hoc explanations that build on implicit constructivist assumptions.

The integration dilemma

Kölliker (2001; 2006) explains the prevalence of differentiated integration
more generally by arguing that if we assume that states act according to
calculated costs and benefits, we can use public goods theory to uncover
the logic of differentiated European integration. This logic implies that
the character of a 'good' (e.g. security, money, information) produced in
a policy area determines whether opt-outs from that policy area are
likely to create permanent or preliminary divisions between the member
states. Kölliker essentially argues that the long-term consequences of
any instance of differentiated integration depend on the nature of the
'good' that it aims to generate.[9] Different kinds of good generate different
incentives: excludable network goods provide the strongest incentive to
join, whereas the regulation of common pool resources is costly to those
contributing most (insiders), as others (outsiders) can merrily exploit
the resource while contributing little or nothing, thus making it unlikely
that new states will join such a co-operation agreement.

The problem is this: when considering the two areas which are of
special interest to us here, the EMU and the AFSJ, Kölliker's theory

---

[9] Some goods have 'centrifugal' effects (that induce initially unwilling outsiders to
join the group of co-operating states), whereas others have 'centripetal' effects
(that drive states further away from co-operation or leave them indifferent).
Whether centrifugal or centripetal effects ensue is largely determined by the degree
of excludability and the rivalry of consumption.

performs somewhat poorly. From the perspective of a cost–benefit calculus, one would expect the member states to have an interest in bringing the UK in as a full member of Schengen (see Kölliker 2006: 59). The free movement of persons can be seen as a 'club good', meaning that its value increases as more actors use it, and excluding others from using it remains simple. In Chapter 6 I will seek an explanation for why the UK is not allowed to participate in parts of Schengen as it wishes.

Kölliker's theory is also unsatisfactory as regards the EMU. According to Kölliker, the potential network effect (the value of a product or service increases with the number of users) would also have us see the UK and Denmark (and Sweden) joining the EMU. The common currency can be conceptualised as an excludable network good where additional users add to the benefit that other users draw from it (Kölliker 2006: 58). This has not happened. Furthermore, if the euro area members were interested in attracting more members, why have they formed the euro-group, which deliberately excludes the non-euro ministers (Puetter 2006)?

While the literature on flexibility and co-operation in international organisations suggests that a multispeed Europe may lead to increased co-operation by offering both sceptical and pro-European states options within the same organisation, the rationalist bargaining literature, based upon Hirschman's (1970) influential exit, voice and loyalty framework (e.g. Bednar 2007; Dowding et al. 2000; Gelbach 2006; Slapin 2009), offers insights into how the creation of a multispeed Europe is likely to affect bargaining power among member states. When faced with a proposal on integration that they oppose, member states have the option to voice their discontent, perhaps by vetoing policy change, or to opt out of the policy, akin to a partial exit from the EU. Which of these strategies states choose (and, indeed, which strategy is even available) depends on the costs associated with allowing the reluctant states to opt out (Slapin 2009). Generally, this literature suggests that the sceptics and EU-sceptics alike must weigh the costs and benefits of deeper integration against the costs and benefits of pursuing integration in smaller groups. It does not, however, explain in detail how these cost–benefit calculations are performed.

This is where Leuffen, Rittberger and Schimmelfennig's (2012) syn-thetic framework fares better. It is essentially an intergovernmentalist approach that seeks to explain and predict when the EU develops vertical (policy-area) and horizontal (number of states) differentiation.

To explain differentiation, they argue that we need to look at governmental preferences (demand) and negotiation processes. The clue to the framework is the introduction of important scope conditions. First, as they argue, governmental preferences change over time as the member states become more deeply involved in a policy area, which becomes centralised. This makes it 'more likely that the preferences of governments are shaped and constrained by integration' (Leuffen et al 2012: 263). Overall, at the initial stage of integration, Leuffen, Rittberger and Schimmelfennig expect intergovernmentalism to provide most of the explanation whereas supranationalism and constructivism gain in strength 'once a critical stage in integration is reached' (Leuffen et al 2012: 264). Adding to this is the degree of politicisation: the more a policy touches upon a 'core area of state autonomy and national identity', the more likely we are to see differentiation. Overall, the approach provides a useful overview of the important factors that lead to differentiated integration. However, the framework does not look at how differentiation works in practice once it has been established.

A number of researchers have enquired into the effects of opt-outs on the position of member states (Larsen 2000; Petersen 1998; Tonra 2000; Wallace 2000; Williams 2005). The most usual conclusion is that states such as the UK and Denmark are experiencing a real loss of influence due to their opt-outs. This account of a how opting out can leave a country on the periphery lends support to the concept of an 'integration dilemma'. This implies that all states (and especially small states) face a dilemma when reaching a certain stage in the process of supranational political integration. This involves an uncomfortable choice between becoming entrapped in the EU by surrendering substantial political authority and being abandoned by the integration system by insisting on preserving formal, state-based sovereignty (Petersen 1998: 35). From this perspective the UK and (perhaps even more so) Denmark have, by virtue of their opt-outs, moved along the continuum towards autonomy and away from integration.[10] In short, the concept of the integration dilemma relies on the assumption that member states with opt-outs have traded some of their influence for increased autonomy.

---

[10] Studies of associated members or quasi-EU members, such as Norway and Switzerland, have richly demonstrated this trade-off associated with differentiated integration (Church 2007; Emerson et al. 2002; Kux and Sverdrup 2000).

From a rationalist perspective, participants in regional integration are expected to act in a value-maximising manner and will naturally attempt to find the point where they have the greatest influence and autonomy. But there will inevitably be a trade-off between the two 'goods': integration and autonomy (Petersen 1998: 37). According to this approach, autonomy and influence can be seen in black and white; either the country is allowed to participate in the adoption of a given measure or not (assuming that, by adopting legislation, a state may participate in the decision-making process). The integration dilemma is based on an assumption of a hard-bargaining game, but the consensus-oriented EU decision-making process may enable states to influence policy decisions despite the loss of their right to vote. The EU is not simply an institutional framework; it has developed into a distinct social community with its own rules of play. If more than 70 per cent of the decisions in the Council of Ministers are taken by consensus (Hayes-Renshaw et al. 2006: Heisenberg 2005; Lewis 2003; Häge 2012), this challenges the clear-cut integration dilemma between autonomy and influence.

The integration dilemma is founded on a narrow conception of influence: the understanding that influence capability is the 'ability to influence other actors to do what they would not otherwise do' (Wivel and Mourtizen 2005: 53). However, scholars who apply the integration dilemma in empirical analysis unwittingly end up presenting the dilemma between influence and autonomy as being (at least partly) intersubjectively constructed. Thus, for example, an opt-out earns a state a reputation as 'a naughty boy' (Mouritzen 2003: 309). As Petersen explains, 'the limited identification with Union goals and the associated "footdragging" image has limited Denmark's influence on Union affairs although it is difficult to prove by how much' (Petersen 1998: 48). Reputation and impressions enter the rationalist equation to help to explain marginalisation. How exactly this reputation is earned remains unclear. Moreover, if reputation and impressions matter, then influence must be analysed differently. Influence instead becomes linked to epistemic power – that is, the ability to shape the understandings of others and the ability to engender specific understandings of the situation. This suggests that differentiation works rather differently from how rationalists assume. Indeed, I will argue that we must look at other aspects of the integration process to understand the inclusionary and exclusionary dynamics within the EU.

The implicit intergovernmentalism of multilevel governance

For many observers, rationalist state-centric approaches such as liberal intergovernmentalism and public choice theory have not sufficiently helped an understanding of the radical nature of European integration. Multilevel governance approaches are usually perceived as the main challengers to state-centred interpretations of the EU and, one should think, also the traditional vision of integration (Aalberts 2004; Marks et al. 1996). In the multilevel governance approach, the state is but one of many actors or levels in a multidimensional order characterised by increasing specialisation and the socialisation of national representatives (Héritier 1999; Hix 1998; Scharpf 2001).

From this perspective the EU is not seen as an ordinary multilateral setting but rather as a partly supranational one, in which actors such as the European Commission and the European Parliament are included in the negotiation process (Bátora 2005: 56). Nevertheless, multilevel governance scholars usually assume that national representatives defend particular national interests and speak solely for their states. The Council of Ministers apparatus – consisting of the Council of Ministers, the EU presidency and COREPER (the Committee of Permanent Representatives) and its working groups – is seen as being responsible for defending individual national preferences. The assumption is that the territorial principle predominates in the Council of Ministers, while the functional, or 'European', principle prevails in the supranational institutions (Laffan 2004: 84). This second principle requires that the supranational institutions, which are formally independent of the member states, are responsible for policy initiation and promoting the common European interest. Consequently, and also according to the multilevel governance interpretation, an opt-out constitutes a political decision based on a wish to protect national interests.

Somewhat strikingly, while recognising the complex character of EU decision-making, multilevel governance scholars still see the Council of Ministers as representing national interests and traditional diplomatic bargaining. Although multilevel governance scholars have pinpointed the changes in the governance structure of the EU, including informal contact between public and private actors and technocratisation, they have generally refrained from exploring identity formation processes within the Council of Ministers (Hix 1998; Marks 1996).

So while the supranational institutions are seen as powerful, most multilevel governance-inspired scholars are inclined to assume that the member states' diplomatic practices remain fundamentally unchanged. Indeed, Council of Ministers negotiations can be said to uphold the sovereign order in Europe. Yet if state interaction in the EU is viewed only from this perspective, a number of important qualitative changes will remain underexposed.

Socialisation

Most government reports and investigations support the argument that the opt-out states are marginalised because they are perceived as unwilling by other European member states. The Swedish Calmfors Commission report of 1997 argued that by choosing not to participate in the Community's most important project to date, Sweden would be removing itself from the EU's inner core, and Swedish representatives would be regarded as reluctant Europeans. The country would ultimately lose influence, even in areas not covered by the opt-out (Calmfors et al. 1997; Gamble and Kelly 2002: 102). In a 2000 report to the Danish government, the Danish Foreign Policy Institute (DUPI) concluded that not only did the opt-outs hinder participation in ever larger parts of concrete policy areas but:

[t]he opt-outs also have consequences in a wider sense for Denmark's influence on the [European] cooperation, and these consequences will increase in the years to come. Not least when it comes to the continued development of the cooperation such as agenda-setting, there is a close connection between *co-responsibility* and *co-influence*. In all forms of international cooperation, the participants that are perceived as interested in taking responsibility for the whole, ceteris paribus, will have greater influence than those who are perceived as only being occupied with their own interests. (Dansk Udenrigspolitisk Institut 2000: 264, my translation and italics)

If systematically re-exploring this argument today, one would have to examine the concrete ways in which the opt-outs marginalise the UK and Denmark by giving them a bad name. How are 'co-responsibility' and 'co-influence' linked? And how is 'ceteris paribus' to be understood? It would become necessary to analyse the connection between the opt-out protocols and respective abilities of the UK and Denmark to be accepted as 'good and constructive Europeans'.

Perceptions arguably play an important role. But how? Some research-ers examining perceptions and opt-outs on the European scene claim that the reason why member states with opt-outs lose influence is not because they have lost their voting right but because the opt-outs represent a breach of the established norms in the Council of Ministers (e.g. Allen 2005; Geddes 2005; Kelstrup 2006; Rosamond 2004: 197–198; Teague 2000). Accordingly the opt-outs affect member state influence by contri-buting to an image of the UK and Denmark as member states which fail to participate wholeheartedly in the EU. Here, influence is linked to the ability to be accepted as a 'good and constructive European'; to gain a reputation as a core country (Larsen 1999; Wæver 1995).

Andrew Geddes thus finds that, because the UK has not followed the norm of consensus-seeking and has not shared the same convictions as other member states, it has not been a 'particularly effective player of the EU game' (Geddes 2004: 228). If reputation as a 'good European' is so important, it is striking that there is no distinction drawn between voluntary and involuntary euro-outsiderness (see also Howarth 2005: 134). While some member states do not wish to be part of the currency union, others, notably the new EU members in Central and Eastern Europe, have been more determined to gain entry to the euro area. It is also well known that Ireland only opted out of Schengen because of the common travel area with the UK (Meehan 2000a: 96). Does it matter whether an opt-out from Schengen or the EMU is voluntary or involuntary?

Helen Wallace has criticised the idea that opt-outs represent govern-ment preferences, suggesting that interparty politics may be just as decisive for the negotiation and permanence of the British opt-outs (Wallace 1995). Indeed, we need to deepen our understanding of the complex process of promoting national interests – and sovereignty claims – if we are to grasp the dynamics of European integration. Studies of public debates on the EU in the UK and Denmark provide valuable insights concerning the 'tensions' and 'awkwardness' charac-terising British and Danish EU policy (Flockhart 2005; Haahr 2003; Hansen 2002; Schmidt 2006). Flockhart, for instance, sees opt-outs as expressions of a gap between a Europeanised elite and a eurosceptic population (Flockhart 2005: 258). Yet this view has not been applied in studies of how opt-outs are managed. Instead, what is meant by opting out is taken to be static and unambiguous; a representation of the reluctant UK or Denmark, preoccupied with national sovereignty

(Hedetoft 2000: 300; Padoa-Schioppa 2006: 86–87; Peterson 1999: 268; Pilkington 1995: 109ff; Wallace 1997). Opt-outs continue to be analysed as crude expressions of a national interest, which is assumed to be an identifiable, agreed-upon 'thing'.

In fact, the original motivation behind an opt-out (which in itself may be widely contested domestically) need not be shared by the politico-administrative elite (Miles 2005a: 6). While national representatives are key managers of opt-outs in the Council of Ministers, our focus on conventional diplomatic actors should not entail a simplistic reading of their practices and how they handle opt-outs. Instead, to obtain a deeper understanding of how opt-outs function in practice, and how they may impact on the position of a member state, we must explore the numerous legal objections to the introduction of opt-outs and how the formal opt-outs may contribute to moulding British and Danish officials as certain types of player. Of course – and this is a key point – for a national representative attending meetings in Brussels, national interests have a very concrete meaning. Indeed, for governments and their administrations, the EU continues to represent a clearly different level of negotiation, demarcated from the domestic. British officials must still go to Brussels for working group meetings and do not come empty-handed (or -headed); they inevitably come armed with instructions from London about specific goals and interests that they are expected to defend during the meetings.

As mentioned in Chapter 1, constructivist research has contributed greatly towards understanding socialisation, particularly by suggesting the scope of conditions necessary for the socialisation of national representatives in international organisations (Checkel 2005; Zurn and Checkel 2005). However, socialisation approaches have hitherto seen this development of 'dual loyalties' as unproblematic; they help the integration process but do not transform the position of the state (Wong 2011). I propose to go one step further by arguing that learning processes are only effective when embedded in a greater understanding of what makes them meaningful. If the state is an abstraction given life and meaning through social action – that is, through the practices of human beings – we must give attention to how this representation is formulated. For instance, do national officials experience the 'integration dilemma'? How do they handle the many objections raised against the opt-outs? How is integration experienced by those negotiating in Brussels?

Remarkably, researchers with a constructivist slant seem to fail – just as rationalists do – to acknowledge the possibility that there need not be an inevitable consequence of opting out. Legal scholars have gone to great lengths to map the legally challenging effects of opt-outs, but how rules matter politically beyond their legal implications depends on the social context (the Council of Ministers) and actors who interpret and manage them (see also Curtin 2006). Methodologically, the focus should encompass situations where perceptions of national interests are transformed. This means analysing not only the causal but also the constitutive effects that opt-outs may have on member state diplomacy. In this context, national exemptions may affect national strategies by contributing to a particular self-understanding among British and Danish officials – for instance, as national representatives who do not participate wholeheartedly in the EU (Kassim and Peters 2001).

Conclusion

EU research projects a murky image of the EU under threat of disintegration. There are a number of reasons why opt-outs are seen as problematic – for example, they undermine the EU's unified legal order and breach the solidarity between member states. So differential integration is detrimental to the already problematic state of affairs concerning democracy and legitimacy in the EU.

In contrast to these objections to opt-outs, representing the dominant view, a pro-differentiation camp celebrates the EU as a multilayered and late-sovereign political order. From this perspective the notion that opt-outs threaten the legal and political order of the EU must be mitigated by the knowledge that new modes of regional governance are necessary and may even help to resolve the so-called democratic deficit. This is the broad idea that EU institutions lack democratic accountability and legitimacy compared with the national governments of its member states. In other words, opt-outs are part of a solution. However, there is no compelling body of evidence available to settle the dispute between the sceptics and the advocates of differentiated integration. Rather, the dispute rests on the underlying differences in perspective.

Strikingly, whether they believe that opt-outs are harmful or helpful, scholars continue to see them as paradigmatic expressions of national sovereignty. Opt-outs are seen to reflect what Neil Walker refers to as an 'ideological assumption of ultimate authority over the internal operation of the polity' (Walker 2003: 26). Yet by focusing strictly on their original motivation or how they appear to express a principled claim to national sovereignty, existing approaches to European integration – whether they belong in the anti- or pro-differentiation camp – ignore the fact that sovereignty is not merely claimed but also managed. Remarkably, scholars of different convictions suggest that an opt-out is a relatively stable institutional arrangement or collective identity position on the European scene. In contrast, I believe that it is necessary to question the assumed unitary character of the state's interest in order to really understand how the EU works.

European integration studies have generally refrained from looking at the role of national opt-outs in the integration process, and only a few scholars have analysed how measures of differentiation have been negotiated. This is surprising given the role that differentiation continues to play in public debates about the EU. As should be clear from the above, previous research – to the degree that it engages with the areas of research addressed here – suffers predominantly from being overly focused on the theoretical assumptions about how a state is influential in daily negotiations (e.g. due to its voting power), instead of grounding these assumptions in real-life practice.

Chapter 3 will offer an alternative political sociological approach to European integration. To do this it is necessary to consider those responsible for European integration, and, as a consequence, the state and its national interests become more fluid than in the approaches already discussed. With this approach, however, we may begin to understand the everyday dynamics of European integration.

3 | A political sociology of European integration

Introduction

This chapter develops a political sociological approach to European integration. It focuses particularly on the EU's Council of Ministers. Instead of regarding the EU as a result of the ongoing promotion of different national interests, I argue that member state diplomats and officials are not just representatives of their masters (the states) but also defenders of a particular European order. By exploring this European order in detail, this chapter reveals the smoke and mirrors employed in top-down theories that are characteristic of both IR theory and European integration studies. The everyday processes of negotiating and working together, including the virtually hidden social hierarchies, are crucial to how the EU functions. They give both form and content to overly abstracted concepts of national interests. The basic idea of this chapter is that diplomacy in the EU should be understood as a world of its own.

In this chapter I draw on the work of Pierre Bourdieu and Erving Goffman. My aim is to help us to visualise the EU as a transnational field where national representatives share a particular Europeanised *sens pratique*, a feel for the game (see also Pouliot 2008). Within this field there is a power struggle to define new legislation and projects for the EU. It is in this environment that an opt-out becomes a stigma – a discrediting mark on national representatives. The chapter concludes with an analytical model, and outlines the limitations and possibilities that diplomats face when managing stigma. This model highlights the links between diplomatic microstrategies and international macroprocesses of inclusion and exclusion. It focuses on how to uncover hierarchies and exclusion from the professional, day-to-day negotiations between states.

Bringing political sociology into IR and EU theory

Political sociology provides a fruitful alternative to existing integration theories. Specifically, it provides a deeper understanding of why opt-outs are so controversial and why member states are punished for them. Political sociology reveals that international organisations (such as the EU) do not merely revolve around positive community values and co-operation. The definition of those states that deviate from the norm is also important to the constitution of the EU. As I will explain in more detail below, member states produce, strengthen and consolidate particular perceptions of normal state behaviour through stigmatisation within a particular diplomatic field.

Political sociology is interdisciplinary and can be found where political science and sociology intersect.[1] Within IR, political sociology and the so-called practice turn has been promoted by scholars such as Emanuel Adler, Iver B. Neumann and Vincent Pouliot (Adler and Pouliot 2011; Pouliot 2007; Neumann 2002). They build on the work of French political sociologist Pierre Bourdieu (1977) and the British sociologist Anthony Giddens (1984), who, in different ways, have insisted that there is a mutual relationship between social structure and social action. In EU studies there has been a real buzz around political sociology, culminating in Adrian Favell and Virginie Guiraudon's 2009 programmatic article in *European Union Politics* and the edited volume *Sociology and the European Union* from 2011. This has led to an increasing number of sophisticated and empirically grounded analyses of European integration.[2]

Of course, political sociology's focus on social norms and control as intrinsic to the construction of order is far from unique. Constructivists (Finnemore and Sikkink 2001) as well as critical theorists and post-structuralists, have been interested in disciplining processes for many years (Edkins 1999). In addition, literature about socialisation in international organisations, such as NATO and the EU, has helped us to understand the disciplining of states and their diplomats, particularly by suggesting the scope of conditions for when socialisation takes place (Zurn and Checkel 2005; Checkel 2005; Ghieco 2005). Socialisation can be interpreted as a 'process of inducting agents into the norms and rules of a given community' (Checkel 2005: 804), which results in the agents following the logic of appropriateness (i.e. norm-guided behaviour). However, the question of what happens when these norms are

---

[1] A major focus of political sociology is the description, analysis and explanation of the state. For an introduction to political sociology, see Faulks (1999).
[2] For an overview, see Saurruger and Mérand (2010).

contested or rejected (such as when states choose to opt out of an organisation) has not been thoroughly investigated (Johnston 2001: 492–439). Scholars have researched the use of social rewards, punishments or shaming to socialise agents into acceptance – for example, human rights (Risse and Sikkink 1999). They have focused on how states can be encouraged to demonstrate 'pro-normative' behaviour, but have downplayed the rejection of social norms (Johnston 2001: 510). In other words, there is a need for a theory that looks beyond the one-way disciplining process. Therefore the aim of this chapter is provide an account of European integration that emphasises interaction and change in an more unplanned way. Instead of interpreting European integration as a one-way process, I will explore the negotiation of social order in the EU as an interactive process.

In his sociological work, Bourdieu attempted to overcome the division between structuralism and individualism, and he demonstrated the importance of social hierarchies that connect social and mental structures. He argued that social and mental structures are interlinked by a twofold relationship of mutual constitution and correspondence, rather than a dialectical relationship. This does not mean that people are less constrained than they are in a rationalist framework, but the constraints that people are facing are often socially produced, including through stigma. Compared with Giddens' structuration theory (Giddens 1984), Bourdieu offers a more concrete toolbox, which includes the concepts of field, habitus, capital and doxa. In *The State Nobility: Elite Schools in the Field of Power* (1989), for instance, Bourdieu presents a form of total anthropology, which surpasses the opposition between exploration and explanation, combining a range of methods, including interviews, statistics, auto-anthropology and participant observation. *The State Nobility* analyses the practical taxonomies and activities through which teachers and students collectively produce the French elite schools' everyday reality as a meaningful life world. Bourdieu argues that educational titles become a prerequisite – a capital – for ascent to the apex of private corporations and public bureaucracies. The educational system, despite its formalised meritocracy, becomes a mode of domination whereby the ruling class maintains itself in France (see also Adler-Nissen 2012).

While Bourdieu's theory corresponds, to a large degree, with the IR version of social constructivism (see Guzzini 2000; Leander 2005; Pouliot 2007; Kauppi 2003; Jackson 2008), there are also huge differences, particularly in analytical strategies: IR constructivists tend to focus on norm transfer, socialisation and localisation, but they avoid connecting these phenomena to the lived and embodied individual experiences at an everyday level, be it as a European Commission official, a consultant for an interest group or an unemployed EU citizen testing their case for social benefits in another EU member state at the ECJ. Experience, however, is a strong element in political sociology, specifically in Bourdieu's method. He links daily human experiences of taste, knowledge and humiliation (and its intersubjective character) with the more permanent structures of domination, such as the education system, which partly determines the individual and collective ways of thinking (Mérand and Pouliot 2008: 610). He studied microsociological practices such as marriage, graduation and gift-giving rituals to understand how structures of symbolic power and exclusion are reproduced. Such rituals have been overlooked in much IR theory despite their importance in international negotiations.

The diplomatic field

Bourdieu's political sociology was originally devised for the domestic level, but it also fits well with politics beyond the state. In order to develop this argument, it is necessary to address the concept of field, which is central to Bourdieu's work. This concept supports a key statement in this chapter: diplomats and national representatives need to be separated analytically from the abstract notion of state. The result is that member state diplomacy in the EU must be understood on its own terms, not as an extension of the state.

Bourdieu's concept of field can be defined as a relatively autonomous social system comprising a pattern of practices and beliefs, which encourage conforming with rules and roles. A field is a historically derived system of shared meanings, which define agency and make action intelligible (Moi 1991: 1021). Within any field, agents develop a particular sense of the social game, including what is considered to be appropriate and inappropriate and how to be strategic (Lamaison and Bourdieu 1989).

There are many fields (e.g. the academic field, the artistic field and the political field) in which different practices take place (Guzzini 2000: 165). Each field can be divided into sites or sub-fields.[3] The stratification

---

[3] Bourdieu used the concept of sub-fields to designate the division of the French field of education into sub-fields of *les grandes écoles* vs. the sub-field of state

of a field is based on different forms of capital (e.g. economic, social and cultural capital; the concept of capital is discussed in more detail below). Agents compete for certain specific types of capital within the field; each field has a particular mix of relevant capital, and power cannot be easily imported into a new field. For example, having considerable economic capital in the cultural field does not (necessarily) help you to become an esteemed artist (Guzzini 2000: 165). People who occupy social positions inside the field take on roles of domination, subordination or equivalence by virtue of the access that they have to the capital that is at stake in the field.

While Bourdieu developed the concept of field for analysing power structures within a national society, it has also been used in a number of studies of inter- and transnational issues (Dezalay and Garth 1995). Some migration scholars use field theory to describe migrants as people who neither belong completely to their home state nor totally assimilate into the new state:

> Individuals within transnational social fields combine ways of being and ways of belonging differently in specific contexts. One person might have many social contacts with people in their country of origin but not identify at all as belonging to their homeland. (Lewitt and Schiller 2004: 1010)

What if British and Danish representatives, like some migrants, feel loyal to both their own state and its opt-outs, and to the transnational diplomatic field in which they are attempting to achieve influence? Of course, unlike migrants, diplomats identify (at least formally) with their own country, as their professional task is to defend national interests abroad. However, when national representatives meet in Brussels, the state is no longer the structuring and dominant field of power (as is the case of Bourdieu's work). It is the transnational field in which they meet that defines their positions.

The idea here is to take neither the 'internal' nor the 'external' perspectives on the state. Instead, I propose that we think of the diplomatic interaction in and through the field, because member state interaction cannot be described simply as the mediation between the domestic and the European levels. The European diplomatic field, as a site, thus becomes the centre of the analysis. In this site, the state cannot be understood in the same way as in the 'domestic' analysis of, for example, French

universities (Bourdieu 1989: 74). See also Niilo Kauppi's application of the concept of sub-field in his article on the EU and political sociology (Kauppi 2003).

culture production or educational systems. It is within this diplomatic field that the stakes are defined and power positions are distributed among national representatives. By thinking in terms of a field, one may develop more nuanced understandings of the interaction in the EU's Council of Ministers and raise questions as to how the national interest is promoted in the EU.

To what degree national societies and state apparatuses (with their particular social hierarchies) fade into the background when national representatives meet in Brussels is an empirical question, but a struggle does take place here – a struggle that is relatively autonomous from those within the member states. I will discuss the question of dual loyalties in the Council of Ministers in the subsequent subsection on habitus.

Building on the above, we can visualise the Council of Ministers and its working groups (the key intergovernmental decision-making forums in the EU) as a field in the Bourdieusian sense. The Council of Ministers comprises a relatively homogenous international group of bureaucratic and political elites, including ministers and officials from all member states. It constitutes a social system, which follows its own laws and logics in formal and informal hierarchies – from the rotating Presidency to the working group lowest in the hierarchy.

The entry criteria are quite strict. The field is reserved for official representatives from the member states and EU institutions; experts are occasionally invited. For example, it would not be possible for an Iranian diplomat to participate in a Strategic Committee on Immigration, Frontiers and Asylum (SCIFA) meeting. SCIFA is a working group of senior officials under the Council of Ministers. The same applies to a representative from a refugee non-governmental organisation. In this sense the Council of Ministers is an exclusive institution with a limited number of participants, most of whom have accepted that the setting (the EU) is important in its own terms and not merely considered to be a vehicle for reaching specific agreements (Lewis 2005).

As in all fields, nothing is more important than sticking to the rules of the game (Bourdieu 1992: 179–180). Indeed, participation in the field requires unspoken acknowledgement of both the existence and the logic of its structures. Crucially, not all negotiators accept this idea. British Conservative ministers have argued that the setting is merely a means to promote British interests (Hayes-Renshaw and Wallace 1997). However, the day-to-day work in the Council of Ministers, particularly in the Committee of Permanent Representatives (COREPER) and council working groups, is characterised by a method of bargaining in which joint problem-solving is a prominent feature (Beyers 2005: 123).

The Council of Ministers is made up of the ministers and officials of the member states. It meets in ten different configurations depending on the subjects under discussion. For example, the 'Foreign Affairs' configuration is made up of foreign affairs ministers and officials; the 'Agriculture and Fisheries' configuration of agriculture and fisheries ministers and officials; and so on. The configuration of the EMU is different from that of AFSJ. Evidently the two areas are different when it comes to their regulative norms and what they 'produce'. In the EMU, co-operation on economic and financial policies takes place predominately through policy co-ordination; and in AFSJ, co-operation in the areas of migration, refugees, civil law, criminal law and police is carried out predominantly through hard and soft legislation. As discussed in Chapter 2, some policy areas are potentially better 'suited' to differentiated integration than others. As a result, opt-outs may have different outcomes in the various sub-fields.

Brussels beyond socialisation – habitus

The previous section referred to the possibility that national representatives feel bound by the official positions of their home state and the informal values of the field in which they negotiate. While a rationalist image of international negotiations assumes that formal decision rules and utilitarian interest calculations determine bargaining outcomes, a sociological perspective emphasises the importance of informal norms as a crucial factor in negotiations (Lewis 2000: 265–266). Iver B. Neumann has called for the use of Bourdieu's concept of 'habitus' to explain diplomatic culture. He encourages us to explore the extent to which a particular habitus is shared across national cultures or is specific to each foreign ministry (Neumann 2002: 23). The habitus can be defined as the unconscious adoption of rules, values and dispositions gained from an individual and collective history. It functions like the materialisation of collective memory and is a disposition to act, perceive and think in a particular way that conforms to the field over time (Bourdieu 1994: 163). This raises a number of intriguing questions: is there a common identifiable habitus among national representatives working in Brussels? To what extent do British and Danish representatives share a particular 'European' habitus? And can that be used to shed some light on their management of the opt-outs? While the concept of field provides an understanding of the social system of the Council of Ministers, the habitus is directly linked to practice and is useful to understand how opt-outs relate to the diplomatic strategies of the national representatives.

There are different views regarding the degree to which national officials are socialised when they engage in international negotiations. Arguably, social interaction between nation-state representatives is much more intensive in the EU than anywhere else in the world, and it increases the possibility of loyalties being transferred. In addition, 'social learning is more likely where a group meets repeatedly and there is a high density of interaction among participants' (Checkel 2001: 26). A number of studies of the Council of Ministers support the understanding that national representatives overtake supranational allegiances in Council working groups and COREPER meetings. This could result in adherence to the EU system, meaning that officials develop 'dual loyalties' (Trondal 2004: 22; see also Kassim and Peters 2001: 298; Bátora 2005).[4]

Scholars such as Uwe Puetter go even further and argue that what goes on in the Council of Ministers is neither hard bargaining nor pragmatic negotiations according to informal norms, but deliberation (Puetter 2006: 17–29; see also Aus 2009; Niemann 2009). Deliberation (or what some call the logic of arguing) can be defined as 'trying to reach agreement through the force of the better argument – convincing others of the right thing to do – rather than bargaining via threats and promises' (Naurin and Wallace 2009: 10). However, in their landmark volume on the Council of Ministers, Naurin and Wallace (2009) conclude that while deliberation certainly takes place, it only happens under specific circumstances. A tougher bargaining attitude becomes evident, especially when the subject is highly politicised.[5] Arguments about both dual loyalties and deliberation remain controversial. Most scholars still claim that member state interaction represents defined national interests, which do not change during the negotiation process.

---

[4] As a result, national actors become stakeholders with shared responsibility for the collective output of the Council (Lewis 2009: 168).

[5] The limits to deliberation are probably a general feature of international politics. As Antje Wiener argues, despite deep institutionalisation in multinational arenas, it is uncommon to have a situation in which all actors share the same life world and understand the meaning of a norm in exactly the same way (Wiener 2007b: 61–62).

Insights from both the logic of appropriateness and the logic of arguing can be used in a political sociological approach. However, such a translation implies that the meaning of concepts (such as appropriateness and arguing) changes considerably. While socialisation scholars accept that international norms carry social content and provide agents with an understanding of their interests through, for example, learning processes (Checkel 1999: 90), they have refrained from asking what makes the negotiations meaningful in the first place.

A political sociologist would argue that it is necessary to put the concept of 'norm following' and 'reason following' into context: we need to integrate social hierarchies in a framework of how norms, roles and dispositions are understood. While the logic of appropriateness is a perspective that interprets human action as being 'driven by rules of appropriate or exemplary behaviour, organized into institutions' (Olsen and March 2004: 3), the habitus gives individuals room to manoeuvre. They can manipulate common understandings and situations to their advantage. People do not just do what is appropriate; they do not 'stand before objective structures and rules which determine their actions, but in networks of relations which they virtuously manipulate' (King 2000: 421).

The myth of clashing national interests, which is common in both IR and EU theory, distracts us from seeing that the real world of diplomacy is both constrained and open to creation and improvisations. I will show that social codes of conduct (particular in the diplomatic field, and not written instructions from the capital) are sometimes more important regarding how national representatives interact in Brussels. For instance, Danish officials will prepare for meetings, but may remain silent to avoid attracting attention to their opt-outs. For national diplomats in the EU, the aim of their negotiations is pieced together not only by ministries and parliament back home but also by their habitus.

Tough bargaining certainly takes place in Brussels and deliberation in a Habermasian sense is rare. However, contrary to what rationalists would have us believe, such bargaining is based not only on conscious calculation but also on results from unconscious dispositions towards practice: the habitus. Therefore strategic practice comes from people's own experience of reality – their practical sense of logic (Jenkins 2002: 72). This logic of practice indicates that people can develop what Goffman calls 'a feel for the game', which they learn in a partly conscious and partly unconscious way. As a result, while diplomats identify themselves with their countries, they are also placed in a socially structured situation – a diplomatic field – in which their perception of national interest is defined.

Goffman's 'sense of one's place'

There has been much criticism of the concept of habitus due to a lack of proper clarification (see Ignatow 2009). In this section I propose that the concept of habitus is quite close to what Goffman calls 'the sense of one's place', which suggests that people tend to internalise their relative positions in the social game (see Goffman 1951: 297). My argument is that Bourdieu's theory can be developed further by linking his 'field-habitus' approach to Goffman's analysis of face-work and role-playing. This is not to say that either sociologist would have liked the result of these two ideas merging. On the one hand, Bourdieu was heavily influenced by the symbolic interactionist understanding of strategy and games; and on the other hand, his whole *oeuvre* has been interpreted as an attempt to distance himself from a subjectivist interpretation of agency (Liénard and Servais 1974). However, Bourdieu was greatly inspired by Goffman's interactionism and dramaturgy (Bourdieu 1982). Many of Goffman's insights are reproduced in Bourdieu's work (i.e. the game metaphor and the idea that actors can improvise and struggle within and with social constraints; Lamaison and Bourdieu 1989; Jenkins 2002: 19).

The EU distinguishes itself from other diplomatic forums because of the regularity and intensity of face-work between states. Previous studies have demonstrated the existence of particular rules and internalised values in the Council system below the level of ministers. Arguably, 'relationships are structured, institutions rather well rooted, rules of procedure operate, judicial settlements of disputes are embedded, and many informal understandings support the arrangements' (Hayes-Renshaw and Wallace 1997: 264). Jeffrey Lewis has demonstrated that when national representatives meet to prepare Council meetings and take decisions, the members adopt roles that are appropriate in that particular setting (Lewis 2005: 949–950). This role-playing is typical of diplomats and offers the national representatives a range of diplomatic resources (Lewis 2005: 950). Lewis identifies five informal norms that characterise diplomatic interaction in the EU (Lewis 2005: 949):

1. *Diffuse reciprocity* refers to the balance of concessions over an extended shadow of the future.

2. *Thick trust* means the ability to speak frankly.
3. *Mutual responsiveness* is a shared purpose in understanding each other's problems.
4. *Consensus-reflex* refers to an instinctive choice to behave consensually and 'bring everyone on board'.
5. *The culture of compromise* is based on a willingness to accommodate different interests, which includes self-restraint in the calculations and defence of interests.

The search for consensus has been highlighted as characteristic of the Council of Minsters – irrespective of the formal rules of decision-making, qualified majority voting or unanimity (Hayes-Renshaw et al. 2006). As Naurin and Wallace observe, 'explicit voting is relatively infrequent and almost certainly does not give us hard evidence about either the nature of contestation or about relative success' (Naurin and Wallace 2009: 18). They argue that to fully understand the relative power of member states, one must adopt a close-up qualitative approach.

To summarise, while literature about socialisation in international organisations and institutions focuses on individual learning processes (Beyers 2005; Checkel 2005), we need to go a step further. Learning processes only work because they are embedded in a greater under-standing of what makes them meaningful. To fully grasp diplomacy in the EU, the next section suggests that we must identify the undiscussed premise that makes negotiations in the EU meaningful in the first place.

The integration doxa

There are things that are so obvious to us that we are not consciously aware of them. For example, in most parts of the Western world, democracy is seen as the only possible form of legitimate government. Also in the EU there are assumptions that are almost never questioned. Apart from the everyday internalisation of rules in the habitus, there are more fundamental rules that national representatives do not even think about. These informal and unspoken structures constitute the prevailing 'doxa': the silent experience of the world (Jackson 2008: 167). Agents in a field work within the doxa, which operates as if it were the objective truth across social space in its entirety (Bourdieu 1990).

The doxa is the undisputed and taken-for-granted premise or 'truth'. To identify the integration doxa, one must reveal the 'unspoken rules' that are fundamental to the European project. Apart from a few valuable exceptions (Manners 2007; 2010), research into the normative project informing the EU has not been carried out sufficiently. This is partly due to the methodological problem of how to visualise the invisible. Identifying the doxa requires someone to ask the questions that those in the field do not ask.

I propose to recall from Chapter 2 some of the ideas that are taken for granted by many EU scholars. One prevailing idea is that opt-outs are problematic because they breach the solidarity between the member states and threaten the unity vision expressed in the Treaty of Rome's notion of 'an ever closer union'. As a result, the *acquis communautaire* is seen as expressing the very meaning of European co-operation. No other international organisation has proved to be as demanding as the EU when it comes to the political obligations and legal constraints that it places on its member states. If law is not only regulative of behaviour, but also plays a constitutive role in the formation of actors' identities and interests, the development of the EU can be understood as a result of a normative 'integration through law' (Wiener 1998: 301; see also Shaw and Wiener 2000). Indeed, the *acquis communautaire* has been interpreted as being more than the legal provisions, procedures and rules of the Treaty of European Union. It is viewed as 'an embedded acquis', which is 'an institution which forms part of an ongoing process of constructing meaning and applying knowledge [...] the acquis represents a certain world view' (Wiener 1998: 302). This insight is generally ignored in studies of diplomatic interaction in the EU, but it could help us to identify what makes the diplomatic field meaningful to the extent that this world view is an important part of the identities of national representatives. To the extent that this adherence to the development of the *acquis* is reflected in the interaction between national representatives, the opt-outs may be seen as deeply problematic.

Diplomatic capital: rethinking power

Rather than attempting to provide a fixed definition of influence, I propose a particular method of conceptualising power relations between member states. I do not share the assumption that there are certain material resources that – across time and space – make one state more powerful than another. My take on influence also rejects forms of naïve constructivism that would suggest that influence is what states make of it (see also Adler-Nissen and Pouliot 2014). The influence that one diplomat may exercise in a concrete negotiation depends on an indirect or structural form of power, which can be understood as 'intersubjectively shared understandings of the world, discourses, specific social practices which sediment as social "structures" and systematically empower and dis-empower actors' (Leander 2005: 811). Power and influence can only be understood relationally; they are neither objects nor things that people 'have'. People 'possess' power only in so far as they are relationally authorised to do so (Clegg 1989: 207). Whereas most analysis of international negotiations places power at the agent level, this type of power is not developed intentionally; it is produced as knowledge.

More specifically, and borrowing from Bourdieu, I suggest that the position of diplomats (and the states that they represent) depends on the volume and type of capital to which they have access. Capital is derived from the different resources that can count as a valid currency for exchange in a field. Any field is characterised by inequality and an unequal distribution of capital. Some groups have a lot of capital and others have less capital, and there appears to be an acceptance in the field that this is just the way it is. Much of Bourdieu's work concerns the establishment and reproduction of inequalities and how inequality is reproduced without any apparent violence – that is, through symbolic violence. In some senses, symbolic violence is much more powerful than physical violence in that it is embedded in the very modes of action and structures of cognition of individuals, and it imposes the sense of the legitimacy of the social order.[6] Cross notes with regard to intra-EU diplomacy:

Internal diplomacy has worked well in large part because of the similarities in the ways member-states select and train their diplomats. Diplomats typically come from the same top universities, they tend to share a similar social background, and they undergo the same type of formal and on-the-job-training. (Cross 2011)

This has helped the development of common ideas about what constitutes a good diplomat, which postings are most prestigious and so on

---

[6] Symbolic violence is the imposition of particular perceptions upon social agents who then take the social order to be just. It is the incorporation of unthought-of structures that tends to perpetuate the structures of the action of the dominated individuals or institutions. The dominated then take their position to be 'right'.

(Mérand 2008). For instance, a posting in the Permanent Representation in Brussels is regarded as a high-status post, increasing your diplomatic capital. To be a COREPER ambassador gives a great deal influence and expertise, sometimes even superseding the position of Ambassador to the USA (Adler-Nissen 2014b).

Why are some states seen as being more powerful than others? One source of power in the EU's Council of Ministers that is most frequently mentioned is member state size. It has been indirectly translated into the number of votes and the size of the majority threshold, but there are many other indices that are also taken into consideration (see Heisenberg 2005).[7] Despite there being tomes about power indices (including game theoretical approaches that look at situations where voting rights are not necessarily divided equally among the voters or shareholders), there is a lack of agreement about the importance of voting weights for member state influence.

Another frequently mentioned power resource is the length of EU membership (Naurin and Wallace 2009). The UK and Denmark became members of the European Community in 1973. The length of their membership does not differentiate them from each other, but it may affect their positions in relation to the dominant and subordinates in the field. While many agree that this division between new and old member states is apparent (see also Wiener 2007b), there is no consensus as to what effect the length of membership in the EU has in this context.[8]

A third power resource in negotiations is arguably the personal experience or expertise of the representative (Lewis 2005). However, this claim fails to explain how personal experience is employed strategically and when, for example, bullying rather than expertise is rewarded.

---

[7] Power indices are frequently used to investigate the distribution of voting power among member states in the Council of Ministers and the European Parliament, the effect of proposed institutional changes, and the EU enlargement on that distribution (Nurmi 1997).

[8] According to Moravscisk, new member states are no different from old member states. They seek the same economic benefits from the co-operation process as other states have done before them (Moravcsik and Vachudova 2002). Others argue that the new member states that joined in the 2004 enlargement round are profoundly different from the original 15 – in terms of political history, economic systems and cultural heritage. Others further argue that while this may be true, officials from the new member states are quick learners and have adapted surprisingly quickly to the formal and informal norms of the COREPER (Lempp and Altenschmidt 2008: 519).

I would argue that all of these proposed sources of power can be exchanged for diplomatic capital if they are accepted as being valid in the field (i.e. the power that comes with social standing affords prestige and attention). If decision-making were based on pure voting power, British and Danish officials would have no influence when an opt-out applied. However, capital in the Bourdieusian sense is founded on the belief and recognition of the person, and it represents the product of subjective acts of recognition.

When considering the political field (i.e. the field of the state), there is a particular form of social capital that Bourdieu labels 'political capital'. This is the political power enjoyed by politicians and leaders, a power derived from the trust expressed in a form of credit that a group of followers places in them. Whenever this trust increases or decreases, the political capital of a politician changes accordingly (Bourdieu 1992). Obtained through social competences, reputation and personal authority, it is an inconspicuous form of capital that is not as exchangeable as economic capital (Everett 2002: 62–63). The political capital of a politician must be renewed constantly:

> This supremely free-flowing capital can be conserved only at the cost of unceasing work, which is necessary both to accumulate credit and to avoid discredit: hence, all the precautions, the silences and the disguises. (Bourdieu 1992: 193)

Negotiations in the Council of Ministers enable state representatives to accumulate capital. Diplomatic capital is similar to political capital, but with the nuances that come with being a diplomat, working below the level of ministers.

Bourdieu argued that the supply of political options does not develop in direct response to popular demand 'but to the constraints peculiar to a political space that has a history of its own' (see also Wacquant 2004). Bourdieu maintains that a key implication of the relative autonomy of the national political field vis-à-vis other fields 'inside' the state is that political professionals say and do things not in direct reference to voters or constituencies but in reference to other political professionals holding different positions in the field. The same (or perhaps a more important) relative autonomy could be seen as characteristic of the Council of Ministers. The Council has its own rules, forms and loyalties. Everyone in the Council system will know that a certain ambassador must return to his capital city with 'a black eye' in order to obtain new and more collectively acceptable instructions for the negotiations – and his fellow ambassadors will help him do so (Lewis 2005: 951). Yves Dezalay and Brian Garth's (1996) analysis of what they call the 'double games' of universal brokers applies just as well for the national representatives in the Council of Ministers system. As Dezalay and Garth have demonstrated, professionals in law and economy act as double agents, promoting both the interests of their constituencies and the international community of professionals, by promoting the long-term dominance of the international community (Dezalay and Garth 1996).

What counts as capital is never set in stone. The translation of capital into power requires legitimacy. To understand how this is achieved, one must examine the institutions that legitimise the power and contribute to making a historically arbitrary social order seem inevitable and natural. The degree to which 'objective' systems of measurement (such as country size or length of membership) feed into the diplomacy of opting out depends on how the status and hierarchies are distributed in a particular field. Opt-outs are embedded in a diplomatic field in which complex hierarchies (where material and the symbolic markers are interwoven) affect the relative positions of the diplomats.

Playing the negotiation game

Given the above, how should we understand the integration process? Diplomatic strategies can be explored in day-to-day tactics, as they are applied in meetings and working groups, and they are loosely coupled with the overall positions of the state. The link between individual representative and state is clear: national representatives literally represent the state. This is where all of the abovementioned factors (such as size, voting power and economic strength) can convert into diplomatic capital for the individual negotiator. When governments and officials travel to Brussels for formal meetings, they are the personification of their state in the negotiations. Or as practice theorists would say, they instantiate the 'state' – they produce praxeological examples of or public embodiments of macrosocial phenomena (Coulter 2001: 36).[9] This does not mean that person and state become one, but rather that

---

[9] Lebow argues that while Goffman's actors are individual human beings, the rituals and interactions that govern face-to-face interactions are also visible in diplomatic practices and interstate relations (Lebow 2008: 566).

by, for example, representing France to a foreign state or an international organisation, a French diplomat performs as France. Goffman saw the state as only being 'loosely coupled' with face-to-face encounters (Goffman 1983: 11). However, complex and collective organisations such as states can become dependent on particular personnel, which means that when these people are injured or humiliated, their organisations suffer too (Goffman 1983: 8).

Diplomats have a variety of strategies for gaining influence; however, they do not necessarily perceive them as strategies. Instead, the field generates its own unarticulated common sense, which gives both meaning and purpose. For example, diplomats from new member states must learn to operate effectively in a small and intimate group such as the COREPER: '[its] intricate codes must be learnt, credibility needs to be built, and an understanding of how the other members of the club operate must be developed' (Kassim and Peters 2001: 307). These norms do not indicate that strategic calculations and external sanctions disappear, or that voting weights are not important, but officials and ministers need persuasive arguments that lean towards a reasoned consensus and what is 'best for Europe' (Lewis 2005: 950). The idea of explicitly furthering one's own national interests may be considered inappropriate in the Council of Ministers and its working groups, as their focus is on problem-solving and common interests (Lewis 2003).

As an informal norm, the consensus reflex is fully consistent with the member states' interest not to be outvoted in any current and future policy issue that is important to them. In a Bourdieusian sense, strategies are the continual interactions between the disposition of the habitus and the constraints and possibilities of reality. To summarise, the unwritten logics of the diplomatic field can create openings for national representatives that are invisible to the outsider (i.e. a person outside the field). The strategies of national representatives only make sense if we understand how the field functions, and what is considered 'good' or 'bad' behaviour.

Opt-outs as stigma

Stigma is a Greek word that originally referred to a kind of tattoo or identifying mark cut or burned into the skin of animals. In Christian mysticism the word 'stigmata' refers to bodily marks, scars or pains corresponding to those of the crucified Jesus Christ, interpreted as a miraculous sign from God. In ancient Greece, branding animals was a universal practice, while branding criminals, slaves and traitors was rare (Jones 1987). In its modern usage, however, stigma is associated with the belief that certain individuals should be avoided or shunned, particularly in public places, as they are regarded as blemished or morally polluted. A stigma can undermine all other claims to normality, rendering the individual less than human.

Goffman systematically developed the concept of stigma as a sociological concept in the 1960s. Despite his enormous impact on sociology and social psychology, IR scholars have neglected much of his thinking.[10] However, his reflections on society as being highly heterogeneous, and his focus on the dramaturgical and strategic aspects of human interaction, are useful in our understanding of social dynamics in IR.

In his book, *Stigma: Notes on the Management of Spoiled Identity* (1963), Goffman described stigma as follows: 'In its most general socio-logical sense, the term stigma can be used to refer to any attribute that is deeply discrediting and incongruous with our stereotype of what a given type of individual should be' (Goffman 1963: 3). Building on Goffman, numerous sociologists and social psychologists have used stigma theory to analyse the circumstances of, for example, the unemployed (Link et al. 1991), transsexuals (Kando 1972), immigrants (Kusow 2004), the homeless (Roschelle and Kaufman 2004) and HIV-positive people (Sandelowski et al. 2004). They paint a complex picture of discrimina-tion as well as strategies for fighting back.

According to Goffman, 'the function of stigma processes is to enlist support for society from those who aren't supported by it' (Goffman 1963: 138). Therefore stigmatising someone who challenges the norm reinforces the concept of normality. This refers to an aspiration for the future and a factual situation in which there are no 'immediate external or internal threats to society's stability' (Misztal 2001: 313).

---

[10] For the few valuable exceptions, see Michael Barnett (1995), who draws on Goffman to argue that symbolic politics is crucial in explaining interstate relations in the Middle East. In addition, Ben Mor (2009) employs Goffman to analyse impression management in Israeli public diplomacy, and Frank Schimmelfennig (2004) builds on Goffman to describe frontstage and backstage logics in the EU-enlargement process. Before constructivism became an established IR approach, Jervis' (1976) landmark volume on perceptions and misperceptions in foreign policy referred to Goffman.

Stigmatisation can help to establish order by distinguishing 'us' from 'them': the normals from the deviant. Bourdieu's concept of classification reveals his intellectual similarity to Goffman. Inspired by Goffman, Bourdieu conceptualises stigma as a distinctive mark that helps to determine the relative positions of agents and groups. Bourdieu maintains that a stigma is the result of negative capital (Bourdieu 1985: 733). He perceives classification as a multidimensional process: it involves the self-classification of a group, the exclusion of others through different symbolic actions and a hierarchical relation in which some social classifications are more powerful than others. The way in which stigmatisation works can be seen in the classifications built around a stigmatised feature which, like the preconception of homosexuals by heterosexuals, isolates the deviant trait from all of the rest (i.e. all other forms of sexuality). The strategies of coping with classifications and discriminations form the core of an analysis of stigma management. Any individual or group that is a potential target of categorisation can only defend themselves against the partial perception. Everybody struggles to classify themselves according to their most favourable characteristics (Bourdieu 1985). This logic of categorisation is crucial for an understanding of stigma, because it is from these categorisations that a social struggle for recognition begins.

In the EU, while opting out is regarded as deviant among national representatives it is not the only source of stigma; other marks are also regarded as problematic. For example, in the stories that diplomats tell in the corridors of the Justus Lipsius building, and in the media, the Greeks are perceived as laggards who lack motivation; the Italians are perceived as being unprofessional negotiators; and the newcomers arguably lack knowledge of the EU system. Therefore it is important to understand more generally what constitutes deviant behaviour in the Council of Ministers.

Stigma imposition

Stigma is not automatically assigned; it results from a process of stigmatisation. Goffman argues that everybody has the potential to become stigmatised; even the most fortunate of 'normals' are likely to have a half-hidden failing (Goffman 1963: 127). Some norms 'take the form of ideals and constitute standards against which almost everyone falls short at some stage' (Goffman 1963: 128). Therefore stigmatisation is not a result of the violation of social norms about normality but a product of the failure to establish normality in the first place. In the EU the deviant state highlights the challenges posed by the question: what is good and acceptable state behaviour? Ironically, ontological insecurity is the original impetus for relegating particular groups to the margins of society. States that appear to reject European co-operation are considered to be intolerable because they expose the illusionary elements in the European project.

Normal and deviant states are differentiated by stigma imposition, which involves classifying certain states as deviant. The sociologists Link and Phelan (2001) define the process of stigma imposition as the co-occurrence of the following components: labelling; stereotyping; separation; and status loss and discrimination. Therefore full stigmatisation requires a social process that goes beyond labelling or 'othering'.

Regarding the first component of stigma – labelling – the critical issue is how culturally created categories develop and are sustained. Why are some human or social differences highlighted while others are ignored? What are the social, economic and cultural forces maintaining the focus on a particular social difference? The second component of stigma occurs when labelled differences are linked to stereotypes. A third feature of stigma imposition occurs when social labels indicate a separation of 'us' from 'them'. This idea that the individuals from the labelled group are fundamentally different results in stereotyping. The 'us' and 'them' component of the stigmatisation process indicates that the labelled group is slightly less human or, in extreme cases, not human at all. In the fourth component of stigma imposition, the labelled person experiences status loss and discrimination. When the label is linked to 'undesirable characteristics', a rationale is created for devaluing, rejecting and physically excluding the stigmatised. Link and Phelan (2001) believe that the members of the labelled groups can be disadvantaged in areas such as income, education, housing status, health and medical treatment.

Not all forms of labelling and classification are linked to stigmatisation. In the EU, states can be labelled, but these labels might never develop into a genuine system of social differentiation, or attempts to label particular states may prove futile. Although stigma should be understood as a consequence of structural relationships, individuals manage their stigma in a microinteractional manner. As the stigma discredits the individual, they attempt to control and manage the discrediting attribute.

Stigma management

This section creates a typology of stigma management and examines the different strategies that are available to the stigmatised (for a broader argument about stigma management, see Adler-Nissen 2014a). As mentioned earlier, research on diplomatic sanctions or interventions tends to focus on the discriminatory process without looking at how states and diplomats cope with it; if coping is addressed, it is often only suggested that these techniques are part of the discrimination process and reinforce the marginal position. Instead of automatically accepting stigma, representatives from stigmatised states may attempt to modify the exclusionary effects of stigma by altering how the 'normals' perceive them and their willingness to co-operate through recognition or rejection of stigma.

Representatives from stigmatised states tend to perceive themselves as belonging to the particular categories assigned to them. However, while some use this affiliation to their advantage and value their exclusion, others pursue strategies to become accepted as part of the 'normals'. These strategies are not necessarily mutually exclusive. Diplomats can adopt several strategies simultaneously or shift between strategies in different situations.

Goffman described two available strategies for a group of stigmatised people: out-group alignment (stigma recognition), where representatives identify with the audience of 'normals' and the wider society; and in-group alignment (stigma rejection), where representatives identify with the stigmatised group (Goffman 1963: 112–123).

Stigma recognition

We can expect states to try to conform with the 'normals' for two reasons. First, as Peter Katzenstein explains, 'governments crave the diplomatic recognition by members of the international society of states because it bestows upon them the legitimacy they may need to secure their existence' (Katzenstein 1996: 24). Diplomatic interaction operates through shared codes of conduct and a high degree of self-control, which is common among stigmatised groups and individuals seeking to pass as 'normals'. If this is correct, we can expect diplomats to use strategies that help to excuse a stigma.

Second, the primary objectives of interstate negotiations are usually influence and status. Therefore state representatives will seek acceptance from the audience of 'normals', and struggle to hide, or work to remove, the stigma. When diplomats manage stigma, they must continuously justify their position to other states and the EU institutions. Interestingly, stigma can initially be a source of embarrassment that later turns into pride, which underlines the ambiguous social identity of the stigmatised and the continuous cycle of stigma. I will demonstrate that this circular dynamic of transforming stigma can also be found in the EU.

Stigma rejection

States may even appear to thrive in the EU despite being stigmatised. They may be politically shunned, but ideologically, governments may gain from stigmatisation. In some cases, stigmatisation may lead to empowerment; it does not necessarily represent a loss of status or exclusion if managed in a way that strengthens the position of the state. This is where the public mark is transformed into an emblem. Through stigma rejection, the stigmatised selectively devalue the performance dimensions on which they/their group fares poorly, and value those dimensions in which they excel (i.e. they turn vice into virtue) (Crocker and Major 1989: 616).[11] There are cases where stigmatised groups of migrants have rejected stigma, such as Somali immigrants who have settled in the USA and Europe. They have created a separate system of honour, with the Somali women wearing colourful, non-Western dresses (and, in most cases, the *hijab*) and avoiding the dance clubs that typically attract young members of mainstream society (Kusow 2004). A selective valuing process protects the self-esteem and status of the stigmatised individual or group. In this example there is no doubt that the stigmatised chooses to fight the negative attitudes, turning the stigma into an attractive attribute.

It is important to emphasise that not all actions by stigmatised individuals and groups are related to stigma. Therefore not everything that a

---

[11] Goffman suggests, parenthetically, that those with more obvious, physically observable stigmas are more likely to embark on in-group alignment than those with less noticeable stigmas (Goffman 1963: 41ff). This suggestion, while it may be intuitively convincing, is problematic from a constructivist viewpoint (and I would claim also for Goffman's own theory). Although physical visibility is important for whether someone may pass as normal, a stigma results from discursive and non-discursive practices. What counts as stigma may change over time and we cannot a priori determine what becomes stigma.

British or Danish representative does or says in the course of a working-group meeting is related to stigma management: asking for a coffee refill or taking notes during a meeting are (usually) not stigma management. However, bilateral contacts and attempts to win over other member states for one's own position can relate to stigma management.

To summarise, part of the stigmatisation process involves stigma being internalised or accepted by the stigmatised. Opt-outs can contribute to a specific diplomatic identity and potentially constitute a certain type of identity and strategy. They can affect state image and reputation, as well as impact on how state representatives view themselves. The stigma management processes are summed up in Table 3.1.

Table 3.1. *Types of stigma management*

Types of stigma management		
	Stigma recognition	Stigma rejection
Stigma management	'Maturing' through good adjustment, self-discipline	Turning the stigma into an emblem
Consequence for stigmatised state	Transforming stigma	Separate system of honour
Consequence for EU	The moral cohesion of the social order is strengthened	Split in competing visions or modification of the moral foundation of the social order

Operationalisation

By bringing together the above mentioned concepts of field, habitus, capital, doxa and stigma, it is possible to develop an analytical framework for studying of the diplomacy of opting out. Of course, any attempt at modelling the world can be criticised for reducing complexity, and I do not claim to cover all aspects of European integration with this model. I aim to provide an understanding of the key social mechanisms of diplomatic interaction in the EU through a political sociological analysis. There are four central aspects:

1. the diplomatic field, understood as the structural normative environment of the particular configuration of the Council of Ministers, and its capital, understood as the resources that achieve status and power;

2. the diplomatic common sense, understood as people's dispositions, which are largely unarticulated;
3. the stigmatisation of 'deviant' states and their representatives;
4. stigma management by national representatives.

The model is dynamic – the different elements may influence one another, leading to a change in strategy as shown in Figure 3.1. Given the above factors, capital is presumably affected by opting out. The success or failure of certain stigma management strategies is likely to have implications. Over time it is likely that the diplomatic field, understood as the European norm environment, will change because of the practices employed by diplomats. However, while both the field and the habitus are historically inherited, the field remains as a social structure more or less independent of individual life, whereas the concept of habitus is linked to the individual national representative.

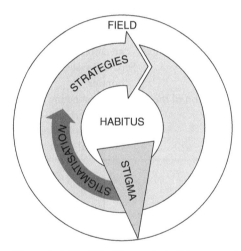

Figure 3.1 Model of the analytical framework

I analyse the diplomacy of opting out through a four step process. The first step maps out the diplomatic field, capital and doxa – focusing on the structural positions and distributions of capital and its formal and informal rules. To unravel the social hierarchies, rules, informal norms and what is taken for granted, the key question is: what count as valid resources for status and power in the relevant Council of Ministers constellation?

The second step goes beyond structural elements in the field and examines the national representatives' common sense. The key question is: what are the roles, values and dispositions of the national representatives?

The third step looks at how national represenatives in the field perceive opt-outs and how that impacts on the distribution of capital. It also focuses on the imposition of stigma on British and Danish representatives. The key questions are: how have the EU institutions and member states interpreted the opt-outs, and have there been conflicting interpretations? How is an opt-out perceived, and how is a particular status imposed on and accepted by the national representatives from the states with opt-outs?

The fourth step asks how British and Danish representatives deal with the opt-outs and whether they identify with the in- or out-group during negotiations in the Council of Ministers. The aim is to analyse diplomatic stigma management. This enables us to explore how the diplomacy of opting out is actually played out. The key question is: what strategies do national representatives adopt when managing opt-outs?

Conclusion

This chapter presented a political sociological framework for studying everyday European integration from the perspective of national diplomats. I argued that interaction between the EU member states cannot simply be described as mediation between domestic and European levels. Building on the work of Bourdieu and Goffman, I developed an alternative theoretical framework for studying member state interaction in the EU. This approach can be used to explore the links between everyday diplomatic practices – from awkward handshakes to group photos – and the macroprocesses of inclusion and exclusion in international organisations. Diplomats are still the key mediators between the national and European levels, but the European diplomatic field, as a site, becomes the centre of the analysis. It is within this field that the stakes of negotiation are defined and power positions are distributed among national representatives.

The theoretical framework focuses on how diplomacy works in the EU. It is summed up in Table 3.2. It concentrates on processes through which states battle for influence and recognition in the EU, and how conceptions of normal and deviant state behaviour are negotiated. I interpret the opt-outs as a leading to a stigma, which British and Danish

Table 3.2. *The analytical framework*

The analytical framework

	Sub-field and capital	Diplomatic habitus	Stigma	Stigma management
Definition	Social system, suggesting competent action in conformity with rules and roles	Disposition to act, perceive and think in a particular way in conformity with the field	Discrediting attribute, incongruous with stereotype of how an individual should be	The continual interactions between the disposition of the habitus and constraints, and possibilities of the field
Analytical focus	Structure, formal and informal rules and norms of a social sub-system	Dispositions and intersubjectively shared values	Logics of categorisation and stigmatisation. The meaning of 'normal'	Diplomatic practices, microprocesses of strategising
Key analytical questions	What are the social hierarchies, rules, informal norms? What counts as a valid resource for status and power?	What are the roles, values and dispositions of the national representatives?	How is a particular deviant status imposed on and accepted by state representatives?	What strategies do national representatives adopt when managing stigma?

representatives must deal with. This is due to opt-outs being seen as openly undermining the solidarity between the member states. Stigmatisation represents an attempt to establish, if only momentarily, a shared moral order in the EU. Bourdieu's structural account of the field, and his understanding of stigma as negative capital, complements Goffman's notion of stigma because Bourdieu weaves the social and economic conditions into his argument. In this way the small everyday stories of groups and individuals coping with stigma are linked to the bigger issue of marginalisation. In this sense, subsequent analysis of how British and Danish diplomats handle their opt-outs serves as a prism for understanding how European integration works.

4 | *The stigma of euro-outsiderness*

Introduction

'No one should think that a further half century of peace and prosperity is assured. It isn't. And that's why I say if the euro fails, Europe will fail, and that mustn't happen.'[1] German Chancellor Angela Merkel did not mince her words when she addressed the German Bundestag in October 2011 and secured a 'yes' to a new euro rescue package. Known for her cautious, understated approach, Merkel opted for unusually grand rhetoric in her brief address to Parliament, underlining the historic significance of the euro crisis. For Merkel and her European colleagues, the euro was the key to European integration.

One decade into the new millennium, an economic crisis haunted not only Europe but most of the world. Huge budget deficits tested European solidarity to its limits, and European leaders openly discussed the possibility of ousting Greece and other countries from the single currency due to their enormous financial difficulties. The euro survived, but its future remains uncertain. The International Monetary Fund and the EU forced Greece, Italy, Portugal, Spain and Ireland to undergo severe austerity measures in exchange for rescue packages worth hundreds of billions of euros. If the euro survives, closer co-ordination of economic and financial policy appears inevitable. Economic government or management of some sort now looms large on the horizon.

Euro-outsiderness is a pressing concern for anyone interested in the future of Europe. The UK and Denmark, together with Sweden, appear to have slid into a semipermanent position of outsiderness. Several of the newest member states are also becoming sceptical of joining the euro. Marine Le Pen, leader of the Front National in France, wants her country to leave the euro, and in Germany the liberal Free Democratic Party is increasingly critical of economic and monetary integration. And

---

[1] www.spiegel.de/international/europe/0,1518,794141,00.html.

yet there are few systematic evaluations of how member states handle euro-outsiderness.

Currently two interpretations compete. The marginalisation camp argues that euro-outsiderness is increasingly excluding non-euro members (Mulhearn and Vane 2005: 255; Puetter 2006). The inclusionist camp, on the other hand, argues that membership of the single currency does not necessarily change the status or influence of its representatives (Marcussen 2005; Miles 2005a). The inclusionist camp believes that what matters is less whether a state has adopted the euro and more whether its economic policy and arguments are sound.

These opposing understandings of the implications of euro-outsiderness raise many questions. For instance, does it matter whether euro-outsiderness is voluntary or involuntary? Whether adhering to the marginalisation or inclusionist camp, existing research suggests that euro-outsiderness is a stable position. In this chapter I wish to venture a different interpretation: that the meaning of and implications of euro-outsiderness are in fact constantly negotiated.

As the EU moves towards a closer economic co-operation, some member states are relegated to the margins. This chapter examines what it means to be a euro-outsider. I will show that the British and Danish representatives are systematically punished for their choice to remain outside the eurozone, a zone that has developed into an exclusive club where the most important deals about Europe are made.

Stigmatisation of euro-outsiders results partly from a failure to discipline the eurozone in the first place. As a monetary union, it is far from cohesive. As such, the shutting out of British and Danish representatives is crucial to ensure the ongoing symbolic stability of co-operation on the euro. Interestingly, however, representatives from these two member states react differently to stigmatisation. While British officials are satisfied with the pound and turn their stigma into an emblem, Danish representatives identify with the insiders, feel frustrated and seek to compensate for their euro-outsiderness. This helps explain why, in December 2011, British Prime Minister David Cameron vetoed the treaty amendment that proposed to strengthen economic and fiscal co-operation, while the Danish government welcomed the treaty and asked to be included as much as possible.

In this chapter, I will first analyse the British and Danish positions and the tacit knowledge and hierarchies that make European economic and monetary co-operation possible. I will then explore how euro-outsiders are stigmatised and demonstrate a more ambivalent diplomacy than is often acknowledged. Choosing to stay outside the euro means that you are not a 'good European' and fighting back cannot remove the mark of deviance.

Negotiating monetary sovereignty

The single currency is now the most important distinction marker in the EU. This is not only how it appears in media coverage of the big EU summits; it is also the everyday experience of British and Danish representatives. When asked to rate the most significant opt-outs, European diplomats all point at the decision to stay out of the EMU.[2] As one Dutch diplomat explains, 'For me, it is really the euro which defines whether you are in or out. If you're not part of the euro, you're not part of the real thing'.[3] The 'real thing', then, has to do with the willingness to give up monetary sovereignty.

The euro plays a tremendous role in the transformation of sovereignty in Europe. As French Finance Minister Laurent Fabius put it when the euro was launched, 'Thanks to the euro, our pockets will soon hold solid evidence of a European identity. Political union is inseparable from economic union'.[4] Despite continued attempts by both British and Danish governments to 'de-sovereignise' the euro, and regardless of the increasing difficulties of imagining and practising monetary autonomy in a globalising world, national currencies continue to symbolise sovereign statehood. Yet it was always assumed that the exclusion of some member states from the single currency would only be temporary. So why did the UK and Denmark not follow the other member states when they surrendered their national currencies?

British Euroscepticism

During the 1990s, ideas relating to a political union in Europe had become increasingly popular. However, the British government – and

---

[2] Interview, Spanish Permanent Representation (Brussels), 26 March 2008; Interview, Belgian Permanent Representation (Brussels), 16 February 2007; Interview, Former Senior Official Council, Copenhagen, 7 February 2006.

[3] Interview, Dutch Permanent Representation (Brussels), 16 February 2007.

[4] For a sophisticated analysis of the ideas shared among the economic and political elites in Europe that helped to create the EMU, see Marcussen (2000).

in particular the Treasury – was critical of the very idea of an EMU (Blair 1998: 175–176). As then – Chancellor of the Exchequer Nigel Lawson argued in 1989,

Economic and monetary union implies nothing less than a European government ... and political union: the United States of Europe. That is not on the agenda now, nor will it be for the foreseeable future. (Lawson, quoted by La Malfa 2002: 86)

Lawson's reading of the political climate could not be more wrong. The other member states soon proved willing to take the momentous step towards a political union and a single currency.

After the fall of the Berlin Wall there was widespread fear that a unified Germany would dominate Europe. Prime Minister Margaret Thatcher was not alone in candidly expressing her opposition to unification – French President François Mitterrand was also highly sceptical. The difference between the British and French positions was that the French found a solution to their fears, while the British never came up with a clear answer to the 'German problem'. The French demanded a high price for German unification: that Germany should engage itself even more deeply in political and economic co-operation (Bozo 2007). The idea of a monetary union had been mooted time and time again throughout the post-war period, but it was not until German unification that it became politically possible. During the Maastricht Treaty negotiations in 1991–1992, Germany sacrificed its strong Deutschmark for a common European currency and was allowed unification, and, later, participation in the creation of a common European military dimension (Berger 1997: 57). On 1 January 1999, the third and final stage of EMU commenced with the irrevocable fixing of the exchange rates of the currencies of the 11 member states initially participating in monetary union, and with a single monetary policy under the responsibility of the European Central Bank (ECB).

Margaret Thatcher was most unhappy about German unification and the European monetary bargain that went with it (see also Thatcher 2000). However, in the course of the negotiations it became clear that the other member states were prepared to go ahead with a treaty on the EMU without the UK (Wall 2008). Consequently the British government had to content itself with an opt-out clause granted in exchange for not vetoing the monetary union (Berger 1997; Blair 1999). The British protocol on the single currency guarantees that it is for the British government and Parliament alone to initiate procedures for adopting the euro. Moreover, the UK remains outside the ERM II. However, the UK is covered by many of the requirements of the EU fiscal policy framework. In particular, it must 'endeavour' to avoid excessive deficits, though only by joining EMU could sanctions be imposed if British budget deficits were judged to be excessive and the government failed to take corrective action.

To fully understand why the UK could not join Europe's single currency, we need to look beyond the general British scepticism, and briefly examine the specific reasons why the UK still has fundamental problems with the euro.

First, the UK has traditionally clung to its doctrine of national sovereignty in monetary affairs, a doctrine centred on ideas of domestic political control, with the monetary instrument and the pound as a global reserve currency (Gamble and Kelly 2002).

Second, the UK has had a particularly painful experience with monetary co-operation in Europe. An initial scheme for the European currencies to fluctuate jointly vis-à-vis the dollar was launched in 1972–1973, followed in 1979 by a more ambitious system. This was the European Monetary System (EMS), based on a set of fixed but adjustable bilateral exchange rates. Each member state had a responsibility to enforce these exchange rates by pursuing appropriate economic policies and backing them with their currency reserves. The EMS continued with varying membership and degrees of success until 1999, when the EMU eventually superseded it.

From 1990 to 1992 the UK was an EMS member, a brief membership that saw British scepticism towards the single currency intensify. The weak point of the EMS was its vulnerability to exchange rate speculation; it proved difficult to enforce co-operation between central banks when currencies occasionally underwent severe bouts of speculation. This was the case with the Italian lira and the British pound on 16 September 1992, also known as 'Black Wednesday'. On that day the sterling's membership of the EMS had to be suspended. Despite spending billions of pounds and raising interest rates to 15 per cent, the British government failed to prevent the pound from falling lower than its agreed minimum level. The resulting devaluation was a national humiliation. The suspension of the sterling's EMS membership following this crisis consolidated the extreme hostility towards the euro in British politics.

Third, there is London's position as a global financial centre. The City comprises a vast, critical mass of markets and financial services in commercial and investment banking, securities and so on, including an extraordinary concentration of the strongest financial businesses from all around the world. Some 600,000 people are estimated to be employed in finance and other business services in Greater London. This goes some way to explaining why Cameron found it necessary to use the veto in December 2011 against a treaty change that he feared would threaten the British financial services industry. These factors, and no doubt others, may help to explain why not only the British population but also the politico-administrative elite has remained sceptical of joining the EMU.

With the election of Tony Blair and the pro-euro Labour government in 1997, the anti-euro position changed into one of 'prepare and decide'.[5] In 1998, the Bank of England gained formal independence from Parliament, a development that brought the UK more or less in line with those countries that were planning to adopt the euro at the outset (Schmidt 1997: 35). The decisive move, however, was made in October 1997 when the Labour government announced the introduction of five economic tests which had to be passed before any decision to join could be made. The tests were:

1. sustainable convergence between the UK and the economies in the euro area;
2. whether there is sufficient flexibility to cope with economic change;
3. the effect on investment;
4. the impact on the British financial services industry;
5. whether it is good for growth and employment.

For an account of the five tests, see, for instance, Howarth (2007: 50). When the government completed its initial assessment of the tests on 9 June 2003, it found that the euro did not pass at the time (HM Treasury 2003). This evaluation process was repeated ritually every year with the same negative result until the election of a Conservative-Liberal government in 2010, which brought the UK firmly back to its traditional eurosceptical position.

---

[5] Arguably, Blair's 'prepare and decide' policy is not fundamentally different from Major's 'wait and see' policy, but it sends more EU-positive signals (Wall 2008: 171).

Denmark's 'unofficial marriage'

Summing up the Danish position on the euro, former Central Bank President Bodil Nyboe Andersen said: 'as long as Denmark is outside the euro, we continue our "unoffial marriage"' (Andersen 2003: 177, my translation). This unformalised relationship reflects that most of the parties in the Danish Parliament, the various Danish governments and the politico-administrative-economic elite are, at least in principle, favourable to joining the euro. The economic crisis did not fundamentally change this. As a result, Denmark is not the same kind of euro-outsider as the UK.

During the Maastricht negotiations, the Danish situation differed from that of the UK in that most of its political parties supported the EMU. The Danish constitution, however, prevented it from making an advance commitment to a single currency. Because the UK essentially fought the battle over the EMU in the early 1990s, Denmark hid behind the UK during the negotiations, and its reluctance passed almost unnoticed (Ryborg 1998: 21).

The Danish government had already accepted the Maastricht Treaty when it was rejected by the referendum held in Denmark in June 1992. The 'Protocol on certain provisions relating to Denmark', annexed to the Maastricht Treaty, provided Denmark with the guarantee that it would not automatically proceed to the third stage of the EMU, so the Edinburgh Decision (which gave Denmark the three additional opt-outs) merely specified the EMU opt-out (Krunke 2005: 348–349).

If we look more closely at the Danish protocol, however, we see that the Danish position on the EMU is fundamentally ambiguous. Unlike the UK, Denmark accepted an unconditional start to the second stage, endorsed an important role for the ECB and was prepared to have the Council of Ministers play a role (Dyson and Featherstone 1999: 766). The difference between the Danish and British positions becomes clear when we look at a primary feature of Danish monetary politics since 1982: the fixed exchange rate policy. This provided monetary stability by linking the Danish krone to the Deutschmark. The introduction of the euro did nothing to change this, as it locked the Danish currency into the ERM II framework, which allows currencies to float within a range of ±15% with respect to a central rate against the euro. Member states that have not adopted the euro are expected to participate for at least two years in the ERM II before joining the eurozone.Until the economic crisis, Denmark also remained well within the constraints stipulated by the Stability and Growth Pact.

At the end of the 1990s, a clear majority among the mainstream political parties in Denmark favoured adopting the euro and began preparing the Danes for the single currency. During the campaign leading up to the referendum of 28 September 2000, the government promoted a 'yes' as sound business sense and stressed the importance of 'a place at the table' at the Governing Council of the ECB (see Marcussen and Zolner 2001). In May 2000, as opinion polls began indicating a decline in support for the euro, Prime Minister Poul Nyrup Rasmussen made a desperate attempt to appease doubters by asserting that Denmark could join the eurozone and withdraw at a later date if the country so desired, thus arguing that Danish sovereignty would remain fundamentally untouched by the decision to surrender the opt-out. However, Nyrup Rasmussen's statement caused confusion when it was contradicted by European Commission President Romano Prodi, who said that joining the EMU was 'by definition permanent'. Prodi thereby articulated the constitutional character of the EU and the principle of solidarity. He later suggested that Prime Minister Rasmussen was correct from a political point of view, although there were no treaty provisions for joining and leaving the EMU (Miller 2000: 15). Consequently, the government's appeasement strategy failed: 53.1 per cent of Danish voters rejected the euro compared with 46.9 per cent who voted 'yes'. Together with the flourishing Danish economy, the 2000 referendum put a lid on the domestic debate on the euro for almost a decade. It did not resurface until the end of 2008, when Danish Prime Minister Fogh Rasmussen saw a window of opportunity for a new vote on the opt-outs.

Because of the British and Danish opt-outs, only 11 of the 15 EU members were initially included in the euro area when it was introduced on 1 January 1999. Sweden and Greece were excluded on the grounds that they did not fully comply with the Maastricht convergence criteria. Greece was admitted to the EMU in the course of the following year, while Sweden, which still had doubts about the EMU but had not negotiated an opt-out clause, intentionally persisted in not fulfilling one of the clauses.[6] The remainder of this chapter will show how states

---

[6] So far Sweden has evaded the obligation to join the EMU by failing to satisfy certain criteria, but it does not have a formal opt-out similar to those of the UK and

that deliberately choose to remain outside the euro area are seen as defectors from the EU.

Creating a common mindset

In her study of convergence and variations of economic knowledge in the USA, the UK and France, Marion Fourcade has shown that 'not only do economists in different countries generally support different ideas and policy positions, but their claims to expertise about the economy are justified in very different ways' (Fourcade 2009: 5). While this is also the case in the EMU, there is an increasing convergence around particular ideas about economic policy. Various fields of knowledge have helped to produce the EU as we know it today. However, economics is perhaps one of the more striking examples, helping to build economic theories not only promoting harmonisation of the single market and establishment of the EMU, but also participating in their legitimation and sometimes gaining from their establishment in practice (Barry 1993; Rosamond 2002; Ryner 2012).

British and Danish representatives obviously identify with their countries. However, they also become integrated into a multinational group of officials in Brussels. The co-ordination of economic policy transcends mere networking; in Europe, economic policy-makers have developed into a relatively autonomous community.

Economic and monetary co-operation in Europe is managed by a distinct group of people: national ministers and officials from the ministries of finance and economy. They have developed a shared way of thinking, which involves an attachment to analytical capacity, budgetary discipline and a hostile view of 'irresponsible' politicians (Jensen 2003). Indeed, the emergence of the EMU is inseparable from the professional monopoly over the production and management of economic policy that economists have acquired. This monopoly means that when economic and monetary politics are discussed in the EU, it is done among a relatively homogenous transnational group of economists. To understand European economic co-operation, we need to understand what drives these people.

Compared with other EU policy areas such as agriculture, the environment or climate, there is little co-operation with non-state actors

Denmark. Sweden is formally considered a 'member state with derogation' as long as it does not fulfil the conditions as defined by Article 122 of the TEU.

(Mak 2003: 191–195). The Economic and Financial Affairs Council (ECOFIN) and its committees and working groups form a closed organisational structure. Entry into this field is reserved for those representing the economic authorities of a member state, so their representational authority depends on their holding a post in one of the finance ministries in addition to a master's degree in economics or, in some cases, the social sciences. Over the last two decades, this group of people has discussed issues such as economic policy co-ordination, economic surveillance, monitoring of national budgetary policy and public finances, and the euro. Of course, the recent credit crisis has sparked interest in the enforcement of stricter sanctions on profligate member states. It is, however, the gradual forming of a common mindset that has led to countries now accepting supervision of national budgets by the European Commission, as well as quasi-automatic sanctions. This would have been inconceivable 20 years ago, but intense co-operation has paved the way for ever-stricter rules on budgetary discipline.

In this field, as in all other political fields, nothing is more important than a fundamental adherence to the game itself. To join the game – to agree to play it according to the rules – means that the player tacitly adopts a mode of expression and discussion that implies the renunciation of 'bad arguments'. Despite the complex web of codes of conduct, conflicts are widespread, and insults and bullying are not uncommon. Today, economists are in charge of the economic and financial aspects of European integration and are thus also the daily managers of euro-outsiderness. The foreign ministries and the prime ministers' offices have generally been relegated to the sidelines.

The ECOFIN is one of the busiest Council formations in the EU. It discusses and decides on reforms and policy results, exchanges information and implements decisions. The European Commission (the DG for Economic and Financial Affairs (ECFIN)) is responsible for reporting, monitoring, preparing and advancing proposals to recommendations and binding decisions. Crucially, it has the power to sanction member states that fail to live up to the rules and guidelines. The Economic and Financial Committee (EFC) consists of senior officials from the ministries of finance and national central banks, and prepares the work of the ECOFIN. The EFC and COREPER are officially equal in status; in practice, however, the EFC calls the shots. A Danish official explains:

COREPER is only a rubber stamp. Some countries are frustrated because they would like the COREPER to play a greater role. But there are good reasons for why the EFC is so powerful. Firstly, the finance ministries agree on wanting to remain powerful vis-à-vis the foreign ministries [in COREPER the ambassadors come from the foreign ministries]; and secondly, the EFC deals with rather technical issues such as an inner market for finances and cross-border trading with bonds.[7]

These comments confirm the image of a brother- and sisterhood of economists who may not agree on everything but who are keen to consolidate and legitimise their dominant domestic position in Brussels.

Naming, praising and shaming

Financial policy touches upon what a sovereign state can decide for itself (see also Dyson 2000a). This is why negotiations have been oriented towards co-ordination rather than surrendering national competencies. However, an increasing number of rules have been negotiated. Some of these rules have been written down and are now legally binding – although not necessarily followed – while others are shared tacitly. Notwithstanding the fiscal compact and new legislation on budgetary restraint, the unwritten rules regarding co-ordination are the most important. They are the true indicators of how far the integration process has gone.

The objective of EU fiscal policy co-operation is officially to secure sound government finances, price stability, and sustainable growth and employment.[8] This has been the case both before and after the economic crisis. There is, however, no central control of fiscal policy. Instead, the treaty requires the co-ordination of economic, fiscal and employment policies with a system of guidelines and multilateral surveillance. A key element of the governance of economic policy is the 'European Semester', which came into effect in January 2011. Under this process, both economic and fiscal policy co-ordination – that is, the two strands of economic surveillance in the EU – are aligned. Macroeconomic, structural, and competitiveness developments, as well

---

[7] Interview, Danish Permanent Representation (Brussels), 5 September 2007.
[8] Resolution of the European Council on the Stability and Growth Pact, Amsterdam, 17 June 1997.

as overall financial stability, are examined simultaneously in order to enhance the overall consistency of policy advice to member states.

The European Commission and ECOFIN monitor the national fiscal policies and plans of all member states. A system of classificatory schemes has been developed in the context of the Lisbon strategy and the Broad Economic Policy Guidelines (BEPGs), agreed by the ECOFIN each year. The latter includes recommendations for the overall stance and direction of fiscal policy alongside a description of monetary policy and detailed plans for reforming structural policies. The BEPG Implementation Report is the central periodic EU policy document and key instrument for economic policy co-ordination, relying on naming, praising and shaming.

Besides the BEPG reports, there are a small number of essential rules that serve as central reference points for this hierarchy in the EU. The Excessive Deficit Procedure, agreed as part of the Maastricht Treaty, which together with the Council Regulations makes up the Stability and Growth Pact, sets overall limits for deficit and debt levels in all member states.

Such instruments for classifying the member states offer a powerful means to rank them in terms of their economic performance. The processes of surveillance, benchmarking, best practice and peer pressure have facilitated cognitive convergence around a paradigm of 'sound economic policy and soft co-ordination' (see also Dyson 2002b: 14). Decisions regarding taxation and public spending are still a matter for national governments, but the Euro Plus Pact of 2011 and the fiscal compact of 2012 include tax and labour market reforms as well as competitiveness.

If the ECOFIN judges the deficit of a euro area member to be excessive, and if that member state does not take action to rectify the excessive deficit, the Council of Ministers can ultimately impose sanctions on the country concerned (but only if that deficit has not been caused by exceptional and temporary circumstances which have been defined in the Stability and Growth Pact). This can culminate in an adverse Council of Ministers recommendation (or ultimately a fine under the excessive deficit procedure in relation to fiscal policy). As previously mentioned, member states not participating in stage three of the EMU are expected to 'endeavour' to avoid excessive deficit, but cannot be subject to sanctions. Members of the euro area have a legal commitment to avoid excessive deficits.

Yet, again, the most important rules are the unwritten ones. In fact, they are sometimes entirely instinctive. This is where the concept of doxa proves highly useful. As argued in Chapter 3, any field is structured around a particular doxa: a 'truth' that is taken for granted and undisputed (Bourdieu 1977: 164). The doxa is the self-evident 'objective' knowledge upholding the symbolic order of a field.

Participation in serious negotiations in Brussels implies a tacit acceptance of a fundamental law of the field: that conflicts between member states can only be resolved through dialogue in economically rational terms. One Danish official explains this rationalism:

> The atmosphere in my working group is very good. Our task is to solve the detailed technical questions and in my group it is really the good argument that counts because we work together to solve problems. We also stand together because we all represent the finance ministries so we think we solve the problems best together. We don't want to bother the ambassadors.[9]

First, the Danish official carves out a space for economic knowledge, which is clearly different from that of foreign policy, for instance. Second, and perhaps more importantly, the official's statement suggests that success at the negotiation table is dependent upon the adoption of a technocratic discourse (see also Bourdieu 1987: 831).

In this light, Puetter's (2006: 18) characterisation of negotiations in economic and monetary affairs as 'reflexive deliberation' seems somewhat problematic. We should avoid equating technocratic discourse with deliberation (in the Habermasian sense), as deliberation is never entirely free or unconstrained. While the force of the best argument is what counts in Brussels, debates on economic policy co-ordination in the EU take place within a narrow understanding of what constitutes legitimate knowledge.

Thus, for instance, no representative from any country would even consider objecting to the paradigm of 'responsible and sound' economic policy as it is represented in the Stability and Growth Pact. It is within this paradigm that all new proposals are made. As Bourdieu reminds us, every 'established order tends to produce (to very different degrees and with different means) the naturalization of its own arbitrariness' (Bourdieu 1977: 164). While national representatives think of their work as a technical, economic exercise, the objectives surrounding

---

[9] Interview, Danish Permanent Representation (Brussels), 5 September 2007.

EMU have always been political.[10] After all, the aim of their work is to promote the surveillance and co-ordination of economic policies and to facilitate the functioning of the single currency.

Stabilitätsphilosophie versus gouvernance économique

The paradigm of sound government finances does not stand uncontested. Much of the thinking in the field reflects the so-called *Stabilitätsphilosophie*, which has been inherited from the German ordo-liberal economic culture. However, this idea competes with the French attachment to *gouvernance économique*, which empowers elected state representatives rather than officials, since it places emphasis on visionary leadership and economic interventions (see Puetter 2004).

The ideological clash between these two positions has also become apparent in a practical sense during negotiations. For instance, the monetarist and stability-oriented coalition led by Germany promotes nominal targets when assessing the budgetary situations of member states. In contrast, a regulatory coalition driven by France (and Italy) argues that structural indicators should also be taken into account in any evaluation of the soundness of an economy.

The ideological division seems, at first glance, to leave the field rather fragile. Yet I will argue that co-operation is actually promoted by this division. The differences between *Stabilitätsphilosophie* and *gouvernance économique* can be neatly divided into two categories: orthodoxy and heterodoxy as shown in Figure 4.1. This opposition between right (orthodox) and wrong (heterodox) only makes sense within a discursive universe comprising that which can be taken for granted (see Figure 4.1). Put differently, member states clash only within the framework of what is considered possible. This universe can be understood as 'a range of ideas which is either expressed or understood as containing the whole matter under discussion' and works in opposition to that which is admitted without scrutiny (Bourdieu 1977: 170). It creates a basic stability built on tension. So *gouvernance économique* is a heterodox position that challenges the German vision of the economy – but paradoxically, the conflict helps to secure continued co-operation.

In order to defend doxa against heterodoxy, it is necessary to admit that the given doxa is no longer self-evident. This is where a common enemy

---

[10] Interview, Danish Ministry of Finance (Copenhagen), 31 August 2007.

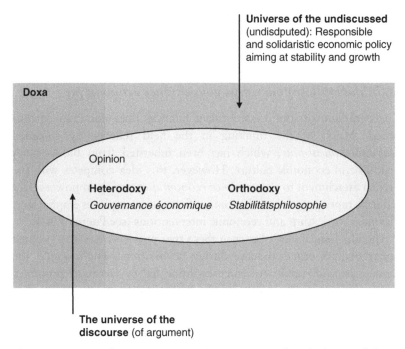

Figure 4.1 Heterodox *gouvernance économique* and orthodox *Stabilitäts-philosophie*
Source: Adapted from Bourdieu (1977: 168)

may be helpful. In other words, when divisions within the euro area become too deep, it helps to remind oneself that there are countries that are even further gone. This is where the notions of orthodoxy and heterodoxy become important; by choosing to stay outside the euro, Denmark and the UK appear to reject not only the euro project but closer co-operation per se. They expose the fragility of the EU's common monetary policy.

National interest and 'credit in the bank'

What makes one country more powerful than another? Over the years, a certain consensus on what counts as power resource, or capital, has been established through the mutual exchange of views. Officials often use the metaphor of 'credit in the bank' to describe power dynamics.[11]

---

[11] Interview, German Permanent Representation (Brussels) 10 May 2006; Interview, HM Treasury (London), 22 August 2006.

This metaphor confirms the suitability of the concept of capital for an analysis of diplomacy in the EU. Officials explain how all member states have 'an account in the bank'. The more they deposit, the more they can later withdraw what they need. The credit deposited in the bank is professionalism and competence – or at least this was the case until euro membership became an important divider. Because the negotiation game never stops (in what some would call repeated games – officials meet several times a month), collective memory is important and representatives are aware of the credit balance in all accounts. The accommodation of a request that other representatives find difficult to accept requires more goodwill than a trivial demand.

A good example is Luxembourg's significant struggle during the five-year-long negotiations on value-added taxation (VAT) intended to prevent distorted competition between member states with different VAT rates.[12] Any changes to EU tax laws require unanimous consent from the member states. With its 15 per cent VAT, Luxembourg has become a popular location for international e-commerce businesses such as eBay, Skype and iTunes, so the Grand Duchy's government was determined to negotiate a better deal to protect its revenue base. A Danish official explains how Luxembourg's blockage was 'without substance':

The pressure is implicit, but it is never pleasant to be the only country out of 27 to be exposed. Luxembourg has also been grilled in the press because it is clear that they were the blocking country and they had no reasonable argument apart from wanting to 'steal' money, which in reality is ours. So they are under pressure. They draw on their account and impose a great strain on their own goodwill. This will be punished next time they have a problem and they need help; they will have less goodwill.[13]

This view not only reflects that good arguments are necessary if a state wishes to influence negotiations but it also suggests that officials do not want to stand out from the crowd. Agreement on the EU's VAT laws was finally reached in December 2007, which somewhat satisfied Luxembourg: community rules covering the VAT on the purchases of goods and services electronically will not come into force until 2015. Being influential requires economic expertise, good arguments and decent economic results.

---

[12] Archival source, May 2007.
[13] Interview, Danish Ministry of Finance, 31 August 2007.

Interestingly, country size does not matter as much as the good argument. Economic performance and knowledge are a crucial power resource, even at the highest level in the Eurogroup (Puetter 2006).[14] Finland, for instance, is regarded as very influential.[15] This focus on good (rational) arguments means that references to national interests, let alone identity, are taboo:

My experience is that constructive, professional, solid answers to the challenges give goodwill and influence. You can get very far if you argue reasonably for a case and have no ulterior motives or national interests to be catered for, which everybody can see through immediately because we know each other so well. You can get far, irrespective of your relative size.[16]

Paradoxically, national interests are a hindrance to the quest for influence. This is a striking rejection of the idea of hard bargaining. It also presents an entirely different picture of EU diplomacy than has been hitherto presented by existing theories. The 'reasonable argument' is obviously also a way of imposing a particular way of thinking. That the argument is not directly linked to size but to more subtle forms of capital does not mean that there is no power struggle or that no marginalisation takes place.

For a considerable number of diplomats, the EU offers the possibility of educating the domestic population about good economic policy. Indeed, the Maastricht convergence criteria and the Stability and Growth Pact have strengthened a particular view of financial policy in countries such as Italy and Belgium (Hallerberg 2000). The 'ideational consensus' in Brussels is perceived as helpful for economists and bureaucrats from countries such as Greece and Italy who receive European backing for their domestic reforms. Meanwhile, for representatives from rather well-functioning economies (e.g. Finland), the EU provides the opportunity to set the agenda and transform competence and good economic performance into diplomatic capital. As a Greek senior official makes clear:

I need the EU to push our agenda [the agenda of the Greek Ministry of Finance vis-à-vis the other ministries], but we also invest a lot of energy in the meetings because the real debate takes place in Brussels.[17]

---

[14] Interview, Danish Permanent Representation (Brussels), 7 February 2008.
[15] Interviews, DG ECFIN, European Commission (Brussels), 25 March 2008; Interview, Spanish Permanent Representation (Brussels), 28 March 2008.
[16] Interview, Danish Ministry of Finance (Copenhagen), 8 August 2007.
[17] Interview, Greek Ministry of Finance, 15 March 2008.

Given this community of like-minded economists and the status that comes with good economic performance, one would expect euro-outsiderness to be a minor detail. The UK, Denmark and Sweden have all performed above average and hence should be rewarded in terms of influence and good position. However, as we will now see, such expectations have been misguided.

Stigmatising euro-outsiders

Increasingly, competence and professionalism are not enough to influence economic co-operation in the EU. The economic crisis has made euro-outsiderness an important marker of difference. As shown in the previous chapter, stigma is not automatically ascribed: it is actively imposed. It involves the co-occurrence of labelling, stereotyping, separation, status loss and discrimination. I will now consider these components one by one. Perplexingly, the uncertaintly of the future of the euro is the underlying motivation for relegating the UK and Denmark to the margins.

Labelling and stereotyping

According to most British and Danish officials, euro-outsiderness significantly influences the way in which others perceive them. When asked to describe the implications of the Danish EMU opt-out, the standard answer from European Commission officials is clear: 'Getting rid of the euro opt-out would be a great step forward for Denmark's image. Right now it is basically a free-rider.'[18] The first component of stigmatisation, labelling, is clearly at work.

There is a widespread assumption that something is lost by not participating in the euro area. As an Italian representative explains:

Denmark could have a much stronger voice if it was in the Eurogroup. With Germany in the euro area, Denmark has an interest in participating to influence its biggest neighbour.[19]

British and Danish officials know that their European partners generally consider their status to be undesirable. Interestingly, though, the British and Danish representatives are not perceived in the same way. First,

[18] Interview, DG ECFIN, European Commission (Brussels), 28 March 2008.
[19] Interview, Italian Permanent Representation (Brussels), March, 2008.

everybody in the field is aware of the fact that the UK has a 'stronger' opt-out than Denmark.[20] Second, the UK is recognised by the European Commission and the Council of Ministers secretariat as a major international power, and its independent monetary policy and its position vis-à-vis the euro area is acknowledged as having some logic. The Danish position, by contrast, is considered to be fundamentally absurd given that Denmark is locked to the euro area.[21] But as long as the Danish opt-out is perceived to be temporary, representatives from Denmark can compensate for their outsiderness. This point will be developed further in the section on stigma management.

The 'outsider' label is linked to the second component of stigmatisation – stereotyping – which ascribes a set of undesirable characteristics to the stigmatised. Denmark is referred to as 'reluctant' and the UK as 'traumatised'.[22] Diplomatic interaction tends to cultivate clichés about nationalities. Also in the EU, there is a tendency to ridicule particular national traits – for example, Greek officials are described as having a 'chaotic negotiation style' and a 'scandalous handling of the euro entry'.[23] However, this national characteristic or trait is countered by a strongly shared feeling of community, which in turn reduces the problem of being Greek. But, by the same token, it also increases the problem of being British or Danish.

Voluntary and involuntary outsiders

The labelling and stereotyping of the UK and Denmark become even more evident when comparing the two countries with new member states that have yet to adopt the euro. While some do not wish to be part of the currency, others, notably some of the members from Central and Eastern Europe, are determined to gain entry to the euro area, as shown in Table 4.1.

Involuntary euro-outsiders, such as Lithuania, are not stigmatised; rather, they are perceived as being on their way to becoming good

---

[20] Interviews, Dutch Permanent Representation (Brussels), 16 February 2008.

[21] Interview, DG ECFIN, European Commission (Brussels), 28 February 2008; Interview Council Secretariat (Brussels), 26 February 2008.

[22] Interviews, Finish and Belgian Permanent Representation (Brussels), 16 February 2007.

[23] Interview, DG ECFIN, European Commission (Brussels), 28 February 2008. For a discussion of the problems of stereotyping nationalities in diplomatic theory, see Sebenius (2002).

Table 4.1. *Types of stigma management*

Types of stigma management

Insiders	Involuntary outsiders	Voluntary outsiders
Austria, Belgium, Cyprus, Estonia, Finland, France, Germany, Greece, Ireland, Italy, Luxembourg, Malta, Netherlands, Portugal, Slovakia, Slovenia, Spain	Bulgaria, Croatia, Czech Republic, Hungary, Latvia, Lithuania (will adopt the euro in 2015), Poland	UK, Denmark, Sweden[24]
17 member states	8 member states	3 member states
'Good Europeans'	On their way to becoming 'Good Europeans'	'Bad Europeans'

Europeans, although they are seen to be 'less well behaved than the Danes' as the former Eurogroup secretary stressed in an interview.[25] Euro area representatives encourage the new member states to make the necessary reforms and help them into the club (Puetter 2006: 170). The euro area is not just a mode of co-operation; it is a 'family with a common destiny', as former ECB President Jean-Claude Trichet likes to put it (Trichet 2008).

The distinction between Danish euro-outsiderness and new-member-state-outsiderness is even more striking because the new member states occupy the same formal position as Denmark in the ERM II; yet they are perceived differently. This is because Danish euro-outsiderness appears to be more permanent. Indeed, the self-disciplining process, which is part of the preparations to become a euro area member, must be credible.

The Eurogroup: Separating 'us' from 'them'

When Slovenia joined the euro area in January 2007 as the first member state from the former Eastern bloc, a festive though solemn reception

[24] As mentioned in Chapter 1, Sweden does not have a formal opt-out but it has voluntarily chosen to remain outside the euro area.
[25] Interview, Eurogroup Secretariat (Brussels), March 2008.

was held. Quite deliberately, no euro-outsiders were invited. The long process of preparation and rapprochement to adopt the single currency culminates in a *rite d'institution*, when a state is welcomed into the euro club. As one senior European Commission official explains, 'such initiatives expose the exclusivity of the Euroclub'.[26] The third component of stigmatisation, the separation of 'us' from 'them', is manifest. Over time, euro-outsiders have gradually been excluded from an intimate club in the field: the Eurogroup, despite British officials fighting long and hard to avoid this. The establishment of the Eurogroup marks what increasingly counts as capital in the field – euro membership:

> In the beginning, it was actually quite spectacular because the meetings of the Eurogroup and ECOFIN were held on the same day. The British, Swedish and Danish finance ministers had to wait outside the meeting room in the lobby until the euro-insiders were finished with their meeting. The political exclusion was quite clear. Now it takes place the day before, but only because you cannot let 12–15 ministers wait.[27]

The formalisation of the Eurogroup – where the ministers meet the day before the ECOFIN Council meeting and not just in the hours before the it – began in 2000. The Eurogroup is the smallest forum in which ministers participate: around 40 people (ministers and officials) are present at these meetings.

But the Eurogroup is only the tip of the iceberg. A veritable 'exclusion zone' with a parallel system of meeting forums that only include euro-insiders has been created (Danish Institute for International Studies 2008: 206). To prepare the meetings in the Eurogroup, for instance, an EFC working group has been established: the Eurogroup Working Group (EWG). With this exclusion zone being replicated at all levels, the division between euro-insiders and euro-outsiders becomes more important than ideological divisions over monetary policy. As such, the exclusion of euro-outsiders reduces the importance of the clash between the *Stabilitätsphilosophie* and *gouvernance économique*.

ECOFIN remains formally responsible for making decisions[28], but the informal Eurogroup has gradually obtained a certain level of

[26] Interview, DG ECFIN, European Commission (Brussels), 25 February 2008.

[27] Interview, DG ECFIN, European Commission (Brussels), 25 February 2008.

[28] The composition, methods and functions of the Eurogroup were first described by the Belgian presidency in a so-called general orientation note published on 10 January 2001 (Danish Institute for International Studies 2008: 210).

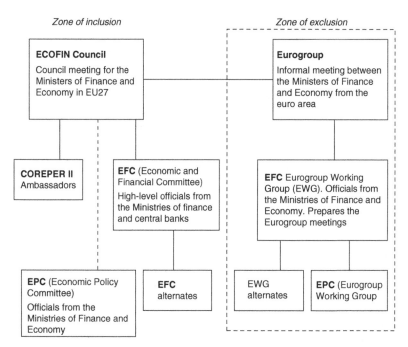

Figure 4.2 The EMU and the exclusion zone

authority and formalisation and has expanded its agenda, culminating with the Treaty of Lisbon, which consolidates the forum as the de facto engine room of integration.

In 2004, Luxembourg's Finance Minister, Jean-Claude Juncker, was elected President of the Eurogroup. The president's area of responsibility is wide-ranging: he is responsible for drawing up meeting agendas and work programmes for the Eurogroup; chairing the meetings; circulating informal conclusions (the so-called 'Letter of the President'); briefing ministers on the outcome of Eurogroup discussions; presenting to the public; and representing the Eurogroup in meetings with third parties and in international forums (Danish Institute for International Studies 2008: 211).

France promised the euro-outsiders that they would be allowed to participate in the preparatory work for the Eurogroup. However, since 2001, they have been permanently excluded from the EFC working group that prepares the Eurogroup agenda (Coeuré 2003: 5). The EFC drafts brief discussion papers, identifies implications of policy proposals and actions, and generally provides input to the Eurogroup (Danish Institute for International Studies 2008: 211). Consequently, euro-outsiders have been de facto excluded from all preparatory work. As a Dutch representative explains:

> It's a great handicap for the British and Danish representatives. In a way it's a shame that they cannot participate with their knowledge and expertise. But think of the signals it sends! We are always very careful about what we say, but the British and Danish positions are not expressing solidarity.[29]

As euro-outsiders, British and Danish officials lose status. Economic competence and performance remain essential, but euro-outsiderness has increasingly become a way to classify member states and to distinguish between those that dominate the field and those that struggle to achieve recognition.

Much to the frustration of the euro-outsiders, the Eurogroup's agenda has evolved over the years into areas that are not directly euro-related. During the first years of the Eurogroup's existence, its members primarily exchanged views on the basis of economic forecasts produced by the European Commission; followed the budgetary situation of euro-insiders; undertook monetary dialogue with the ECB President; and discussed and analysed the exchange-rate developments of the euro, and issues related to global imbalances and the international use of the euro (Puetter 2005: 80–111).

When French President Nicolas Sarkozy succeeded in establishing summits exclusively for the heads of state of the euro area, now formalised by the fiscal compact of 2012, he was completing a process of separation that had been evolving for over a decade. Already in July 2000, the French presidency introduced a routine whereby the Eurogroup held longer meetings and could distinguish euro-area issues from the ordinary agenda of the ECOFIN Council (see also Elgström 2003: 25). Following the December 2000 European Council of Nice, the Eurogroup began to deal with structural reforms related to the Lisbon strategy in a more systematic manner. The group now issues specific advice on labour market reform, product market reform and financial markets. Moreover, it debates overarching macroeconomic policy, international economic and energy policy. Even climate and environmental issues are discussed in the Eurogroup. In other words,

---

[29] Interview, Dutch Permanent Representation (Brussels), December 2007.

euro-outsiders are now excluded from substantial discussions about EU decisions and legislation that will later be binding on them.

Nearly all compromises are reached during the Eurogroup's Monday meeting and are not discussed in the ECOFIN on the Tuesday. It is therefore difficult for non-euro members to have a say on issues discussed in the Eurogroup. As a senior official from Luxembourg states:

> Of course we are polite, but the Eurogroup always reaches agreement before the ECOFIN meetings. At the ECOFIN, the euro-ministers are bored and just want to get things over with as soon as possible and go home.[30]

Euro area ministers sometimes do not even bother to show up for the ECOFIN meetings. In the section on stigma management, I will discuss how Brown's behaviour may relate to the UK's missionary strategy. Moreover, euro countries rarely send their most well-briefed representatives to a meeting where everything has already been decided.[31]

Of course, not all euro area initiatives are deliberately crafted to exclude euro-outsiders. Apart from strengthening cohesion among the euro-insiders, the exclusion of euro-outsiders also serves practical purposes. The ECOFIN adheres strongly to the notion that Europe 'needs to function' and that everyone has to be on board. However, as new member states join, formal decision-making forums have continued to grow in size. With well over 150 people present in an ordinary ECOFIN Council meeting, the scope for negotiations and effective interaction has diminished significantly. This is why the parallel system is so valuable. It stands to reason that it will only become more difficult to reach agreement with the UK, Denmark and Sweden, as well as the involuntary outsiders, all in one room.

Managing euro-outsiderness

Euro-outsiderness destabilises the uniform monetary order in the EU and the solidarity between member states. This is why euro-outsiders are excluded from meetings – not just because it is easier to negotiate without them but because they represent a threat. Instead of automatically accepting outsiderness, British and Danish diplomats attempt to

---

[30] Interview, Luxembourg Permanent Representation, February 2008.
[31] Interview, Danish Ministry of Finance, April 2007.

modify the exclusionary effects. This section looks more closely at the management of euro-outsiderness. The analysis focuses on how it affects British and Danish representatives, and how the field authorises and favours certain voices over others.

I have identified four distinct sets of strategies for managing euro-outsiderness. The first aims to actively renegotiate the lines of distinction between the 'ins' and 'outs' in an attempt to reduce the exclusionary effects of the opt-outs. I label these efforts strategies of challenging exclusion.

The second set of strategies aims to create harmonious relations with the other member states – it is a form of stigma recognition, involving camouflage (deflection) and compensation (normalisation). This strategy reflects a desire to eradicate the boundary between the 'opt-out' identity and the diplomatic *sens pratique*. Through these strategies, officials hope to be recognised simply as hardworking officials.

The third set of strategies also involves an attempt to gain social acceptance, but it is not necessarily aimed at creating a harmonious atmosphere. I refer to these as missionary strategies because officials use them to distinguish themselves from the 'normals'. With these types of strategy, officials attempt to redress their spoiled identity by presenting themselves as being better than the rest of the EU.

These three first sets of strategies are active, while the fourth represents a passive avoidance of attracting attention, whether good or bad. I refer to this fourth set as self-restraint strategies because officials deliberately abstain from seeking influence to avoid sustaining further damage to their image. In the following, I will explore these four ways of managing euro-outsiderness in greater detail.

Challenging exclusion

Most Europeans are now familiar with the images of European bridges that decorate the euro banknotes. What is puzzling, however, is that the precise design of the euro banknotes and coins should be of interest to British and Danish representatives.

For a long period it remained uncertain whether the UK and Denmark would eventually join the euro. It was expected that all states would do everything in their power to fulfil the convergence criteria for introducing the euro, and the British and Danish strategies gave good reason to believe that they might one day join. Not only did British officials engage actively in the negotiations on the procedure for excessive deficits[32] but they also took part in the preparatory committee's lengthy discussions about the design of the single currency coins and banknotes. For instance, they criticised a passage in the European Commission's proposal about national symbols on the notes being 'very discreet'. Instead, they suggested that national emblems should take up at least 20 per cent of the individual coins and notes.[33] Still today, British and Danish officials tend to negotiate as if they were bound by the same rules as the euro area. David Cameron's veto of the treaty changes in 2011 – which would never fully apply to the UK – is just one illustration.

In fact, euro-outsiders have not passively accepted their gradual exclusion. The establishment of the Eurogroup and the expansion of exclusion zones have been severely criticised by the UK and Sweden; Denmark to a lesser extent. When British and Danish representatives feel unjustly labelled and excluded, they advocate their right to receive information and to influence the decision-making process. British officials often feel obliged to remind their European colleagues of the UK's status as full member state. This struggle draws on a discourse about 'fairness'. Despite the frustration, the European game itself is never questioned. As such, the British struggle is reminiscent of what minority groups have done for years: claimed their rights as equal citizens.

British and Danish officials find exclusion unfair when the Eurogroup discusses issues that have implications beyond the euro area. Needless to say, what constitutes 'implications beyond the euro area' is difficult to agree upon. Even before the Eurogroup had been conceived, British diplomats questioned the division between what they called 'ins' and 'outs'. They argued that it was problematic if only the 'ins' had the right to vote when decisions could materially affect the 'outs'.[34] This struggle continues. British officials regularly challenge the division of labour between the Eurogroup and ECOFIN:

We have always been clear that when it's an issue of economic importance to the EU as a whole, then it should be rightfully discussed in the ECOFIN Council.

---

[32] Archival sources, 24 April 1997. The UK was very active in the development of the pact and voted against it in the ECOFIN meetings because of the position of its Parliament and its general position on financial policy.

[33] Archival sources, 10–15 June 1995.

[34] The British officials find that Article 109 (3) is unacceptable. Thus the European Commission should consult the 'outs' under Article 109 and avoid taking decisions that may create 'institutional divisions' between ins and outs, cf. archival source, 17 April 1997.

ECOFIN should be the main decision-taking body, and the Eurogroup should not in any way impinge on that.[35]

British officials recall the revision of the Stability and Growth Pact in 2005 as a defining moment for their exclusion:

> We were quite vocal about our exclusion and we felt it was wrong because the revisions would affect us and it would affect the non-euro members equally.[36]

Decision-making is sliding from ECOFIN into the Eurogroup, thereby confirming the rubberstamp function of the ECOFIN meetings, which are presented with decisions as a *fait accompli*. Despite British protests, the Treaty of Lisbon recognises the Eurogroup as an official EU institution – not just a private dinner club – and it will have the ability to set a formal agenda for itself. This further strengthens the division between insiders and outsiders. Euro-insiders are able (among other things) to use a qualified majority on budgetary discipline; economic policy guidelines and the views of outsiders will no longer be taken into account when the euro area is enlarged. The formalisation of the Eurogroup was deliberately sought to get rid of the bothersome British interventions. As one European Commission official comments,

> We do not want outsiders such as the UK to use disagreement in the Eurogroup to make a big mess, and this is why we expanded the questions that are only dealt with by the euro area. We also want them to feel frustrated.[37]

British representatives, by drawing attention to their own situation, have consolidated the public image of their deviance, thereby legitimising the very exclusion that they contested in the first place. Generally, strategies of challenging exclusion have been futile. The good argument and expert knowledge remain the key to influence, but euro-insiderness or euro-outsiderness increasingly plays a role in the positioning of a member state representative.

The first big crisis

The Stability and Growth Pact is an understanding adopted by all EU member states in 1997 about the soundness of a national economy and

---

[35] Interview, UK Permanent Representation (Brussels), 15 October 2007.
[36] Interview, HM Treasury, 17 April 2007.
[37] Interview, DG ECFIN, European Commission (Brussels), 25 March 2008.

how to react if an economy is likely to breach the convergence criteria. The pact is one of the most important rules in the field and was also the centre of one of the first big crises in the EMU, which took place in the second half of 2002. At that time the excessive deficit procedure was initiated in the cases of Portugal, Germany and France.[38] At a meeting on 25 November 2003, however, the Ministers of Finance decided against imposing any sanctions on France and Germany and plunged the EU into a crisis. Neither France nor Germany had accepted the defining rules of the field. Professional complicity collapsed. The very idea of a monetary union was at stake when European Commission President Romano Prodi subsequently described the Stability and Growth Pact as 'stupid' (Castle 2002).

Doxa had to be restored. The guardian of the treaties – the European Commission – took charge. It launched an action in the ECJ about whether ECOFIN was legally entitled to act as it did – that is, whether it was allowed to refrain from imposing sanctions on Germany and France despite agreeing with the European Commission's recommendation. In its ruling of 13 July 2004, the ECJ annulled the November 2003 Council of Ministers decision.[39] Stating that ECOFIN has the right to reject any recommendation from the European Commission, the ECJ made it clear that ministers do not have the right to accept a recommendation and subsequently fail to act accordingly.

Having sought to restore temporary order, the European Commission knew that the rules of the field had been breached and that this was likely to be repeated unless the rules were changed. In light of this it decided to launch a wide-ranging discussion on a reform of the pact.[40] Euro-outsiders were not considered to be the right states to rewrite the rules of the game, although these rules would also impact on them. Instead, reform proposals were discussed intensively in the Eurogroup in late 2004 and early 2005. It was the Eurogroup – not the ECOFIN – which de facto reformed the pact and re-established order. The handling of the reform process made the division between insiders and outsiders even more pronounced. The euro crisis has only accentuated this development.

---

[38] When the Council decides that an excessive deficit exists, the country concerned is formally obliged to reduce its deficit below 3 per cent of the gross domestic product or ultimately face financial sanctions.

[39] Case C-27/04, Commission vs Council, [2004] ECR I-6649.

[40] Interview, DG ECFIN, European Commission (Brussels), 25 February 2008.

The division is also apparent in everyday negotiations. British officials challenge exclusion on a daily basis, as a leading senior official explains:

I don't think we have any sort of grand strategy of any kind, but we do tend to take a defensive position and argue much more in the committees. We are always very prepared and we draw on the legal texts to argue that ECOFIN should be the centre of decision-making not the Eurogroup. We feel that we have the right to say more about the criteria for membership and the Stability and Growth Pact.[41]

Danish officials also engaged in the ongoing struggle to limit marginalisation. One Danish official explains how they protested against attempts to transfer responsibility for issues related to structural policy – a key priority for the Danish government – to the Eurogroup. Although they succeeded in persuading the others to change the text, 'it never ended up the way it should'.[42]

Sending the right signals to Brussels

Euro-outsiders describe an interesting phenomenon: extra activities carried out in order to compensate for lost influence due to an opt-out. This involves playing the 'model state' – that is, being extra prepared, helping member states which have domestic difficulties with a proposed article of legislation, developing constructive suggestions for compromises and so on.[43] These strategies reflect that British and Danish officials are often split between their eagerness to be good Europeans and their loyalty to the government of the state that they serve. While the UK is outside the euro area, its representatives still seek influence and compensate for their euro-outsiderness. For instance, British officials have been very active on the Lisbon strategy as an alternative route to influence the EMU and to combat stigmatisation. As a high-ranking Treasury official explains,

For me, the Lisbon strategy is a way to say that the EMU is actually a British policy; that it is not difficult or dangerous for us. I think it works in Brussels. The problem is that no one in Britain knows about the Lisbon strategy.[44]

---

[41] Interview, HM Treasury (London), 17 April 2007.
[42] Interview, Danish Ministry of Finance (Copenhagen), 31 August 2007.
[43] Interviews, Danish Permanent Representation (Brussels), Ministry of Finance (Copenhagen), December 2005 and March 2008.
[44] Interview, HM Treasury (London), 17 April 2007.

Denmark has benefited from having obtained a position as a 'model country' when it comes to economic performance (see Marcussen 2007: 17). Consequently, it has acquired a speaking platform that would otherwise be difficult to obtain given its opt-out status. Through relatively good economic performance, the UK, Denmark and Sweden have had greater influence on policy-making than some other euro-outsiders of equal size, and even greater influence on certain aspects of the European economic agenda than some euro-insiders. This, combined with the fact that Danish and British civil servants are considered to be competent and well prepared, partly compensates for their exclusion from the euro area. However, it is unlikely that the two countries will be able to maintain their respective positions as model countries in the EU.

British diplomacy has been particularly complex in this respect, reflecting a very ambivalent attitude towards handling euro-outsiderness. During the Labour term from 1997 to 2010, the five economic tests regarding the UK and the euro were used to signal to the EU that the UK was open to the idea of adopting the euro – some day. Domestically, however, they had an almost opposite purpose, serving as guarantees that the UK would never adopt the euro.

The Labour government continually claimed that the UK's official position remained unchanged since being set out by the Chancellor in his Statement to the House of Commons in October 1997. This position was also repeated on official British websites:

The determining factor underpinning any government decision on membership of the single currency is the national economic interest and whether the economic case for joining is clear and unambiguous. (BERR 2008)

When I asked a senior Treasury official if the five tests were merely a cover for the fact that the UK would never adopt the euro, he looked firmly at me and said:

They are not just a cover! The tests are analytical and profound economic analyses by the best economists and experts in the UK and from elsewhere. I would say that it is probably the most substantive and serious analysis that the Treasury has made in the last 10–15 – maybe even 20 years. Maybe even in the whole of Whitehall.[45]

---

[45] Interview, HM Treasury (London), 17 April 2007.

His answer reveals that solid economic arguments are the only valuable arguments. The British duplicity was, not surprisingly, unconvincing in the long run. The ritual of annually repeating the five tests only serves to consolidate the image of being an outsider.[46]

Moreover, with the advent of a Conservative-Liberal Democratic government under the leadership of David Cameron in May 2010, this signal was bound to change. The new government had no intention of replacing the pound with the euro (despite Deputy Prime Minister Nick Clegg being openly in favour of the UK joining the euro). Instead, Chancellor George Osborne announced (to laughter) in the House of Lords that he had abolished the Treasury's Euro Preparations Unit. 'Yes, one does exist, and the officials concerned have been redeployed to more productive activities', he said.

The productive potential of the Euro Preparations Unit lies perhaps more in what it says about the tensions created by British stigma management. It was set up in 1997 to devise a National Changeover Plan to prepare the different parts of the British economy for a change-over to the euro. It published guides for business managers and hosted a website to inform the public. Even after Prime Minister Gordon Brown took over from Tony Blair, when it became clear that the government had no intention of adopting the euro, the Euro Preparations Unit remained in place. It continued to work hard, organise conferences for British companies and improve its website. Its work, however, was primarily about sending the right signals to Brussels, thereby camou-flaging the staunch euroscepticism. It sought to lend credibility to the government's 'prepare and decide' policy.[47] This strategy brings to mind those cases where individuals conceal the fact that they have lost their job by dressing for work and leaving the house each morning so that their family and friends believe that nothing has changed (Letkemann 2002: 516ff). To some degree, this strategy can be self-deceptive. As one Treasury official explained:

The Euro Preparation Team really believes in the 'prepare and decide' policy. No one in the Treasury would ever challenge their vision openly; and to some degree I think we all feel sorry for the Preparation Team. We all know that the UK is very far from adopting the euro.[48]

---

[46] Interview, HM Treasury (London), 17 April 2007.
[47] Interviews, HM Treasury (London), 17 April 2007.
[48] Interview, HM Treasury (London), 17 April 2007.

Strikingly, even within the Treasury, the meaning of euro-outsiderness is constantly renegotiated.

Camouflage and compensation

Danish representatives also make use of compensatory and camouflaging strategies. And unlike their British colleagues, the Danes have enjoyed some success. One reason for this is that the Danish government actually tried to abolish the euro opt-out in 2000, thereby demonstrating a genuine willingness to 'join the club'. Denmark is bound to the euro area by its fixed exchange rate policy, meaning that Danish officials do not experience the same degree of hostility as the British from their European colleagues. On the contrary, Danish representatives are met with more understanding, even humour:

My colleagues often ask me if and when there will be a new referendum; if there is any news. They are teasing a bit. Sometimes when we take a *tour de table* in the working group on preparation on the euro and external communication led by the Commission, teasing remarks are made.[49]

Generally, Denmark's goodwill in ECOFIN is greater than that of the UK: 'We do have quite a bit of goodwill because we have not drained our account and do not intend to do so [...] instead, we have contributed with compromises, and this is noticed'.[50] The language of draining the account is striking. Indeed, capital is not merely a theoretical abstraction; it is used by diplomats in their everyday negotiations.

Danish officials see themselves as 'the best euro country that never was'. They are proud when ECB President Jean-Claude Trichet says that Denmark should count as a member of the euro area in future statistics.[51] As one official underlines, 'Remember we do not live up to the Stability and Growth Pact because we have to, but because it is sound policy. It is our policy!'[52] In this way the Danish strategy of normalisation clearly differs from the British strategies.

Interestingly, it appears as though the Danish camouflage strategy successfully removes a portion of the stigma. At least the other member

---

[49] Interview, Danish Permanent Representation (Brussels), April 2007.
[50] Interview, Danish Ministry of Finance, April 2007.
[51] Interview, Danish Permanent Representation (Brussels), September 2007.
[52] Interview, Danish Ministry of Finance (Copenhagen), 31 August 2007.

states and EU institutions confirm the image of a constructive Denmark. As one former Eurogroup Secretary explains,

Because of Denmark's relationship to the euro and the way the Danish officials negotiate, I see Denmark as a more interesting and 'warmer' non-euro member state than Sweden and the UK. You know that most euro member states are aware that the Danish government is very interested in introducing the euro, but it just does not yet have its voters on board.[53]

However, there are limits to the extent to which one can 'play' at being a real member. The Eurogroup represents a closed club and rapprochement must be credible:

As long as I can say that the political and economic elite and the government is interested in participating, we appear positive; but if it becomes too obvious that Denmark does not intend to adopt the euro, I fear that we will be perceived as Switzerland, which enjoys the benefits without paying the costs.[54]

Switzerland, then, is seen as an extreme case and evokes the image of the 'free rider'. Abstract ideas of solidarity are central to everyday negotiations in the Council of Ministers system.

Danish officials do not seek to influence the Eurogroup; this is deemed impossible. They are, however, interested in obtaining information about what has been discussed in the group. In contrast with the Danes, the British officials do not attend all meetings and have a selective approach to the committees and working groups. One Finnish representative explains that it is not 'too difficult for Denmark to find out what's going on, but they cannot be sure to hear the "whole truth and nothing but the truth". It's much better to be there yourself; to be all in.'[55] This view is repeated when the same official is asked about his perception of Finland's position:

It is of utmost importance for Finland to be in the euro area and I believe our voice is highly appreciated by those inside. Instead of waiting in the corridors to ask, 'What happened?', we are inside.[56]

In striking contrast, a British official explains that loss of influence is not a major issue for him:

[53] Interview, Danish Permanent Representation (Brussels), March 2008.
[54] Interview, Danish Permanent Representation (Brussels), March 2008.
[55] Interview, Finnish Permanent Representation (Brussels), March 2008.
[56] Interview, Finnish Permanent Representation (Brussels), March 2008.

A lot will already have been discussed in the EFC, which sets the agenda for the ECOFIN. Any issue which comes to the Eurogroup or the ECOFIN will have been discussed by the EU27 already in the EFC. So if we feel particularly strongly about something that is coming up for discussion in the Eurogroup, then we will have a chance to speak in the EFC forum.[57]

While Danish compensation increases goodwill, there are clear limits when it comes to influencing the Eurogroup. This is not least because the insiders also have a strategic interest in keeping outsiders out.

Missionary strategies and self-restraint

While compensatory strategies are related to a fear of losing out, missionary strategies stem from an entirely different perception. Here, officials try to convert the stigma into an emblem. This involves stressing the good reasons for opting out of the EMU. The hard stance of the UK during the negotiation of the fiscal compact and the reform of the Stability and Growth Pact crisis is a case in point. One high-ranking European Commission official describes the British positioning:

While Denmark tends to keep a low profile, the UK has generally been very vigorous – also on euro areas. Remember when France and Germany breached the Stability and Growth Pact, the Council chose not to adopt our recommendation, but to *suspend* the treaty! It was the biggest crisis in the history of the EMU. This was why we went to Court. Portugal and the UK supported France and Germany. The UK only did it to block the machine and make a mess. I think the UK were the ones who made the crisis possible; it likes to play these silly games.[58]

The British version of this story, however, is rather different: the crisis and subsequent reform of the Stability and Growth Pact was encouraging, not messy. As the Financial Secretary to the Treasury declares to the House of Lords,

Of course we exercise our power of negotiations and persuasion at all stages. Indeed, I think the evolution of the Stability and Growth Pact to a large extent reflects the UK's own view of the direction in which it should be moving. (House of Lords 2004: 9)

---

[57] Interview, UK Permanent Representation (Brussels), August 2007.
[58] Interview, DG ECFIN, European Commission (Brussels), March 2008.

In a debate in the House of Lords, Angela Eagle, former Exchequer Secretary to the Treasury, echoes the missionary strategy:

We have not discovered that there are any disadvantages to not being in that group [...] we are confident enough in the way that we handle ourselves as negotiators in ECOFIN itself that we can look after our own economic wellbeing and our own economic interests. (House of Lords 2008: Q26)

British radicalism consists not in its position on economic policy but in that it openly argues that sound economic policy is not necessarily achieved through the single currency. While UK officials remain within the doxa of a 'sound economic policy' and are attached to budgetary discipline, they express heterodoxy when they want the UK to remain outside the euro area. As one Danish official explains, 'They take pride in being alone. My impression is that they have a different self-understanding, they regard themselves as an economic big power.'[59]

As Goffman observes, militant attempts to remove stigma may lead to a politicisation of the stigmatised, which renders the stigmatised even more different from the normals. This means that the UK is not even welcome. Obviously it would be a considerable triumph to have the City of London and the pound in the euro area. Given the rigid political position of the British politico-economic leadership, however, it is clear that British participation in the EMU would adversely affect the prospects of any reinforcement of political co-operation on economic policy.

Danish entry into the euro area does not give rise to such concerns because Denmark is a much smaller economy and already abides by all of the euro area obligations. As a Luxembourg representative explains:

Denmark could get much more influence if it were in; but whether Denmark is in or out does not change much for the rest of the EU. This is of course not the case with the UK.[60]

Missionary strategies may be successful at the outset but, in the long run, they only reconfirm the status of the stigmatised. As this British official underlines in relation to the reform of the Stability and Growth Pact, where the UK was particularly active:

[59] Interview, Danish Ministry of Finance (Copenhagen), 31 August 2007.
[60] Interview, Luxemburg Permanent Representation (Brussels), February 2008.

We hoped that the Pact would be revised in our direction, which would apply to all 27; instead, we got special provisions for the UK. We got what we wanted on the Stability and Growth Pact revision, but only in a sense of getting some very particular provisions, which were UK-specific.[61]

Consequently, the attempt made by British officials to push the EMU in a British direction was futile.

When asked about the prospects of enhanced co-operation on taxation among euro member states, a British senior official replies: 'If they really want to create an area with low growth and high taxes, they can go ahead without us.'[62] Indeed, British officials construct a separate system of honour; they praise the assumed special value of being a euro-outsider and advocate a militant, chauvinistic line, 'even to the extent of favouring a secessionist ideology' (Goffman 1963: 113). Remarkably, Danish officials never engage in missionary strategies; instead they see euro-outsiderness as a frustrating constraint on Danish interests.

While the majority of the stigmatised protect their sense of self and attempt to gain social acceptance, there are also cases in which stigma management may result in a further 'spoiling of identity', to use Goffman's terms. It is not easy to provide evidence for self-restraint; it is essentially a non-action, but excessive self-discipline is widespread in Brussels. Intimidated practices are brought about by the belief – particularly prevalent among Danish officials – that some officials are worth less than others due to their euro-outsiderness. One such example is the discussions had by the EU27 relating to the expansion of the euro area, in this case the admission of Cyprus and Malta. Though formally allowed to speak, British and Danish officials exercise self-restraint:

When we discussed enlargement of the euro zone to Slovenia and more recently Cyprus and Malta, we really have not felt comfortable about speaking because we are not a member. It doesn't impact us in anywhere near the same way it does on the euro area member states. So we don't tend to speak up too much on those kinds of issues.[63]

Another statement from a Danish official discussing the enlargement debate also reveals such self-censorship:

[61] Interview, HM Treasury, October 2007.
[62] Interview, UK Permanent Representation (Brussels), 29 February 2008.
[63] Interview, UK Permanent Representation (Brussels), October 2007.

In principle, we could speak. But in the general code of conduct, it would be very unprofessional and strange if Denmark tried to do so in such a case. We wouldn't do it.[64]

Of course, this might simply be due to pragmatism and prioritising, but the word 'comfortable' suggests that it has more to do with tact. Interestingly, British and Danish self-restraint goes largely unnoticed by officials of other member states.

Most officials engage in several different forms of stigma management in the course of their career. Several strategies may be used simultaneously in different situations. Nevertheless, when it comes to the UK and Denmark, a clear trend is visible where UK officials engage in missionary battles, while Danish officials often seek to compensate for, or camouflage, their stigma. Table 4.2 provides an overview of these strategies.

Conclusions: Excluding the euro-outsiders

It can be argued that the UK and Denmark safeguard their monetary sovereignty while the rest of Europe have surrendered their national currencies and monetary self-determination. Yet the choice of opting out of the single currency has its challenges. This chapter has argued that euro-outsiderness becomes a stigma on British and Danish diplomats. The daily management of euro-outsiderness is not based on stable collective national identity or interests but is a diplomatic process that unfolds among economic and financial politico-administrative elites in a dense social field. The analysis has helped to unravel the struggles, exclusions and battles over the stakes defining this field.

The EMU entails a profound, macropolitical transformation of European statehood. It is one of the most ambitious and controversial projects in the history of European integration. Beneath the apparent agreement on 'sound economic policy', there are fundamental disagreements over the balance between economic and political governance in Europe, which have only been intensified by the economic crisis. Heterodox tendencies are on the increase among large member states as well as among the euro-outsiders, giving rise to an extra need to impose orthodoxy. Euro-outsiders are shunned, not just for practical reasons but because they threaten the very idea of a single currency.

---

[64] Interview, Danish Ministry of Finance, 31 August 2007.

Table 4.2. *Stigma management in the EMU*

Stigma management in the EMU

	Challenging exclusion	Camouflage and compensation	Missionary strategies	Self-restraint
Perception	Unfair exclusion due to opt-out	Perceived loss of influence and status due to opt-out	EU goals in an area covered by opt-out are against national interests	Serious loss of status or poor reputation among other member states
Strategy	Claim right to participate and restrict formal exclusion	'Model state', help others, hide opt-out	'Teach Europe a lesson' through examples and threats	Stay silent, be more careful
Outcome	Not efficient	Reduce stigmatisation	Enhance stigmatisation and exclusion	Neutral
State	UK	UK and Denmark	UK	Denmark

British and Danish representatives are stigmatised because they represent a threat to the difficult process of establishing economic and monetary solidarity. Stigmatisation is thus not an outcome of the infraction of 'normality' as much as it is a product of the failure to construct normality in the first place. States that appear to reject the very idea of European integration are ontologically intolerable, because they expose the fragility of the common currency.

For British and Danish officials, euro-outsiderness prevents their diplomatic quest for influence in the EU. However, they react differently to these processes of exclusion. Generally the differences in response stem from the dynamic between the different national dispositions and the formal and informal hierarchies in Brussels. Of course, it makes a great difference how the opt-out is designed in the first place. British officials have on their hands a 'complete' opt-out, while Danish officials manage an opt-out which could be seen as largely symbolic. Beyond formalities, an opt-out contributes to the idea that the member state requires special treatment, which leads to missionary strategies (UK); or that it should somehow apologise, which leads to camouflage and compensation (Denmark). Danish officials are sometimes so uncomfortable about opting out that they will refrain from seeking influence if they believe it to be inappropriate. A 'small state' or 'big state' identity may thus become a self-fulfilling prophecy.

Marginalisation is not automatic: it is socially negotiated and partly self-imposed. In some cases, such as when Danish officials are reluctant to take the floor, excessive self-restraint is at play. Denmark has a room of manoeuvre. Moreover, if British ministers and officials become less confident that the euro opt-out is socially justifiable or economically sustainable, missionary strategies will no longer be attractive. Denmark's most important and successful stigma management strategy is to 'play' at being an insider. This means that, should Denmark (which is more likely than the UK) one day choose to join the final stage of the EMU, the adjustments to the new situation are likely to be swift. The Danish officials are ready to play the role that they have always wanted to play: that of the constructive insider. Both member states compensate via their (relatively) good economic performance – and in the British case, London's role as a global financial centre. This improves their standing in the economic governance architecture.

Yet the division between euro-insiders and euro-outsiders has become the central mode of differentiation in the EU. Choosing not to adopt the single currency is not just a decision about keeping monetary sovereignty; it is about where one stands in the integration process per se. It does not merely mean sitting outside meeting rooms or losing a voting right; it means that one is not a 'good European'. As the euro area continues to integrate, euro-outsiders will become increasingly isolated and will need to invent new strategies to avoid increased marginalisation. To uphold solidarity among euro insiders, euro-outsiderness will continue to be punished.

5 | Through the revolving doors of Freedom, Security and Justice

Introduction

During the 1990s, Europe was hit by mass migration, was struck by terrorists and struggled to combat cross-border crime. The European media reported the Arab Spring of 2011 as an unprecedented migration crisis for the EU. The arrival of several thousand North African refugees and migrants on Italian territory led the former Minister of the Interior, Roberto Maroni, to brand the events a 'biblical exodus'. The Italian government's decision to grant temporary visas to the first arrivals, allowing them to travel within the EU, led to a serious falling out with France, as many Tunisians immediately travelled there to join relatives. France temporarily imposed border checks on trains arriving from Italy, a move that the European Commission confirmed was illegal. Both France and Italy considered opting out of the Schengen zone altogether to make it possible for them to protect their own borders.

This is European integration as seen through the eyes of the outsider, as if external events simply forced European governments to work together to find solutions. But the inside story is just as revealing, if not more so. The fight against cross-border crime and the regulation of migration flow in Europe were – and still are – brought about in part by a particular logic of co-operation. When the human suffering of those fleeing North Africa via the Mediterranean is translated into 'smart borders' and 'the third generation asylum system', we are not just witnessing the pragmatic response of member states to a dire situation; we are looking at the result of a long process of negotiations in a social field with its own rules and logics. These logics help to explain why opting out and the reintroduction of temporary border controls have little to do with our traditional understanding of sovereignty.

This chapter will move us away from the euro debate and onto other contentious areas of European integration: migration, asylum, border control, cross-border crime and civil law – all of which fall under the umbrella of Freedom, Security and Justice in EU terms. Despite the controversy surrounding their opt-outs from EU asylum, migration and civil law co-operation, both British and Danish officials take an active role in shaping new EU legislation – even in politically sensitive areas that are covered by their opt-outs. Opting out does not necessarily imply being out in the cold.

I will start by analysing the development of this high-profile and politically sensitive area of co-operation, as well as the controversial British and Danish opt-outs. I will then explore the partial stigmatisation of British and Danish representatives, and the strategies that they employ to circumvent their opt-outs, with varying degrees of success.

From taboo to totem

Until the end of the 1990s it was unimaginable that British and Slovenian police officers would one day be sitting together in Europol investigating child pornography networks; that the EU would have an agency in Warsaw co-ordinating the common border control; or that authorities in one member state would extradite presumed criminals at the request of another, as is now regular practice with the Common Arrest Warrant. For many years, European states were careful not to let the EU influence policies on asylum, immigration, border control, and police and criminal law. These areas were 'out of bounds' because they were perceived as being deeply rooted in national sovereignty.

However, from the mid-1990s, and particularly since 11 September 2001 and the ensuing global war on terror, member states have been eager to intensify co-operation in AFSJ. This fast-growing area covers the free movement of people, immigration, visa and asylum policy, and external border policy, as well as judicial co-operation in police, criminal and civil law matters. In 2007, on average, ten new legislative proposals were tabled on these issues every month (Monar 2007).

Researchers have discussed the extent to which the rapid increase in co-operation in this area has been accompanied by legal and political harmonisation. They generally hold one of two positions. The first is that national, political and legal authority remains a critical issue. The result of this is that many member states are reluctant to co-operate in this area (Givens and Luedtke 2004). The other maintains that AFSJ is driven by the desire of national officials to co-operate internationally so as to gain freedom from domestic scrutiny (Guiraudon 2003: 168; see also Monar 2003; Trenz and Eder 2003: 123). According to this second position, the reluctance to participate has been supplanted by a problem-solving agenda. While national agendas still play a major role, the second interpretation is the more accurate one as this chapter will show. In less than two decades, co-operation on internal security and justice has shifted from taboo to totem.

Agents (*presque*) provocateurs

The UK and Denmark have been dissidents since the 1980s. When the Schengen agreement was made between five states in 1985, it was only a matter of time before the rest of Europe was clamouring at the door. The free movement of citizens was generally seen as a big success, uniting Europe both symbolically and practically. The UK, however, refused to lift border controls to other member states, with Prime Minister Margaret Thatcher acting as a staunch opponent. She later wrote:

[A unified] 'Europe' is the result of plans. It is, in fact, a classic utopian project, a monument to the vanity of intellectuals, a programme whose inevitable destiny is failure: only the scale of the final damage done is in doubt. (Thatcher 2002: 359)

In Denmark, the prospect of German police officers entering Danish territory was widely propagated by the media, eloquently illustrating the anxieties behind Danish opposition to the Schengen agreement (see also Ryborg 1998). I will later explore why the Danish government nonetheless signed the Schengen agreement in 1996.

During the Maastricht negotiations of 1991–1992, the British and Danish governments, together with the governments of Ireland and Greece, successfully blocked German plans for the full communitarisation of immigration and asylum policy (Manners 2000: 82–123). This blockage resulted in a messy compromise and led to the creation of the so-called 'pillar structure'. The third of these pillars was strictly intergovernmental and dealt with 'justice and home affairs'. It differed from the supranational first pillar covering existing policies on agriculture, trade and the internal market, and EC policies, while the second pillar covered Common Foreign and Security Policy. John Major declared the third pillar a diplomatic triumph and presented the Maastricht Treaty as 'game, set and match' for the UK (Geddes 2000: 93).

When a narrow majority of the Danish population subsequently voted 'no' to the Maastricht Treaty in 1992, it was carefully interpreted by pro-European politicians (and the officials who helped to draft their position papers) not as a refusal of European co-operation but as a rejection of 'the United States of Europe'.[1] The opt-out from justice and home affairs was therefore designed as an exemption from supranational co-operation, leaving Denmark free to participate as long as co-operation remained intergovernmental.[2] While few Danes understand the technical details, the opt-out remains an important symbol of sovereignty for much of the Danish population, and not only those who rejected the Maastricht Treaty. Most observers saw the British and Danish opt-outs as purely symbolic; they reasoned that the other member states' desire to make co-operation supranational would be limited (e.g. Petersen 1993: 93). Therefore the general interpretation in the early 1990s was that British and Danish sovereignty was secure.

A quiet revolution

In 1997 the member states made a radical move towards integrating their asylum and immigration policies, border control and civil law. The Treaty of Amsterdam changed the nature of co-operation by defining the AFSJ. The UK, Denmark and other hesitant member states resisted communitarisation of asylum, immigration and border control right up until the final weeks before the Amsterdam summit (Moravcsik and Nicolaidis 1998: 29). Following exhausting negotiations, the British government accepted the incorporation of the Schengen *acquis* into the Treaty of Amsterdam. For the UK, however, removing national border control was still out of the question. The Schengen zone has since witnessed an explosion of cross-border activity: citizens from 22 member states, together with Norway, Iceland, Liechtenstein and Switzerland now move freely across Europe.

---

[1] For details regarding the Maastricht referendum, see Adler-Nissen (2008a), Møller (2003) and Petersen (2003).

[2] Supranational co-operation implies that EU legislation has a direct effect in member states and a direct effect for EU citizens. In contrast, intergovernmental co-operation – the traditional form of treaty-based international co-operation – means that, to be effective, treaty law must be transposed into national law through national parliaments.

Furthermore, in 1997 a new title was added to the treaty: 'Visas, asylum, immigration and other policies related to the free movement of persons' (Title IV TEC). This covered measures concerning external border controls, asylum, immigration and judicial co-operation in civil matters, bringing these areas under the first pillar. To secure British acceptance of Title IV, the UK was granted a remarkable opt-in protocol, making it possible for the UK to choose whether to participate in a measure on a case-by-case basis. Police and judicial co-operation was still under the jurisdiction of the reshaped third pillar, to which the Treaty of Amsterdam added the fight against racism and xenophobia. The treaty also included new provisions for co-operation against organised crime, such as sexual exploitation of children, human trafficking, vehicle theft, dealing in illegal arms and drugs, fraud and terrorism.

The Danish opt-out from Title IV was a lot less dramatic than the original opt-out, which (as mentioned above) was a rejection of supranational legislation. When elements of the co-operation became supranational, the Danish government had to update its Maastricht protocol to ensure that Denmark would remain exempted. Initially, Denmark was reluctant to give up its national border control, with the domestic debate centring on the possibility of German police officers entering Danish territory and the EU influencing Danish criminal law. Despite this, in order to safeguard the Nordic Passport Union[3] (with Sweden, Finland, Norway and Iceland), Denmark went ahead and surrendered its national border controls by signing the Schengen agreement in 1996. The reason for this controversial move was that Sweden and Finland joined the EU in 1997, meaning that they would also be part of the Schengen system that was now integrated into the treaties. Consequently, to uphold the Nordic Passport Union, Denmark (and also Norway and Iceland, albeit on different terms) would also have to be part of Schengen.

Nonetheless, the Danish opt-out from supranational co-operation still had to be respected. So when the Schengen agreement was included in the Treaty of Amsterdam, a protocol was drafted to ensure that Denmark would continue to participate in Schengen-related measures under the supranational Title IV, while still paradoxically respecting the

---

[3] Since 1958 the Nordic Passport Union has allowed citizens of the Nordic countries – Denmark, Sweden, Norway, Finland and Iceland – to travel and reside in other Nordic countries without a passport or residence permit.

opt-out from 'supranationality'. I will return to this bizarre Schengen protocol later in this chapter.

With the Treaty of Nice (2001), most of those areas covered by Title IV (visas, asylum, immigration and other policies related to the free movement of citizens) would be subject to the codecision procedure (Article 251 of the EC Treaty). The Treaty of Lisbon (2009) completed the 'normalisation' of Freedom, Security and Justice by bringing matters of internal security within the scope of the 'community method'. Within this new legal context, the Union is looking to enhance judicial co-operation through mutual recognition of the respective legal systems of the member states. Qualified majority voting (QMV) now applies to areas such as police matters and crime. Moreover, regarding family law, the EU is promoting common procedures for recognising cross-border marriage and divorce for all EU citizens. This explains why Poland took care to ensure that the Treaty of Lisbon does not prevent it from having particular rules about public decency, family law and morals.[4] This Polish exemption does not change the overall picture of a quiet revolution of European integration, however. As Jonathan Faull – the former Director of Commission DG of Justice, Liberty and Security – explains:

> To have been able to create something substantial from nothing in the relatively short period of just over ten years is obviously satisfying, particularly so when you consider that the area falls within the remit of the national ministries of interior and justice – not famous for their openness to working with the EU.

So just how has this transformation been possible?

The good argument is European

The Freedom, Security and Justice Council of Ministers is top of the pecking order in terms of decision-making. It consists of justice, immigration and interior ministers from the member states. The ministers act as the supreme policy-making body. Sitting beneath them is COREPER (II), where permanent representatives from the member states meet every week to negotiate agendas on behalf of the ministers. In turn,

---

[4] The protocol contains two substantial provisions (see Annex 1 of the Decision of the European Council, 11225/09). The second vote was predicated on concessions agreed by the European Council in December 2008 and confirmed in June 2009 as 'guarantees' to be formalised in a protocol attached to the next accession treaty.

below COREPER and the main committees is a growing number of working groups comprising national officials. Numbering around 25, these groups cover areas ranging from general primary concerns, such as terrorism, police co-operation and external frontiers, to more technical policy areas, such as false travel documents and the international enforcement of driving disqualification.

During the 1980s and most of the 1990s, the decision-making process was secretive, some might even say undemocratic (Hix 2005; Lancker 1997). Co-operation on Justice and Home Affairs developed partly in isolation from broader domestic constraints. Pro-migrant non-governmental organisations have been rather unsuccessful in influencing what Andrew Geddes calls a 'bureaucratic epistemic community' (Geddes 2000: 150; see also Gray and Statham 2005). Intensive co-operation in the Council of Ministers has led to increasing trust between the member states' administrations but has not brought with it much transparency for the general public (Smith and Tsatsas 2002: 79–80).

It is interesting to note that this intensified co-operation has not threatened the dominant position of national governments (Gray and Statham 2005: 890–891; see also Guiraudon 2004). Until recently the European Commission, the European Parliament and the ECJ had limited powers. Even after the Treaty of Lisbon, the ECJ has limited jurisprudence in police and criminal law. This reflects a broader tension between the determination to protect national sovereignty and the sense of urgency in strengthening European cooperation in this area.

A small group of officials work full time with the AFSJ. They all have similar professional backgrounds and are typically lawyers by training. Most are not career diplomats but come from the interior, justice, home office or related agencies or departments. This reflects a general trend that has seen foreign ministries fade into the background, while other ministries have come to the fore in Brussels due to increased specialisation.[5]

This group of officials is convinced that Europe is facing two major challenges: on the one hand, large waves of refugees and illegal migration

---

[5] The notion of 'intensive transgovernmentalism' (Wallace 2000b: 33) provides an idea of the integrated and insular nature of co-operation. The transgovernmental method of policy-making is different from intergovernmentalism, since government actors such as ministerial officials, law-enforcement agencies and other actors have relatively autonomous decision-making functions (Lavenex 2001).

and terrorism, which demand pan-Europe responses; on the other hand, domestic protests against EU co-operation from 'illogical' politicians and 'hysterical' media. In this sense, national officials are like pioneers, trying to develop a new field of European integration.

The Brussels effect

Most national officials share the attitude that Europe 'needs to function' and everyone needs to be 'on board'. In this atmosphere of pragmatism, officials welcome constructive solutions to principled national positions, as one senior Council of Ministers official puts it.[6] States can increase their level of influence in the Council of Ministers system by adopting this problem-solving approach. 'The good argument' is crucial. It is an argument that addresses common problems (as opposed to limited national issues), and which calls for European solutions.

As a result of meeting several times a week, national representatives tend to develop a mutual understanding of the purpose of the negotiations. While they identify with their own countries, they are also placed in a socially structured situation – a field – which frames the way in which the member states identify and develop policies. Of course, this does not mean that domestic agendas disappear or that voting weights become unimportant. There is, however, a clear understanding that the purpose of negotiation is to present persuasive arguments that can lead to what is 'best for Europe'.[7] One junior British official from the UK Permanent Representation explains:

Brussels does something to you. I think of the officials from the other member states as my colleagues; they are not opponents, although of course sometimes we have to defend different interests.[8]

This 'Brussels effect' is not limited to those who are permanently based in Brussels. I asked a senior British official at the Home Office in London to name his closest colleague. The first he could think of was his German counterpart:

---

[6] Interview, Council Secretariat (Brussels), 13 May 2006.
[7] Interview, European Commission (Brussels), January 2007; Interview, French Permanent Representation (Brussels), September 2007.
[8] Interview, UK Permanent Representation (Brussels), May 2006.

We are very close, you know. We are on the phone many times a day. I think I speak with him more than I speak with my colleagues next door. And I also see him more often [laughs].[9]

One British national expert seconded to the European Commission describes the atmosphere of the High Level Working Group on Migration and Asylum:

It is very co-operative. Occasionally, we have, for example, the representative from Malta saying why is all the attention on the West African states when we on our tiny island get hundreds of people a day? They make a lot of noise and then we try to help, but what more can we do? But certainly it's very co-operative, and generally everyone is working towards the same agenda and we agree on the same ideas about creating a common policy.[10]

The metaphor of movement is worth noting: 'Everyone is working towards the same agenda,' she says. It also illustrates that negotiations are geared towards solving problems. This approach has its origin in the legal and technical expertise that is being developed in Brussels (see also Guiraudon 2003: 168). 'Problems' may be experienced nationally – for example, the thousands of North African refugees reaching Malta – but they are increasingly perceived as common European refugee problems.

A European Commission of orthodoxy

For all this camaraderie, the British and Danish opt-outs are nonetheless perceived by other member states, and in particular by the European Commission, to be increasingly problematic. One reason is that, contrary to a position outside the euro, opt-outs relating to borders, asylum, immigration and justice co-operation are legally complicated and difficult to manage. The Council of Ministers secretariat describes opt-outs as 'time-consuming frustrations' and finds them 'damaging' for British and Danish national interests.[11]

European Commission officials go even further and consider opt-outs to be 'extremely worrying' and a 'threat to solidarity'.[12] According to one British diplomat, this is because the Commission 'finds that opt-

[9] Interview, Home Office (London), April 2007.
[10] Interview, European Commission DG JLS (Brussels), January 2007.
[11] Interview, Legal Service of the Council Secretariat (Brussels), 10 May 2006.
[12] Interview, DG JLS, European Commission (Brussels), 24 January 2007.

outs are basically against the idea of a common legal order for every-one'.[13] Moreover, it sets a dangerous precedence, tempting new member states to also ask for exemptions. Indeed, European Commission officials protect what Bourdieu would call the orthodoxy of European integration. The ultimate objective of orthodoxy – which it never actually achieves – is to restore the primal state of the 'innocence of the doxa'. Orthodoxy exists only in opposition to heterodoxy, and opt-outs are heretical – the 'wrong' position. It is no surprise, then, that those who engage in labelling and stereotyping – two of the components of stigmatisation – are largely Commission representatives. As a result, the British and Danish representatives are in a difficult situation when they seek to promote national interests.

The third and fourth elements of stigmatisation – the separation of 'us' from 'them' and discrimination – are less pronounced, however. There are several reasons for this. First, the issues discussed in the Council of Ministers deal with national security and citizen rights, which are delicate issues for all member states. Because negotiations concern matters of national security, there is some understanding of British and Danish 'domestic problems'.[14] All officials have experience of having to handle and cater for a difficult national parliament or particular sensitivities back home. Generally the member states are more puzzled than provoked by opt-outs. A German official explains: 'I don't really understand the protocols. They do not make much sense to me because we are all working towards the same goal.'[15] A Greek representative calls it a 'disloyal mechanism'.[16] Spanish national representatives express why they think the opt-outs are problematic:

From a Spanish perspective, it is very hard to understand the need for an opt-out in this area. Harmonisation in Justice and Home Affairs means stability.[17]

From the perspective of a Spanish Permanent Representation, co-operation produces 'European' results, which are of a higher quality than 'national policy considerations'. New member states (that had no choice but to prepare for Schengen and renounce national border controls when they became EU members) are more alarmed at the special treatment granted

[13] Interview, UK Permanent Representation (Brussels), 22 August 2007.
[14] Interview, DG JLS, European Commission (Brussels), 26 January 2007.
[15] Interview, German Permanent Representation (Brussels), 21 August 2007.
[16] Interview, Greek Ministry of Foreign Affairs, 13 December 2007.
[17] Interview, Spanish Permanent Representation (Brussels), February 2008.

to the UK and Denmark.[18] However, the other member states generally have a more pragmatic view than the European Commission, although there is no agreement on just how problematic the British and Danish opt-outs are.

It is difficult to separate the insiders from the outsiders in internal security and justice co-operation. While the euro area has the Eurogroup and a growing zone of exclusion, as shown in Chapter 4, the co-operation on AFSJ cannot be easily divided institutionally into the 'ins' and the 'outs'. Physical exclusion of representatives from opt-out states would be impractical, since new proposals on the Council of Ministers agenda covered by the opt-outs are invariably linked to other measures covered by areas from which the UK and Denmark have not opted out. Moreover, it is not always clear at the beginning of the negotiations whether a state chooses to opt in or out; British and Danish ministers and officials are present at negotiations even when they have no voting right.

The UK's selective engagement

British and Danish officials are not excluded from any meetings when it comes to internal security and justice co-operation. But why is it that they are still allowed to exercise influence when they have opted out? Have they not, after all, violated European solidarity? To answer these questions, I will take a closer look at how the British government and officials manage the UK's protocols on visas, asylum, immigration and its position outside the border-free Schengen zone. I will show that British representatives regularly influence the policy-making process and can surprisingly transform themselves from outsiders to insiders.

The island mentality

In the UK, large parts of the domestic scene, led by Conservatives and other eurosceptics, have 'securitised' the Schengen protocol. Discursively, the opt-out from the common border zone constitutes a guarantee of the survival of the British nation (Wiener 1999). The Schengen protocol is therefore likely to remain in place for many years. A leading Home Office official explains:

[18] Interview, Polish Permanent Representation (Brussels), March 2008.

It might have to do with our island mentality – but it does mean a hell of a lot if you have you own border control or not. So I would say – sort of as in the euro question – you know when the conditions are right.[19]

However, this does not mean that the UK is passive. In April 2000 the UK joined the part of the Schengen agreement that deals with police and judicial co-operation as well as the Schengen Information System. But it remained outside the core of Schengen: the common border policy. The UK can 'request to take part in some or all of the provisions of this *acquis*' (Article 4 of the Schengen protocol) only with the unanimous agreement of all of the Schengen states. For the UK it is therefore important whether a new proposal builds on the border-related Schengen *acquis* or not.

However, British representatives try to avoid exclusion by challenging the interpretation of the scope of the Schengen protocol – something that Danish officials would not dream of doing. In 2002–2004, the UK supported two new EU measures: regulations on security features and biometrics in passports (Council Regulation 2252/2004), and the Regulation on a European Border Agency (Frontex) (Council Regulation 2007/2004). At the time the British government was engaged in the politically sensitive task of introducing identity cards and biometric identifiers in UK passports. Due to widespread national scepticism about registration and control of personal freedom in the UK, the government had an interest in promoting these issues at the EU level because it believed that this would enable it to promote the issue indirectly. The Labour government participated in the discussions about what to include in the regulation, representing the UK's interests as a 'normal' member state.

However, when both regulations were proposed, they were deemed to be building on Schengen border measures, in which the UK does not formally participate. Therefore the UK was not allowed to adopt the two measures. British legal experts declared that the UK was being 'unfairly' excluded. They argued that the two regulations were wrongly proposed as measures developing the border provisions of the Schengen *acquis*. They lodged applications with the ECJ, which challenged the UK exclusion. By choosing this dramatic route, the UK tested the norms of good behaviour, as a high-level European Commission official pointed out:

[19] Interview, Cabinet Office (London), 17 May 2007.

I think it is a complete shot in the dark. I must say that I was also personally surprised that the UK government, which has excellent lawyers, chose to go to court with such a bad case.[20]

On 18 December 2007, the ECJ ruled against the British challenge on Frontex and passport regulations (ECJ 138/79, United Kingdom v Council). The ECJ therefore backed the position of the Council of Ministers and stressed that the UK and Ireland can only adopt those provisions that build on an area of the *acquis* in which they already participate.

As the European Commission official explains, 'Basically, they try to have their cake and eat it. But you are either in or out of Schengen'.[21] As long as the UK is unwilling to surrender its national border control, it is not perceived as a 'good European' in relation to Schengen co-operation. Strikingly, however, although the UK lost the Frontex and biometrics cases at the ECJ in 2008, the Schengen protocol does not prevent it from adopting national legislation on biometrics in passports, which conform to EU standards. Furthermore, in relation to Frontex, the UK participates 'without question' in all of the European Border Agency meetings and operational work on an ad hoc basis. I will return to this circumvention of the opt-outs later in this chapter.

The opt-in protocol and the reinterpretation of sovereignty

The UK is less exposed when it comes to EU co-operation on internal security and justice. The option of opting in allows the UK to choose whether or not to participate in decisions on a case-by-case basis. Legal scholars have asked how the UK has managed to obtain such a favourable tailor-made protocol (Juss 2005; Tuytschaever 1999). But what matters here is how the UK has exercised this flexible right.[22]

The Blair government was reluctant to use the opt-in at first. However, with an increasing number of asylum-seekers entering the UK via other EU states, the British government recognised the benefit of addressing issues of asylum and immigration through the EU to ensure greater burden-sharing (Fella 2006: 9). Instead of passively accepting

[20] Interview, DGJLS, European Commission (Brussels), 24 January 2007.
[21] Interview, DGJLS, European Commission (Brussels), November 2008.
[22] The opt-in protocol grants Ireland and the UK a higher degree of flexibility than any previous forms of treaty-based differentiation (Monar 2000: 10).

(a self-imposed) exclusion, British representatives have contributed to policies dealing with immigration, refugees and security (see also Harvey 1997: 68). This high level of engagement has been reinforced by the terrorist attacks in New York (2001), Madrid (2004) and London (2005). In this case the EU becomes a window of opportunity for national administrations to develop more ambitious migration and security policies.[23]

The UK has been actively developing a European asylum policy since the beginning of the 1990s. As I will explain later in this chapter, this has been far from uncontroversial. But the effect of EU legislation on the UK goes well beyond its opt-in, though this may not be visible to the public at large. From ideas such as 'regional protection areas' close to refugee-generating countries (Smith and Tsatsas 2002) to mutual recognition of national legislation and practices, the UK is trying to both influence and imitate EU measures (Geddes 2005: 734).[24] To date the UK has opted into most civil law measures, all asylum measures and most measures concerning illegal migration. But it has remained outside all protective measures concerning legal migration, visas and border control. 'The UK does not act like an opt-out state in this field', a European Commission official explains.[25]

Regarding police and judicial co-operation, the UK supports an increase in collective EU measures to fight transnational crime and terrorism. In areas such as civil law co-operation, it has special reservations because of its common law system. The exemptions help consolidate how British representatives think of the national interest:

Civil law is a very sensitive issue for us and that is why we do not like too much co-operation here. Our common law tradition means that we do not refer to foreign legislation in these areas. What we are very keen on is mutual recognition, because it does not mean that we have to change our own legal instruments.[26]

Indeed, British officials have successfully promoted mutual recognition as an alternative to hard legislation:

I see the benefits of practical co-operation more than actual legislation. That has probably to do with our vision of sovereignty, but we do not like

---

[23] Interviews, Home Office (London), 13 April 2007.
[24] Interview, DG JLS European Commission (Brussels), January 2007.
[25] Interview, DG JLS European Commission (Brussels), October 2007.
[26] Interview, Home Office (London), 17 April 2007.

co-operation on these matters. We think that the European Commission tends to have the view that only legislation is a way forward instead of practical co-operation.[27]

One high-level British official involved in the promotion of mutual recognition of national legal arrangements explained that the opt-in has not only protected the UK against interference from the EU but also made it possible for the UK to guide the EU towards a more pragmatic course.

The informal veto and the magic of consensus

To understand the UK's position, we need to take a closer look at the opt-in model. Ireland is the only other member state that follows the same model, but here I will mainly focus on how it has been used by the UK. Figure 5.1 demonstrates how the opt-in protocol works. First, (1) the UK has three months to decide whether or not to participate in discussions once a proposal is presented for legislation. Second, if the UK (or Ireland) decides to participate (2a), the negotiation will continue with their full participation. But the proposal could ultimately be adopted by the other member states without the participation of the

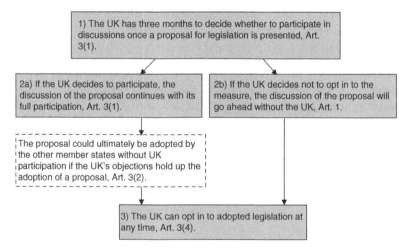

Figure 5.1 The UK's right to opt in to measures under Title IV (Protocol 4)

---

[27] Interview, Cabinet Office (London), 12 April 2007.

UK or Ireland, if these raise objections that delay the adoption of a proposal, as indicated by the broken line. The broken line indicates that this has never been used in practice. If the UK (or Ireland) does not wish to participate (2b), the discussion will go ahead between the other member states, and they can then adopt the proposal without British (or Irish) participation (or either of the two).

Finally, the UK or Ireland (or both) could opt in to adopted legislation at a later stage (3), provided that the European Commission approves. On the whole, the possibility to opt in either before or after the adoption of legislation indicates that the UK cannot easily be excluded.

But these formal rules do not nearly reveal the full significance of the right to opt in. Where the UK has opted in to discussions, it has been able to delay the adoption of legislation that could otherwise have been adopted without the UK's participation (see also Givens and Luedtke 2003: 293). This is remarkable given that Article 3(2) of the protocol allows the other member states to adopt measures without the UK, as illustrated by the broken line in Figure 5.1. Counterintuitively, and contrary to rationalist negotiation theory, the UK has had the right to opt in to legislation from the start, and an informal right to veto anything right up to the end of the negotiations.

The Rome II Regulation on the choice of law in cross-border disputes (Council Regulation 864/2007) is a good example of how British officials have been able to block and influence a proposal despite Article 3(2). Put forward as part of the co-operation on civil law, the UK was against the proposal from the outset. British officials argued that the European Commission had failed to demonstrate that the harmonisation of rules relating to media, privacy and defamation was necessary for the promotion of the internal market (OUT-LAW 2002). Despite fierce domestic criticism, the UK chose to opt in to the negotiations from the outset to 'keep the whole venture away from the harmonisation of substantive law', as former Home Secretary, Jack Straw, explained (House of Lords 2004). According to a Cabinet Office official, 'We opposed the way it was drafted and succeeded in changing it. We were full negotiators on that issue.'[28] This resulted in the UK achieving a positive outcome with the Council of Ministers, which led to the European Parliament finally accepting a regulation where the issues of freedom of the press and defamation had been sidelined.

[28] Interview, Cabinet Office (London), 17 April 2007.

One explanation for this informal veto right is the unwritten rule, whereby national representatives listen to each other's objections until they can agree on a revised measure (Lewis 2005). A European Commission official involved in the negotiations notes: 'I suggested that the others should move ahead, but the Council works like a gentlemen's club where you do your utmost not to isolate any country.'[29]

On the whole, the search for consensus means that British representatives can influence, and also block, specific measures until they can live with the result. Or, as one Commission official bitterly explains, 'The British really don't care whether they have opted in or not. They believe that they have a right to express themselves on everything.'[30]

Yet British officials actually take great care not to breach unwritten rules. When I asked what would happen if the UK permanently blocked a proposal after having opted in (which was possible before the Treaty of Lisbon), a Cabinet Office official said that it would be a 'huge problem – a major situation!'[31] A British official explains this self-restraint:

We would never play the veto card straight out, it wouldn't be cricket. Everybody knows that the other member states could go ahead without us, but we would never say it. Instead, we explain why we want the measures changed and that helps.[32]

This reveals an unwritten agreement between the 'dissenter' and the 'compliers'. The logic is as follows. Once the UK announces that it will opt in, the other member states will endeavour to get the UK on board. In exchange, the UK will be co-operative. Extreme measures should be avoided at all costs, including playing the veto card. If the UK were to 'abuse' its right to opt in, it would not receive this favourable treatment. This 'unspoken rule' is not openly discussed ('we would never play the veto card straight out' the official explains), so it appears to be a true act of goodwill (Bourdieu 1977: 191ff). The 'magic' of consensus must be seen as a natural process, and not enforced. Clearly such negotiations are not two-level game bargains reflecting explicit national win-sets as intergovernmentalism would have us believe. Instead, they resemble exchanges of favours and gifts, 'which owe their infinite complexity to

---

[29] Interview, Legal Service of the European Commission (Brussels), January 2008.
[30] Interview, DG JLS European Commission (Brussels), 24 January 2007.
[31] Interview, Cabinet Office (London), 17 April 2007.
[32] Interview, Department for Constitutional Affairs (London), 12 April 2007.

the fact that both the giver and the receiver pretend that there are no calculations behind' (Bourdieu 1977: 171). This is the essence of the give-and-take game in Brussels.

Fast-tracking national interests

Ladrech claims that the British use of its right to opt in is driven by national interests (Ladrech 2004: 57). But what does this mean? British opt-in decisions are driven more by views held by the government and administration than any broader concern for Parliament or societal reservations. Parliamentary protests against specific opt-in and opt-out decisions have had no significant effect on government decisions to opt in or out.[33]

Tony Blair was often criticised in Parliament for specific opt-in decisions. His response to one of those accusations of 'surrendering sovereignty' illustrates how opt-in decisions have led to a fascinating reinterpretation of sovereignty:

> But it is our complete choice as to whether to opt in; we might as well say that about any measure in Europe [. . .] Obviously, once we opt in, that is presumably because we have decided that it is in our interests to do so. Only the Conservative party could say that a decision whether to opt in is somehow a negation of our sovereignty; surely, it is the expression of it.[34]

Blair's choice of words is revealing in two ways. First, national sovereignty and integration are no longer mutually exclusive in Blair's rationale; it is by opting in that the UK affirms its sovereignty. Second, Blair claims to speak on behalf of a domestic audience, a 'we'. But, in practice, the British government is autonomous in its decisions to participate (or not) in any given measure under Title IV TEC. 'The people' need not be the representation of sovereignty. In the UK the exemptions drift between different entities: 'government', 'parliament', 'people', 'nation' and an abstract 'we.' Here Blair discursively invokes the sovereign people of the UK to

---

[33] The reluctance to renounce the opt-out on border control is not shared by the House of Lords Select Committee, which, on the one hand, criticises the government for its inability to prove that British border control is the most effective way to control immigration and fight illegal immigration, and, on the other hand, finds it 'politically unwise' for the UK to isolate itself from the continuing development of EU-wide policies (House of Lords 1999).

[34] Prime Minister Tony Blair, House of Commons Daily Debate, 8 Nov 2004.

justify decisions to opt in or out, but this 'we' could be interpreted as a void, an artificial referent.

Second, identifying national interests is no mean feat. British officials need to consider whether to opt in or out each time a new proposal is put forward. The three-month time limit puts additional stress on the process:

It is simply a very short time to get everyone to agree. It creates many tensions. Policy-wise – is it something we want? Legally – do we want it? All the ministers have to agree, the officials have to agree both within the department and across the departments.[35]

Tony Blair has claimed that the right to opt in means that 'unless we opt in we are not affected by it and this actually gives us is the best of both worlds'.[36] British officials are less certain:

There are some clear advantages – it is a last resort to protect our sovereignty. But there are also a number of disadvantages. We have to take risks, and it is a very difficult calculation to make.[37]

To understand how the opt-in decision is made, I asked a Cabinet Office official to explain the process:

First, we go for the ideal, which is to opt in right from the beginning, because then we are full members and have full influence. The second best option is to make clear that we would like to opt in eventually and negotiate the condition for that to be possible. The worst case is when we do not opt in.[38]

Generally the UK seeks to opt in as much as possible; only the right to maintain border controls remains non-negotiable. If the UK does not make use of its right to opt in, its image is harmed. According to one British official:

After our choice not to opt in to four measures last year, people have started thinking that the UK has changed position and that it does not want to participate on civil law. That is wrong! We just have a problem with the idea of applying foreign law, but I feel that our position is quite exposed.[39]

[35] Interview, Home Office (London), 21 August 2006.
[36] The Guardian, 26 October, 2004, www.guardian.co.uk/guardianpolitics/story/0,,1336027,00.html
[37] Interview, Cabinet Office (London), 17 April 2007.
[38] Interview, Cabinet Office (London), 17 April 2007.
[39] Interview, Cabinet Office (London), 17 April 2007.

Participants in the Council of Ministers negotiations are hypersensitive to the slightest slur on or breach of the unspoken rules. This impacts on how the British administration makes opt-in decisions. The opt-in decision is not simply a question about the concrete proposal but also about how the UK wants to position itself in the field.[40] British officials may appreciate the flexibility of the British position, but they operate in a field that values participation and punishes national reservations and euroscepticism. Consequently the definition of British national interests may change during the course of the negotiation process.

Ireland's struggle to distance itself from the UK offers a striking example of how the opt-out position is perceived. To maintain the Common Travel Area between the UK and Ireland, Ireland has had to begrudgingly follow the UK's lead and remain outside Schengen.[41] Irish negotiators attached a special declaration to the Irish protocol on the right to opt in, affirming that Ireland would participate to the greatest extent possible. Moreover, to avoid 'contamination' by the British position, Ireland uses the right to opt in differently from the UK to demonstrate its affiliation to the EU. One Irish official explains:

If it wasn't for the UK, where would Ireland be in Justice and Home Affairs? If we had to choose, we would probably go the EU route on most issues. You already see this in our independent opt-ins, which both Parliament and the Department of Justice have approved.[42]

Ireland's considerable diplomatic efforts to distance itself from the UK make sense in the context of Ireland's conviction that a pro-European stance is important for a country's position.

Danish awkwardness

Denmark is a member of Schengen. But ever since the opening of the Danish borders in 2001, this membership has been a hot potato in domestic politics. When the Danish EU presidency term started in January 2012, one of Denmark's priorities was a 'safe Europe', which included working on a common asylum policy, and measures to fight

---

[40] A classic interpretation based on game theory would be that the shadow of the future impacts on the choices of the players (Axelrod and Dion 1988: 1387).

[41] For an interesting account of how Ireland has been forced to follow the UK in the AFSJ, see Meehan (2000a).

[42] Interview, Irish Permanent Representation (Brussels), February 2008.

terrorism and cross-border crime. However, Denmark cannot participate in any of these initiatives because of its opt-out from supranational co-operation within the EU. Denmark's position is ambiguous to say the least.

In 2011, Denmark's right-wing government announced the deployment of more than 40 additional customs control officers to be permanently stationed at the border with Germany. Critics at home and abroad, especially the European Commission and Germany, cautioned that this move undermined the principle of the Schengen border-free zone. European Commission President José Manuel Barroso warned that the Commission 'would not hesitate to intervene' if the principle of free movement was endangered. The Danish Foreign Minister Lene Espersen defended the move, which was the result of a deal with the government's far-right ally – the Danish People's Party. Espersen insisted that the new border checks complied fully with the Schengen agreement, and that the aim was 'to fight the entry of illegal goods and drugs' into Denmark, not to control people.[43] I was working in the Danish Ministry of Foreign Affairs in 2011 when the decision to deploy the additional customs control officers passed Parliament. Most Danish officials knew that this move would cause political problems for Denmark. In October 2011 they breathed a collective sigh of relief when the newly elected Prime Minister, Helle Thorning-Schmidt, abolished her predecessor's border control plan and reintroduced normal Schengen procedure.

One of the paradoxes of the Danish opt-out is the remarkable contradiction between the original motivation behind Denmark's opposition to EU competence within the area of asylum and immigration policy, and its current motivation to maintain its opt-outs. In the early 1990s, Denmark (together with the Netherlands) was among the most liberal countries in Europe, and it feared that community competence within asylum and immigration policy would threaten the high level of protection given to asylum-seekers in Denmark (Manners 2000: 98). However, since the late 1990s, the Danish asylum and refugee policy has become stricter than the corresponding policies of other EU states. This has resulted in special requirements concerning rules about family reunification and attachment to Denmark. Today, Denmark's rules on asylum and immigration are perceived as an essential measure to curb

---

[43] 'Denmark reintroduces custom controls at its borders', EUbusiness, 1 July 2011.

the apparent influx of immigrants, asylum-seekers, criminals and terrorists. According to the influential right-wing Danish People's Party:

No supranational or international body should impose a particular refugee and immigration policy on Denmark. The Danish People's Party will fight to ensure that the refugee and immigration policy remains an area where Parliament is sovereign.[44]

This view bears testament to a domestic debate whereby the opt-out reaffirms the boundary between the state and everything beyond it. However, the opt-out from immigration, asylum and civil law is presented differently to European colleagues.

Denmark and the border-free zone

As mentioned, Denmark signed the Schengen agreement in 1996 despite domestic opposition. When Schengen was integrated into the Treaty of Amsterdam in 1997, a protocol was drafted to ensure that Denmark would continue to participate in Schengen-related measures while opting out of 'supranationality'. The protocol states:

Denmark shall decide within a period of six months after the Council has decided on a proposal or initiative to build upon the Schengen *acquis* under the provisions of Title IV of the treaty establishing the European Community, whether it will implement this decision in its national law (Article 4 of the Schengen Protocol).[45]

At first glance it looks as though Danish autonomy has been formally secured. However, the protocol also states that if Denmark decides not to implement a Council of Ministers decision, the other member states will consider 'appropriate measures'. 'Appropriate measures' is a euphemism for being thrown out of Schengen.[46]

This strange protocol implies that Danish officials fly to Brussels for negotiations but are unable to vote on new Schengen measures. Nothing

[44] Dansk Folkepartis valggrundlag til Europaparlamentet 2004, www.danskfolkeparti.dk/sw/frontend/show.asp?parent=18717&menu_parent=22669&layout=0
[45] This special procedure is criticised by legal scholars for being 'complex [and] illogical' (Tuytschaever 1999: 101). Indeed, it is the result of a hurried agreement, and its legal consequences were probably not fully understood at the time of drafting.
[46] Interview, Ministry of Foreign Affairs (Copenhagen), 24 January 2007.

that a Danish representative utters during meetings will be entered into the protocol.[47] Denmark has formally abstained from influence but is bound to adopt all decisions taken by the Council of Ministers six months after the other member states. This, of course, contradicts the idea that an opt-out guarantees immunity from EU legislation. Instead, the Danish Schengen position is reminiscent of its pegging to the euro, as described in Chapter 4.

Danish officials find the Schengen position 'extremely awkward'.[48] Yet despite the strange legal process, which creates considerable work for Danish officials, there is still room for Danish influence. A European Commission official explains:

Denmark is a normal Schengen state. As long as Denmark does not create any problems, nobody mentions the protocol. There is no voting, so Denmark's position is always taken into account on equal terms with the other member states.[49]

This game relies on an abundance of discretion and diplomacy. Since Denmark automatically implements all legislation, if only on an intergovernmental basis, and because of the norm of consensus-seeking, Danish representatives are permitted to influence new Schengen measures.

Self-restraint

Denmark's 'real' opt-out covers asylum, migration, civil law and police co-operation. This opt-out allegedly implies that Danish sovereignty will not be undermined by supranational integration. While the British have the option of picking and choosing as they please, Denmark can only participate in intergovernmental co-operation. In practice, this gives Denmark much less room for diplomatic manoeuvring than the UK with its right to opt in.

Unlike in the UK, the politico-administrative body in Denmark sees the opt-outs as a 'pain in the neck'.[50] The policy of all Danish governments – right and left – since 1993 has been to abolish the opt-out as

---

[47] Interviews, Home Office (London), 16 April 2007, Interviews, Ministry of Foreign Affairs (DK), 17 January 2006.

[48] Interview, DG JLS, European Commission (Brussels), 11 January 2007.

[49] Interview, DG JLS European Commission (Brussels), 28 February 2008.

[50] Interviews, Ministry of Foreign Affairs (Copenhagen), 2 February 2006.

soon as the conditions are right for a referendum. The opt-out must be strictly observed, of course, but Danish government and officials find that protocols limit their ability to further Danish interests.[51] One senior Danish diplomat uses the word 'treason' to describe the Danish opt-out:

> The difference between the Danish and British opt-outs is that the Danish opt-out is turned against *us*. This is the real treason committed by the Socialist People's Party against the population. The Danes were promised a 'digestible' Maastricht Treaty, and the Socialist People's Party wanted to make it a 'Danish' Treaty. But eventually the aim was not to influence the EU, but to handcuff the Danish government.[52]

Danish officials appear two-faced: they have to respect opt-outs that they perceive to be damaging to the 'real' national interests of their country.

Interestingly, there is an understanding among the more experienced officials in the Council of Ministers, the European Commission and some of the older member states that the opt-out is not the fault of the Danish officials. They feel sorry for the Danes. Unlike their British colleagues, who manage a right to opt in that is tailored to meet the wishes of the British government, these 'insiders' know that Danish diplomats have to manage a very inflexible arrangement that was drafted by a eurosceptical opposition back in 1992.

'I honestly think you should have a psychologist have a look at the harm done by the opt-outs to the Danish representatives', a former diplomat says.[53] Danish officials believe that their opinion carries less weight than that of other member states, and that they have a weaker bargaining position.[54] Danish representatives are worried about making mistakes during meetings, such as overstepping their competences, getting the complex legal nature of the opt-outs wrong, or underestimating the power of the sceptical Parliament and media back home. Fearful of scandal, officials may err on the side of caution in their interpretation of proposed legislation and remain silent during meetings.

---

[51] Interview, Ministry of Foreign Affairs (Copenhagen), 28 February 2006.
[52] Interview, Ministry of Foreign Affairs (Copenhagen), 7 March 2006. It is a point of debate whether the Socialist People's Party had such a key role in the negotiations, but it played a major part in the interpretation of the 'no' and in the framing of the opt-outs (Petersen 2003).
[53] Interview, private (Copenhagen), 7 February 2006.
[54] Interview, Council Secretariat (Brussels), 10 May 2006.

An official from the Danish Ministry of Refugee, Immigration and Integration Affairs explains why she avoids mentioning the Danish opt-out during meetings:

Personally, I think that it is embarrassing when member states argue by referring to national interests and problems instead of trying to find common ground.[55]

In other words, whereas British diplomats are prepared to provoke, Danish diplomats would rather not. A senior official in the Danish Foreign Ministry explains:

The problem with the opt-outs is that they are not legitimate demands; they are difficult for the other member states to understand. If there were a real problem, for instance on fishing quotas, the other member states would take the opt-outs much more seriously because Denmark is a fishery nation.[56]

There appears to be agreement within the Council of Ministers on what constitutes a 'real' problem in negotiations. For Danish negotiators, the opt-out is a 'false' problem because it is 'unnecessary' for Denmark; it is self-imposed. While Danish diplomats try to hide the opt-outs, they nonetheless cannot act as full members:

There are issues I would not push in the working groups because of the opt-out. We take care to inform the minister if it is an area covered by the opt-out, and this also means that unless it is a very sensitive issue, we cannot really take a principled stance on a measure covered by our reservation. This is logical. Certainly, one cannot expect to have the same influence if one has chosen to stay outside.[57]

The reason for this 'self-restraint' is that Danish officials do not see the need for special treatment for what they perceive to be a 'domestic problem'.[58] At least two interesting observations can be made in this regard. First, this intimidated practice of self-restraint does not fit with the theory of an integration dilemma, which excludes such social dynamics where representatives do not identify 100 per cent with the opt-out. Second, there is no indication that British officials demonstrate this type of self-restraint.

---

[55] Interview, Ministry of Refugees, Immigration and Integration Affairs (Copenhagen), 22 August 2007.
[56] Interview, Ministry of Foreign Affairs (Copenhagen), 7 March 2007.
[57] Danish Permanent Representation (Brussels), 12 December 2006.
[58] Ministry of Foreign Affairs (Copenhagen), Interview, 28 February 2006.

Playing the constructive insider

Nonetheless, and despite the legal constraints, Danish officials sometimes try to play the role of a constructive insider. This is possible because Denmark participates in all meetings. As this official describes:

This may also reinforce the impression that we are serious and have an interest in the cause, which means that the other member states will not hold the opt-outs against us in day-to-day management.[59]

But there are limits. A European Commission official explains:

Denmark is not always super active in meetings. I mean, they can't be. The UK and Ireland are more active because of their opt-in possibility and because they are directly affected by the decisions.[60]

However, acting as a constructive insider has reaped real benefits for Denmark despite the legal and social constraints. The negotiations on the Directive on Family Reunification illustrate this well. The directive represents a legal measure that Denmark would never adopt due to its opt-out but which it succeeded in influencing. First proposed in 1999, it is the first directive ever adopted by the EU in the area of legal immigration. On 1 December 1999, the European Commission adopted the initial proposal for a Directive on Family Reunification. After negotiations in the Council of Ministers, and following recommendations made by the European Parliament, the Commission presented the first amended proposal on 10 October 2000. However, the first directive was considered to be 'too liberal'. In response, the European Commission presented a second amended proposal on 2 May 2002. In both directives it was suggested that the age limit for family reunification should be 18.

A compromise was reached during the Danish EU Presidency (July–December 2003). During the negotiations the Danish government promoted its own theory on integration by arranging conferences and initiating informal debates about 'best practices'. By drawing on practical experience and invoking the mutual need to solve problems, Bertel Haarder, then Minister of Refugees, Immigration and Integration

[59] Interview, Ministry of Refugees, Immigrants and Integration Affairs (Copenhagen), August 2006.
[60] Interview, DG JLS European Commission (Brussels), February 2008.

Affairs, together with his team of officials, promoted the hard-line Danish policy. Denmark argued for a stricter directive whereby the age limit of the sponsor and their spouse would be raised from 18 to 21 years, compared with the more liberal stance of France, Sweden and Belgium. As a result, member states can set a minimum age of 21 for both parties 'in order to ensure better integration and to prevent involuntary marriages' (Council Directive 2003/86). This directive had been developed by Denmark and had been forcefully argued throughout the negotiation process. Indeed, Denmark was so committed that a member of the Greek delegation forgot that Denmark had an opt-out.[61]

While Denmark's agenda-setting power in this case can partly be attributed to the 'Presidency effect' (Tallberg 2004), there is still a question as to how Denmark could continue to influence the negotiations down to the last detail, despite never having to implement the directive. Tacit understandings already explored here may explain why the other member state representatives ignored (or chose to ignore) that Denmark was not formally part of the decision-making process. This example demonstrates that, in practice, the management of the opt-out has very little to do with safeguarding national autonomy.

Mimicking

As well as seeking to influence new legislation, British and Danish representatives are sometimes also looking to borrow new EU legislation. This 'mimicking' of policies covered by the opt-outs is quite remarkable. A well-established (but not publicly known) policy of the various Danish governments has been to keep Danish legislation consistent with that of the EU in the field of immigration and asylum – in spite of the opt-out. The most notable form of mimicking, however, is the negotiation of parallel agreements associating Denmark with legislative measures where the Danish opt-out applies. While this is a legally sound practice, one could argue that it represents a political bypassing of the protocol.

If an EU measure is based on a reciprocity principle, it is not enough for Denmark to simply copy the EU legislation. For example, the Dublin regulation is based on a reciprocity principle that commits all member

---

[61] Interview, Greek Ministry of Foreign Affairs, 19 December 2006.

states to receive asylum-seekers referred under the Dublin criteria from another member state. Denmark is, of course, free to copy parts of the Dublin regulation into Danish law and can decide whether to receive asylum-seekers from other member states. But there is no guarantee, for example, that Greece would accept asylum-seekers referred from Denmark. These more advanced forms of co-operation with EU agencies and supranational funding structures have increased over the last ten years.

The Danish government has requested parallel agreements only in areas considered to be of 'vital interest to the country' (Vedsted-Hansen 2004: 67).[62] So far, Denmark has applied for six parallel agreements, but the European Commission has only granted three: two on civil law and one on asylum.[63] The most important of these is the Dublin system on asylum-seekers.

The EU is very reluctant to extend such parallel agreements. For the Commission, the very idea that the EU should enter into a treaty with one of its own member states seems absurd:

Parallel agreements are extremely artificial; the EC has to do an external agreement with one of its own members. This cannot stand as a precedent for any future arrangement with any member state.[64]

This also explains why such agreements have taken up to six years to negotiate, and why some Danish representatives have spent over 50 per cent of their time 'negotiating, preparing and dreaming about the parallel agreements'.[65]

According to the European Commission, the following conditions apply if Denmark is to be granted a parallel agreement:

1. Parallel agreements can only be of an exceptional and transitional nature.

---

[62] If Denmark is granted a parallel agreement, the government copies the EU measure in the form of Danish law, which is then subsequently agreed on by Parliament. The majority of the Danish Parliament has supported the application for parallel agreements (Larsen 2006: 96).

[63] The European Commission refused to grant Denmark parallel agreements with respect to the regulation on insolvency proceedings and the regulation on jurisdiction and the recognition and enforcement of judgments in matrimonial matters (Bruxelles II).

[64] Group interview, Legal Service, European Council (Brussels), February 2008.

[65] Interview, Ministry of Foreign Affairs, (Copenhagen) March 2007.

2. Such an interim solution should also only be accepted if the participation of Denmark is fully in the interests of the EU community and its citizens.
3. Denmark agrees to give up its protocol on Freedom, Security and Justice in the long term.

The conditions built into the parallel agreements act as a disciplining mechanism whereby Denmark promises to forego its disputed exemptions. To be granted parallel agreements, Danish officials must act like representatives from applicant countries asserting that their country is making progress and moving closer to the European core (Wæver 2000: 262–263). By signing the parallel agreements they agree to the temporary nature of the exemptions and accept that Denmark will eventually have to renounce its authority on the areas that it has opted out of.[66] In this sense the opt-out no longer guarantees autonomy because it is transformed into a delay mechanism. Danish politico-administrative bodies promise to work towards lifting the opt-outs 'in a few years' and continually claim that they are just waiting for the conditions to be right before calling a referendum.

The Lisbon impasse

Prior to the Treaty of Amsterdam, the Danish opt-out from supranational legislation was hypothetical. However, Denmark has become marginalised as a result of legislation increasingly taking supranational form. The volume of legislation covered by the opt-out has surged during the period from 1999 to 2012. In 1999, Denmark was excluded from participating in only a handful of measures. In March 2012 the total number of legislative measures covered by the opt-out exceeded 230, ranging from directives on railroad security to common visa rules and trafficking of women. Danish diplomats regularly update this list, and its growth alone is a source of great annoyance.[67]

The consequences of the Danish opt-out has intensified as a result of the Treaty of Lisbon. Since the treaty abolishes the division between intergovernmental and supranational co-operation, Denmark is increasingly excluded from all co-operation on police and criminal matters. This

---

[66] Interviews, Danish Ministry of Refugees, Immigration and Integration Affairs (Copenhagen, August 22, 2006.
[67] Interview, Ministry of Foreign Affairs (Copenhagen), 25 January 2007.

leaves Denmark with a dilemma: should it try to hold a referendum to abolish the opt-out in order to remain part of police co-operation and the fight against terrorism (issues popular with the Danish public), or should it accept a situation where Denmark is completely excluded, not only from sensitive policies of immigration but also from police and security co-operation?

While other member states have been pragmatic up to now, if Denmark continues to opt out it will be viewed as 'unjustified' by the insiders:

Denmark has no justification for staying out of this area. Denmark is already part of Schengen and as such different from the UK. The consequences of continuing to have opt-outs under the Treaty of Lisbon are simply ridiculous to my mind. Think about it: Denmark will have to retreat from Europol![68]

Faced with the possibility of complete exclusion, the Danish government cashed in all of its accumulated goodwill during negotiations on the Constitutional Treaty in order to change its opt-out to an opt-in system, similar to that of the UK.[69] A member of the negotiation team explained the Danish strategy:

This was our only priority. It was now or never if we were to have any chance of jumping on the Justice and Home Affairs train. We simply had to change the opt-out and, at the same time, ensure that the government's immigration policy was safeguarded.[70]

This possibility of opting in can only come into force following a Danish referendum. The modified Danish protocol includes an important declaration stating that Denmark will make use of the right to opt-in; opting out should not be permanent; and the European Commission expects Denmark to participate fully with time. This clearly demonstrates the orthodoxy of a 'unified legal order'. Table 5.1 provides an overview of the ways in which British and Danish officials manage the opt-outs in the AFSJ.

---

[68] Interview, Spanish Permanent Representation (Brussels), February 2008.
[69] Interviews, Ministry of Foreign Affairs (Copenhagen), February and May 2006.
[70] Interview, DANATO (Brussels) (formally at the Danish Foreign Ministry, Copenhagen), 13 December 2006.

Table 5.1. *Stigma management strategies in the AFSJ*

Stigma management strategies in the AFSJ

	Challenging exclusion	Camouflage and compensation	Missionary strategies	Self-restraint
Perception	Unfair exclusion due to opt-out	Perceived loss of influence and status due to opt-out	EU goals in an area covered by opt-out are against national interests	Serious loss of status or bad reputation among other member states
Strategy	Claim right to participate and restrict formal exclusion	Play the 'teacher's pet', help others, hide opt-out	'Teach Europe a lesson' through examples and threats	Stay silent, be more careful with the legal interpretation
Outcome	Not efficient	Reduced stigmatisation	Increased stigmatisation and exclusion	Increased exclusionary effects of opt-outs
State	UK	UK and Denmark	UK	Denmark, sometimes the UK

Conclusion

Migration, asylum and justice are integral to our traditional understanding of what makes a state sovereign. However, AFSJ is the fastest growing area in the EU in terms of new legislation. This is not only due to external pressure; it is also a result of national officials from different member states managing asylum and border policies together. In this increasingly integrated area of policy, we are far more likely to see courteous exchanges of views between close colleagues than hard clashes of national interest. Everybody agrees that constructing viable solutions to international crime, and illegal and legal immigration is an important task. In this sense, national officials create the conditions for a self-perpetuating political system.

Even where they have lost the right to vote, British and Danish representatives battle against marginalisation. In particular, the European Commission sees opt-outs as a threat to the integrity of the political system. Therefore British and Danish diplomats engage in a strategy of stigma management based on different – and sometimes contradictory – understandings of the opt-outs.

In contrast with the situation in the EMU, the UK and Denmark are not necessary perceived as 'bad Europeans' in this field. British and Danish officials appear to identify with the aim of a common immigration and asylum policy, in some cases even being seen as frontrunners.[71] By acting as constructive players, British and Danish officials are adept at 'hiding' the fact that they have an opt-out,[72] their compensatory strategies often proving successful in countering the effects of exclusion. Such compensatory strategies go against the rationalist interpretation that near-core insiders 'have been willing to refrain from some of their insider influence-capability in order to bolster their autonomy in one or more respects' (Wivel and Mouritzen 2005: 37). However, compensation is consistent with the idea that officials value joint problem-solving more than autonomy. Even Danish officials can influence directives that they will never implement. British officials are allowed to change legislation despite there being legal provisions in place that should prevent this from happening. An informal veto can only exist in a system where

---

[71] Interview, DG JLS, European Commission (Brussels), 12 January 2007; Interview, German Permanent Representation (Brussels), 21 August 2007.
[72] Interview, Council Secretariat (Brussels), 10 April 2007.

reciprocity and the 'magic' of consensus are standard logics. Yet while British officials confidently exercise influence almost irrespective of whether it is considered appropriate by others, Danish officials are sometimes so uncomfortable with the opt-outs that they withdraw altogether from debate.

The way in which the protocol is designed makes all the difference. With regard to asylum and immigration policies, British officials have a very flexible right to opt-in, while the Danish opt-out prevents Denmark from adopting legislation in most parts of the AFSJ. The British case-by-case model creates tension between the orthodoxy of a common legal order and the informal rules of pragmatic decision-making.[73] This tension makes opting in difficult to manage and results in British national interests being constantly redefined. Regarding Schengen, the situation is almost entirely the reverse. The UK faces serious obstacles because it does not participate in the core of the Schengen agreement – the common border policy – whereas Denmark acts as a 'normal' Schengen member.

Overall, the more integrated internal security and justice co-operation becomes, the less room for manoeuvre there is for British and Danish officials. In addition to increasing legal constraints, the European Commission will play a more central role and is likely to uphold orthodoxy at every opportunity. As a result, British and Danish officials will face a more clear-cut exclusion, resembling that of the eurozone. As the Schengen agreement continues to develop and gain in symbolic importance, the British position will become more and more difficult to sustain. For Denmark, as co-operation in areas of asylum, immigration, police co-operation and civil law increases, so will Denmark's exclusion. Unless the UK and Denmark change positions, the revolving doors of the AFSJ are likely to be replaced by a wall. Hitherto, however, when it comes to everyday co-operation on matters of internal security and justice, Denmark and the UK have succeeded in getting round sovereignty safeguards and in compensating diplomatically for loss of influence.

---

[73] Interview, DG JLS, European Commission (Brussels), 20 June 2007.

6 | *Late sovereign diplomacy*

Introduction

A few decades ago, diplomacy was thought to be in decay. According to Hedley Bull, the feelings of trust and shared responsibility for peace and good relations were disappearing:

> The solidarity of the diplomatic profession has declined since the mid-nineteenth century when diplomatists of different countries were united by a common aristocratic culture, and often by ties of blood and marriage, when the number of states were fewer and all the significant ones European, and when diplomacy took place against the background of 'the international of monarchs' and the intimate acquaintance of leading figures through the habit of congregating at spas. (Bull 1977: 328)

Building on the previous analysis, this chapter argues that Bull's diagnosis of eroded diplomatic solidarity was misguided – at least with regard to the EU. Instead of the usual picture of clashing national interests, the previous chapters presented a picture of European integration that gave rise to the re-emergence of solidarity among national representatives, which scholars described as lost 30 years ago.

In the EU the member states are united – not by blood and marriage, but by what I call 'late sovereign diplomacy', which results from day-to-day negotiations in the Council of Ministers and its working groups. Late sovereign diplomacy is characterised by an intense integration of national representatives who adhere to what the Treaty of Rome called 'an ever closer union', producing legislation that challenges the sovereignty of their own nations. As I will argue, this selected group shares a collective identity that may be even stronger than that found among the aristocrats in the mid-nineteenth century. The consequence of this collective identity for the EU is that national and European interests are merging. This is in sharp contrast with the systemic conceptions of diplomacy as mediation and representation.

This chapter reflects on the insights rendered by the previous chapters and discusses the features of a differentiated European polity, where the member states do not participate on an equal basis. The chapter falls into three parts. I begin by examining statements from the 'exempted', who tell us something very important about the inner workings of the EU. By exploring processes of stigmatisation in the Council of Ministers, we discover another side of integration. If we look beyond the much discussed formal dynamics (e.g. voting patterns, the role of the rotating Presidencies), it becomes evident that it is, in fact, real people who drive integration. Sociality matters, and national opt-outs serve as a social marker. This explains why British and Danish representatives, with their history of opt-outs, are not always perceived to be good company in Brussels. From the diplomat's perspective, treaty exemptions are not so much safeguards of sovereignty as a handicap that limits the quest for influence.

The second part of the chapter considers how diplomacy operates in the EU. Three interlinked discourses characterise late sovereign diplomacy: the teleological interpretation of the EC and EU treaties; the intense socialisation of state representatives; and delocalising the national interests in the negotiation process, promoting national positions as part of a European cause. The latter discourse proposes an understanding of everyday integration as being partly driven by a relatively autonomous group of national representatives. Thus I suggest that the EU has not rendered national diplomacy obsolete but has profoundly changed its meaning and consequences.

Following this reconceptualisation of diplomacy in the EU, I turn to the need to develop better ways of understanding and managing sovereignty in an increasingly integrated Union. Challenging the dominant assumption that opt-outs actually protect sovereignty – represented by Fritz W. Scharpf among others – I argue that integration cannot easily be 'rolled back'; nor can sovereignty be easily reclaimed through some kind of institutional redesign. While guarantees of sovereignty and increased differentiation may help the difficult ratification of new EU treaties and agreements, I suggest that they will not lead to a more legitimate EU, as many decision-makers and scholars have hitherto argued. Instead, I argue, a more fundamental reconsideration of the integration process is necessary.

Stigma and catharsis in the Council of Ministers

'At the heart of our membership of the EU lies a persistent sense of shame. This is what sets us so apart from our neighbours' (Clegg, quoted in Baker 2005: 34). This is what British Liberal Democrat Nick Clegg wrote in 2005 about the UK's failure to shape its destiny in Europe. The increase in the country's opt-outs in the 1990s contributed to the UK's image as the 'awkward partner' (Rosamond 2004; George 1994; for a systematic analysis of 'awkwardness', see Geddes 2013: 28–41) and a 'stranger in Europe' (Wall 2008). Clegg's use of the word 'shame' highlights the emotional aspect of what is usually portrayed as a dispassionate bureaucracy in Brussels. To understand this sense of shame, I have analysed the ideas that make opt-outs so controversial in the first place. European integration is produced in a social setting in which certain types of behaviour are considered appropriate and others are frowned upon. This is crucial for how opt-outs are managed. An experienced Danish official working with asylum and immigration policies describes their experience of shame:

A few months ago, I was at a working group meeting and raised a point on a specific issue that needed clarification. France then said, 'Thank you Denmark for this comment. It is always good to hear the point of view of someone with an outside perspective'. It was so humiliating. I blushed. I didn't say anything for the rest of the meeting. But of course I was furious afterwards.[1]

Why such embarrassment? Is the French representative's remark not simply a natural reflection of the Danish position? Not quite. As his statement suggests, the incident resulted in humiliation of the Danish representative in front of his colleagues. It is also an example of a 'normal' state addressing a 'deviant' state. In this case, France embodies European interests, while Denmark is reduced to an outsider, who does not fully deserve a right to comment. Anger, shame and pride are part of daily member state interaction in Brussels – and these emotions are sometimes exploited strategically.

The labelling of outsiders is generally a very subtle process, which reflects the pragmatism of everyday negotiations in Brussels. On occasion, however, stigma imposition becomes quite blatant. Through pejorative comments and teasing remarks from other member states, British and Danish diplomats are often reduced to being primitive defenders of national interests – one of the worst epithets that you can get in the EU. This example is one of many stories that illustrate the reality of EU operations: beneath the facade of technocratic

---

[1] Interview, Danish Ministry for Refugee, Immigration and Integration Affairs, Copenhagen, 12 February 2008.

negotiations we find an integration process that is rife with emotions and political positioning.

Beyond a legal interpretation

The British and Danish opt-outs threaten the doxa of an 'ever closer union' of equal members who have solidarity, as described by scholars such as Deirdre Curtin. However, neither legal nor political scholarship has paid attention to the way in which this threat is perceived and managed in practice. National opt-outs do not merely represent a hijacking of the *acquis communautaire* – a threat of legal disintegration – but may also undermine the tacit assumptions that give meaning to EU diplomacy in the first place. This menace of disintegration leads the European Commission, in particular, to seek to re-establish order by stigmatising the transgressors. Stigmatisation involves the distinction between the 'good Europeans' and those perceived to be only catering to their short-term domestic interests – that is, opt-out countries. To understand the daily struggles of British and Danish representatives, we need to consider these social mechanisms of distinction.

The British and Danish opt-outs work differently from each other. They do not lead to the same trade-off between influence and autonomy, and they involve different coping strategies on the part of British and Danish officials. One reason for this could be that finance ministers and officials mainly engage in co-ordination and produce soft law, whereas the ministers and officials involved with the AFSJ produce harder legislation. However, the differences are not only due to the output of the policy area; they are also affected by how negotiators perceive the stakes of their field. In the EMU, participants have a clear understanding of what is at stake when they meet – namely, the production of sound economic policy. Through economic policy co-ordination – in which instruments of classification, benchmarking and sanctions for excessive deficits are practised – member states' statuses are decided. Although the EU has yet to recover from the financial crisis that began in 2008, the positions of the member states are beginning to settle into more permanent hierarchies. The Eurogroup has been cast as the EU's core – probably for good. This feeds into daily diplomacy as the eurozone countries work to demonstrate and uphold their exclusivity. Consequently, British and Danish representatives are labelled, stereotyped and excluded from central forums, despite their record of good economic performance.

The picture is more blurred in the AFSJ. On the one hand, the Schengen members socially and politically exclude non-members, in a similar way to the Eurogroup. Only three member states are not full Schengen members: the UK, Ireland and Denmark. For 'Schengen lovers', as they are often referred to among officials, the British position is particularly provocative: the British do not adhere to the principle of free movement of people, and the Schengen members are willing to punish the UK for this.[2] For instance, the UK was not allowed to participate in two new EU measures: the regulation on security features and biometrics in passports, and the regulation on a new European border agency. So the UK faces a tough choice: either it continues outside a high-profile policy area, or it gives up its national border control, which, domestically, is considered tantamount to surrendering lifeblood.

On the other hand, the AFSJ cannot be easily divided into 'normals' and 'transgressors'. In Council of Ministers agendas, new EU proposals covered by the British and Danish protocols feature alongside other measures that do not touch upon issues where they have opt-outs. This gives them a chance to cope more actively with the stigma and work as a normal member state. Moreover, other member states also demonstrate reluctance towards further integration. This explains why the UK and Denmark, somewhat paradoxically, are seen as active member states in, for instance, the fight against terrorism and migration management. Contrary to the expectations of constructivist research, British and Danish diplomats are not necessarily perceived as 'bad Europeans'. Informal norms do not automatically exclude opt-out member states; on the contrary, pragmatic, consensus-oriented norms enable inclusion. For instance, on the choice of law in cross-border disputes, British officials have been allowed to block and change new legislation despite treaty rules that are devised to prevent this from happening. Even with the less flexible opt-outs, Danish officials are granted the opportunity to shape directives even though they will never be part of their implementation. Currently, national opt-outs are circumvented in the pragmatic AFSJ Council formation to allow integration to continue with everybody on board.

---

[2] Interview, Spanish Permanent Representation (Brussels), 26 February 2008.

Breaking the taboo and repairing the symbolic order

In January 2013, David Cameron broke the ultimate taboo in a speech on the future of Europe held at Bloomberg. What made the speech so important was not just that he promised to renegotiate the terms of British EU membership and put that change membership package to the British people in an 'in or out' referendum, but also that he said that the UK was not committed to the objective of 'an ever closer Union' and instead wanted an 'à la carte Europe'. The reaction from other European leaders, although subtle, was clear. German Foreign Minister Guido Westerwelle stressed that 'cherry-picking is not an option'. French Foreign Minister Laurent Fabius, in an interview with Radio France, went further, harshly criticising the speech, saying that the UK could not take 'Europe à la carte'. He also compared Cameron's views to sports fairness: 'We are like a soccer club, and if you want to join the soccer club, you can't then say you want to play rugby,' he said. As José Manuel Barroso later made clear, the 'process towards an ever closer Union continues'.[3] Yet Cameron is not as isolated as most European leaders would like him to be. His statement was echoed by Dutch Prime Minister Mark Rutte at the World Economic Forum in January 2013, when he said that the EU shouldn't be like the Hotel California described by rock band the Eagles as a place where 'you can check out any time you like – but you can never leave'.

In both academic and political circles there is increasing concern that euroscepticism and an increasing number of claims to sovereignty will lead to a disintegrating Europe. In the quest for European unity, opt-outs represent one of the most direct expressions of this threat. To counter such an unfortunate development, the argument goes, the EU must assert itself as a united and coherent legal and political order (De Witte 2001: 236).

What is too often neglected, however, is that this threat scenario is also present among the daily managers of the Union. In other words, the effects of differentiation are not what we generally assume. Officials are not just messengers or go-betweens; they are active repairmen who always seek to counter or forestall developments that may have a disintegrating effect on the whole. Because opt-outs represent a breach

---

[3] Brussels Think Tank Dialogue: 'The State of the EU in 2013: Heading towards Federalism or Fragmentation?'/Brussels.

of the idea of a united Europe, they threaten not only the legal order but also the *raison d'être* of national representatives working in Brussels, as well as the cohort of Europeanised national officials in the other European capitals.

Stigma imposition serves as a form of catharsis for the EU; catharsis refers to a release of emotions that reduces underlying tensions and anxieties (Gibbons 1997: 73). It requires the stigmatised to work hard to repair their image – in some way cleansing or purging themselves of their sin. In witnessing the ritualised repetition of decisions taken in the Eurogroup, whether directly or through second-hand reports, the 'normal' member states experience the emotional drama of an opt-out and its resulting exclusion. Stigmatisation contributes to clarifying norms and achieving conformity by distinguishing between 'us' (the normal states) and 'them' (the transgressive ones) (Hacking 2002: 99–114). Indeed, most societies not only rely on socialisation (in the form of emulation, learning or persuasion) but also use public sanctioning to construct and display normality. In earlier days, this was the role of the public scaffold. Today the heavy flow of news about criminal deviance serves a similar purpose (Garland 1990: 68).

Repairing and restoring social order require constant effort, as do creating and rearranging it. The EU is not a finished system; rather, it is a *modus vivendi*, which operates only insofar as diplomats take the time and trouble to oil it and keep it going. This may involve a lot of compensations and remedial work in order to support the social order. Just as the unemployed, the disabled or a sexual transgressor may fight stigma, the British and Danish representatives seek to fight the excluding effects of their opt-out status. British and Danish diplomats do not passively accept their stigma; they manage it in order to restore the existing social order of symbolic unity (primarily Denmark) or to promote their alternative visions for Europe (the UK).

Chapters 4 and 5 identified various diplomatic strategies related to opting out, including compensatory strategies, missionary strategies and self-restraint. The identification of these strategies challenges the analysis proposed by most research. For instance, neoclassical realists have argued that near-core insiders, such as the UK and Denmark, 'have been willing to refrain from some of their insider influence-capability in order to bolster their autonomy in one or more respects' (Wivel and Mouritzen 2005: 33). However, most officials value joint problem-solving more than autonomy. Although they formally respect the opt-out, diplomats try to compensate for the loss of influence, often with considerable success.

The compulsion to engage in compensatory strategies relates to a fear of losing out. It also originates in feelings of responsibility for European integration, as well as an urge to bolster their self-perception as effective diplomats. State representatives negotiate on a daily basis in Brussels – not necessarily with the aim of safeguarding sovereignty but often with a view to promoting a particular national position. In practice, this means promoting particular ideas and initiatives in the integration process. From new legislation on counterterrorism to decisions on the Stability and Growth Pact, British and Danish representatives try to leave 'British' and 'Danish' marks on the European edifice, despite their opt-out status.

Missionary strategies stem from an opposite perception: they involve a form of in-group alignment. Officials attempt to convert the stigma by raising their opt-out status into an emblem. They use their opt-out to show the rest of the EU that there are good reasons behind it. British officials generally feel more comfortable with a selective approach to the EU from the European menu than most of the Danish representatives do. Missionary strategies are partly consistent with the realist assumption that a larger state such as the UK can afford an opt-out. However, a country's decision to opt out is not determined by abstract geopolitical considerations but by how defendable the opt-out is believed to be.

Self-restraint is the third strategy adopted by Danish and British officials. When pursuing this strategy, officials acquire characteristics that further 'spoils [their] identity' (Goffman 1963). Self-restraint arises from the belief – particularly prevalent among Danish officials – that they are less worthy because of their opt-out status. This strategy reflects how deeply officials can be socialised into acknowledging the norms of the diplomatic field. According to an experienced official from the secretariat of the Council of Ministers, Danish officials often believe that they are less attractive negotiation partners, despite the fact that other member states believe that the opposite is the case.[4] The Danish officials generally feel embarrassed about the opt-outs. Their spoiled identity results in neither out- nor in-group alignment, just a general sense of inferiority.

[4] Interview, Council Secretariat (Brussels), 10 May 2006.

One might assume that these strategies are mutually exclusive. For instance, trying to hide a stigma suggests a desire to make it less obtrusive. However, diplomats often try to accomplish more than one purpose and may therefore adopt various strategies at a single meeting; if one strategy fails they can always turn to another. For instance, a representative from the Home Office may be embarrassed about the UK's approach to migration control in the Mediterranean and try to frame it as a European interest, but at the next meeting defend a staunch British position on biometrics in passports without trying to hide that the UK is pursuing a particular point, which is important domestically.

Diplomacy from mediation to transcendence

A classic argument in diplomatic theory is that diplomats are essentially mediators. Diplomacy has been interpreted as constituting a third culture – that is, a culture for mediation between political entities with diverse cultures (Neumann 2005: 72). Diplomatic studies from Watson's (2009) *raison de système* to Sharp's diplomatic theory emphasise diplomacy as a question of retaining separateness between entities, individuals, cultures and states. Diplomats, from this perspective, are focused on keeping the world running and manage the consequences of change. The basic idea is that diplomats help to grease the wheels and that 'order is further promoted by general agreements and rules that restrain and benefit all members of the system, and make it into a society' (Watson 2009: 9).

However, the EU's telos or trajectory goes beyond mediation or bridge-building between 'disparate and not necessarily directly connected worlds' (Neumann 2007: 197). The interactions between European states could be seen as the location for what James Der Derian calls 'anti-diplomacy'. If diplomacy is about mediating estranged relations, anti-diplomacy represents an 'aim to transcend all estranged relations' (Der Derian 1987; Neumann 2002). The next section looks at how national representation in the EU differs from traditional understandings of diplomacy.

Three aspects of late sovereign diplomacy

The microstrategies related to opt-outs reflect the dynamics of real-life diplomacy in the EU. In Chapter 3 I argued that officials who represent their member states in EU making (whether formally employed in the diplomatic services or members of the national home civil services) behave in particular ways when negotiating. The empirical findings regarding how British and Danish representatives manage opt-outs make it possible to substantiate this claim. The subsequent sections discuss three interlinked aspects of late sovereign diplomacy: the teleological interpretation of the EC and EU treaties, the social integration of national representatives and the promotion of national interests as part of a European cause.

The teleological doxa

The first feature of EU diplomacy is the teleological interpretation of integration, which invests in negotiations a desire to overcome national differences. From this perspective, diplomacy not only builds bridges but also goes further.[5] The previous chapters have demonstrated that member state representatives in Brussels work within what Bourdieu calls a doxa, which operates as if it were the objective truth across the entire social space. With some variations, the doxa of European integration is captured in the preamble of the Treaty of Rome, which states that the gathering nations of Europe are 'determined to lay the foundations of "an ever closer union" among the peoples of Europe'. Indeed, when the states became EU members 'they also implicitly signed up for more integration, because – in EC rhetoric – law (and obedience to law) has traditionally meant integration' (Shaw 1996: 337).

The doxa of 'an ever closer union' serves to legitimise the EU's actions to its own civil servants in the European Commission as well as to the national representatives negotiating in Brussels. It is simply part of the *raison d'etre* for what they are doing. Even if this self-legitimation has not become a genuine ideology, it does contribute to making diplomacy in Brussels a radical phenomenon. In their negotiations, member state representatives work in a particular direction, more or less consciously sharing the common goal of fulfilling the aims of the treaties. Indeed, the idea that Europe must continue to move forward is a shared assumption that is very rarely questioned by any national representative. They may not always agree on which direction the EU should be moving, or how fast, but they are unanimous that it should move forward.

---

[5] One may recall Goffman's rather peculiar definition of diplomacy as 'the polite encounter between people aimed at eliminating difference' (Goffman 1963: 57).

One of the most important ways to move forward is through law. In the Council of Ministers, diplomats translate the abstract notions of 'an ever closer union' into negotiations regarding secondary legislation in the form of regulations and directives. Even in the EMU, which is traditionally based on soft law, rules such as the Stability and Growth Pact are not just political guidelines but have a legally binding character. In other words, when preparing, drafting and negotiating on an everyday basis, national representatives not only make decisions but also create new legislation that often has a direct and immediate effect in their member states.

A European *sens pratique*

Linked to the doxa of 'an ever closer union' is a *sens pratique* – a second feature of late sovereign diplomacy. Social interaction between nation-state representatives is much more intense in the EU than anywhere else in the world, which increases the possibility of transferred loyalties. From this perspective neofunctionalism might seem relevant to the study of EU diplomacy. Neofunctionalists such as Lindberg stressed that elite socialisation was key to understanding European integration; in the Council of Ministers, problem-solving is dominant and 'the normal practice is to exclude the possibility of not reaching an agreement at all' (Lindberg 2006: 127). However, neofunctionalism failed to link the negotiation processes in the Council with the teleological interpretation of the treaties and the doxa of 'an ever closer union', thereby ignoring a crucial aspect of state interaction in Europe. The EU is a formal international organisation, established by states through international legal rules, but these legal rules in turn affect the self-understanding and practices of its member state representatives.

Negotiations in the EU produce a cohort of officials in every member state – not only those who have worked in the permanent representations but also those participating in the Council working groups. They are spread throughout the national administrations in the ministries of finance, agriculture, foreign policy, defence, justice, home affairs and so on. These officials promote national preferences but are also committed to collective outcomes at the European level. They see themselves as working both for their own country and for Europe, and usually do not see any contradiction between the two. As Brian Hocking notes, the diplomat in Europe is no longer a gatekeeper between the inside and outside of the state; rather, he is a boundary-spanner in a complex, transnational space (Hocking 2005). Following this line of argument, other scholars claim that the European diplomatic service constitutes 'an epistemic community of experts who often exercise their own agency separate from member state preferences' (Cross 2007: 224–225). This claim implies, however, that member state preferences are generated domestically and are subsequently represented in Brussels. Clearly this argument rests on the assumption that forming national preferences and the subsequent negotiations in the Council of Ministers are two different things – in other words, that there is a clear distinction between what is national and what is European. While this argument points to the importance of community, it fails to fully acknowledge the most significant feature of late sovereign diplomacy – that the distinction between the national and the international scenes, a classic phenomenon in diplomatic practice, loses its meaning. In late sovereign diplomacy, the very construction of a national position takes place as part of a struggle for distinction and dominance in a transnational field where the stakes have already been defined.

The merging of national and European interests in the EU goes uncontested in most cases. It has helped the member states to work together peacefully on very advanced regional co-operation projects that demand a high degree of mutual trust. Without close contact there would be no integration when it comes to sensitive issues such as monetary policy, common defence and criminal law (Mak 2003: 205). National representatives' identification with the European project can increase simultaneously with their identification with the nation-state. If this dual identity structure works well, national and European identi-fication can be mutually reinforcing (Herrmann and Brewer 2004: 12). The fact that national representatives assume the role of bureaucrats when they participate in the construction of a new polity – the EU – does not imply that they agree on the type of polity. There are divergences over, for example, which kind of asylum policy should be followed, how much sovereignty the state is willing to give up or how the member states' economic policies should be co-ordinated.

Yet most diplomacy is characterised by a dual purpose. It functions as a means of preserving and cultivating peaceful and orderly relations between states, as well as promoting particular national interests[6]

---

[6] According to Mayall, the underlying rationale of the diplomatic profession is to facilitate orderly and peaceful relations among states (Mayall 2007: 6).

(Berridge 1994: 7). While the integration doxa may sound radical, it is merely a reflection of what Neumann refers to as the general trick to being a diplomat: 'to concentrate on the here and now, on keeping the wheels turning' (Neumann 2005: 90). Being prepared to accept the principles of supranationality and economic integration, and to work effectively together, is not the same as losing sight of national interests. While national officials assume that legitimate authority stems from non-elected supranational bodies, such as the European Commission, as well as state-based elected and non-elected representatives, this does not mean that their loyalty to the common endeavour is a zero-sum game. Rather, it reflects the more pragmatic position that influence is only gained through common solutions.

This explains why it is so difficult for British and Danish diplomats to navigate with opt-outs. Keeping the wheels turning in the EU goes beyond safeguarding an established political order; it also involves participating in the creative construction of new policies – an opt-out makes this more difficult. When the opt-outs apply, British and Danish diplomats represent national positions that do not appear to cater to European interests. The opt-outs breach the ingrained notion of what it means to be a good diplomat in the EU, namely that of acting as custodians of an ever closer union.

Building a polity

A third feature of late sovereign diplomacy is the delocalisation of national interest. The objectives of the national officials' negotiations are pieced together, not only by their ministries and parliament back home but also by their European colleagues. The physical displacement of national representatives in the Permanent Representations in Brussels indicates that an ideational shift has taken place from a focus on national to shared interests. Today, national interests are largely produced in a transnational field among officials sharing a Europeanised habitus. Consequently, national diplomacy in the EU cannot simply be described as mediation between the domestic and European levels.

This brings us back to Moravscik and other scholars working with three- or two-level game understandings of the EU. They see national interests and policy goals as being 'determined by [the] domestic political system and by the preferences of policy makers, technocrats, political parties and interest groups' (Moravcsik 1991: 26). Yet they do not adequately account for the process of these interests being formed, since they ignore the influences of self-legitimation and constitutive effects of social integration of state representatives.

Diplomacy in the EU is still centred on representing the interests of the member states against other member states in the Council of Ministers. However, forming national interests happens in a transnational diplomatic field that is focused on constructing a European polity that limits the sovereignty of its member states. Member state representatives may continue to think in terms of national interest, but they do so in ways that are different from 50 years ago.

Intra-EU diplomacy between member states takes place within a system that contains the fundamental assumption that no member will contemplate the use or threat of force in EU interactions. Yet European integration is something far beyond what Adler (2008) means by a security community. Negotiation, at least below the level of ministers, has developed sophisticated codes of conduct, implying that any reference to national interests must be avoided. Instead, negotiators frame national positions with reference to some kind of common good for the European community. In this process, national representatives assume the role of polity-constructing technocrats, which is evident in the specification level in new EU legislation, which has reached a point that is comparable to national law. Legal instruments such as Directive 2001/43/EC relating to 'tyres for motor vehicles and their trailers and to their fitting', and Directive 2004/24/EC on 'traditional herbal medicinal products', are negotiated in the Council of Ministers system, but they have very little to do with defeat or victory for the nation. Rather, to paraphrase President of the European Commission José Manuel Barroso, they relate more to the creation of a 'Europe of results'.

This suggests something crucial in terms of how we understand influence. As mentioned in Chapter 3, influence in the Council of Ministers (i.e. the power to shape new proposals for legislation or policies) has been measured as a resource in the form of, for instance, voting weights, economic power, expertise or proximity to the position of the European Commission. My analysis suggests, however, that influence is achieved not through a direct and automatic application of these resources but rather by converting them into diplomatic capital. Diplomatic capital is a composite form of capital and its meaning is constantly negotiated. Indeed, the experience of the British and Danish officials demonstrates that part of achieving influence relates to defining what it is. For example, to influence the development of the EMU, officials enter an ongoing classification game about what a sound economy is; and how well – as a member state – one performs as a European economy.

Diplomatic capital can only be translated into influence in concrete negotiations. Thus, while a member state can be said to possess different degrees of objectified power – for instance, the UK has 29 votes and Denmark has seven votes in the Council of Ministers – this resource can only be exercised effectively if channelled through narrowly defined and accepted roles and scripts defined by the Council. To be influential, one must respect the informal norms of problem-solving and consensus-seeking. Indeed, voting power may never apply as an effective resource, as the management of the opt-outs in the area of asylum, immigration and civil law suggests when the British officials have never used their veto or when Danish ministers and officials influence rules on family reunification despite having no voting right due to the opt-out.

The future of a differentiated Europe

There is a new trend in the EU that appears to point in the opposite direction of deeper integration: the shift towards decision-making dominated by the European Council – that is, the heads of state and government. The growing number of bilateral meetings and summits between political leaders of member states could be viewed as a return to classic diplomacy between sovereigns. The heads of state and government are often far removed from the community's supranationalist method. However, this is not a return to the days of state-centric diplomacy but part of a trend that allows Europe speak with one voice.

The financial crisis that hit Europe in 2008 offers an example. At every extraordinary summit between the heads of state and government, the message was clear: Europe must speak with one voice. In 2010 the Greek sovereign debt crisis forced the member states to rethink the co-ordination of their national economic policies, confronting the euro-zone with its most severe test since its launch 11 years earlier. It was largely the member states that invented the rescue plan, and it is the President of the European Council – not the Commissioner for Economic and Monetary Affairs – who is in charge of formulating new rules on economic governance.

As Uwe Puetter (2014) has shown, the increasing number of high-level summits reflects more than the wish to reach concrete decisions; these summits are part of a larger transformation of how good statesmanship is formed in contemporary Europe. At press conferences, French and German leaders express satisfaction with the negotiations, underlining that they reflected a concerted approach. The many attempts to 'speak with one voice' are not just a cover-up for hard bargaining; they are also an effort to disseminate normative and cognitive frameworks. The idea that 'we are doing something together' is an important message to send out to the public. It also perpetuates the myth of a unified Europe as the results of a negotiated consensus among the member states.

From this perspective, Hollande's and Merkel's euro-speak connects those inside the European institutions while, simultaneously, excluding those outside it. Strengthening the European Council can be seen as a government technique, which – like the common foreign and security policy – is legitimised by the attempts to overcome national differences and driven by the wish to play a role in the world. Diplomatic success is largely measured by the ability to find a common position that results in Europe speaking with one voice.

Tempering transformations

If the EU speaks with one voice, what happens to the national voices? If a common diplomatic culture continues to develop in Europe, what will remain of independent national diplomacy? Can we conceive of a Europe without representatives of separate political polities? Not only has the context in which intra-European diplomacy takes place changed, its very meaning seems to be shifting as well. Supranational institutions and national representatives are jointly participating in creating a common European language that shapes their understanding of the negotiations.

It is important, however, to moderate the claims that an intra-EU diplomacy undermines the idea of a sovereign state. Late sovereign diplomacy has inherent conservative features that I will explain below. In other words, one should refrain from assuming that these trends represent the terminal phase of diplomacy in Europe. There are at least two reasons for arguing against the idea that the EU will fundamentally transform national diplomacy.

First, the doxa of integration is intrinsically ambiguous. The fundamental idea behind the EU is that it should never reach the crucial point where one state is the same as another state; when a state can no longer make sovereignty claims to supreme and ultimate authority over its own territory. When Barroso and other European leaders talk of a federalist future, they are using it as a relatively ambiguous term. A federal state, depending on how it was constructed, would be different from an ever-closer Union. If member states agreed to become European *Länder*, the diplomatic task of pushing Europe towards an always moving horizon of deeper integration would no longer be meaningful.

In the current system, however, national representatives accept that other states and entities make competing and sometimes more successful claims to sovereignty. This is a critical element in late sovereign diplomacy: there must be no clear endpoint of integration. The idea of an 'ever closer union among the peoples' requires there to be separate 'peoples', and hence that the EU should remain a polity with separate and sovereign states. An increasing number of areas may become supranational and integration may get so overwhelming that the state essentially loses most autonomy. However, as long as state representatives can make effective calls for sovereignty and the *finalité* debate remains abstract, late sovereign diplomacy will have a long shelf life.

Second, if national representatives forget about the self-limitation clause in the constitutional structure of the EU, others will remind them of the fragility of their project, which is only fully shared by a small European elite. In light of the euro crisis and public protests across Europe, the European Parliament elections in 2014, the British renegotiation plans, the Czech ratification problems in 2009, the French and Dutch rejections of the Constitutional Treaty in 2005 and the subsequent negative Irish vote on the Treaty of Lisbon in 2008, objections to EU orthodoxy are likely to become more vociferous in the coming years. The doxa of 'an ever closer union' will be challenged by calls for increased differentiation in the form of national opt-outs and exemptions. The Polish declaration to the Charter on Fundamental Rights in the Treaty of Lisbon represented a eurosceptic view, which has rarely been adopted among the political and diplomatic elite. New generations of heads of state and government, and their national representatives, now enter the European scene with a different understanding of the purpose of European integration, thereby strengthening traditional sovereign diplomacy vis-à-vis the orthodox integration mode. Future enlargement rounds may also threaten the existing doxa, although, as mentioned in Chapter 5, it has been demonstrated that national representatives from the new member states adapt quickly to the informal norms of the Council of Ministers system (Lempp and Altenschmidt 2008).

Beyond the EU

It could be said that the EU's polity-building agenda is a general feature of contemporary world politics. As Paul Sharp notes in a critique of post-Cold War diplomacy:

Representation – of sovereigns, interests, or ideas – was replaced by metaphors of constructing and building by which issues were to be managed and problems were to be solved. (Sharp 2004: 67)

According to Sharp, the modern diplomat moves from initially representing a sovereign state towards engineering new international institutions. Yet one should carefully specify the area of validity of this claim. A system-wide phenomenon such as diplomacy may not be directly affected by what happens within one unit of the system – that is, the EU. Diplomacy may be changing at a global level, but this debate must be studied at the level of the global system, for instance, as a result of trade liberalisation, technology changes and globalisation processes (see e.g. Cooper, Hocking and Maley 2008).

Are there other international organisations with similar dynamics to late sovereign diplomacy? Outside Europe it is difficult to identify the same degree of integration between national representatives that exists in the EU. Trade organisations, such as the World Trade Organization (WTO), and regional organisations, such as the Association of South-East Asian Nations (ASEAN) and Mercosur (from the Spanish *Mercado Cumún del Sur*), could be interesting comparisons. Unlike the EU, however, these organisations are inter-governmental by nature.

The WTO is possibly the closest construction to the EU; WTO laws can impact national law in a similar way to EU law through the dispute-settlement mechanism. Although the WTO lacks fundamental elements of supranational law – such as superiority and direct effect – it is 'functionally equivalent to supranational law' and has gained a further layer of governance (Krajewski 2001: 171). However, the

WTO does not have all of the features that constitute late sovereign diplomacy: it reaches decisions by consensus among some 150 member states, and no supranational institutions participate in the negotiations. Crucially the WTO does not have a genuine polity-building agenda. Indeed, a key element of diplomacy in the EU is the unprecedented nature of the EU itself and national officials' roles in representing member states while making decisions in the name of a supranational authority.

Making a late sovereign polity accountable

Negotiations in the EU centre on representing member states' interests against each other. However, handling national interests – in the sense of negotiating – takes place within a transnational diplomatic field in Brussels that is focused on constructing a European polity. National interests do not disappear in the EU, but they are far less socially mediated than most accounts of the EU describe. As a Danish senior official said, 'I think it is embarrassing when member states argue by referring to national interests and problems instead of trying to find common ground.'[7]

Does this bring us back to earlier forms of pre-democratic *realpolitik* where actions were taken by individual leaders and their advisors rather than nations or peoples? They are still national positions but they lack popular legitimacy. National interests do not always have the strength and absoluteness of interests with the weight of society behind them. As Chris Bickerton explains, the European integration process has contributed to a paradoxical combination of technocracy and populism, the two mutually enforcing each other (Bickerton 2012: 185). With technocracy Bickerton understands the strengthened role of non-elected experts and managers, following 'reasonable and dispassionate' logics. With populism he understands the increasingly powerful 'discourse that pits "the people" against the elites', promoted by leaders such as Marine Le Pen and Geert Wilders, who embrace the domain of the 'spontaneous and emotional' (Bickerton 2012: 184). The combined effect of these two trends is a hollowing-out of the idea of parliamentary democracy and popular sovereignty.

---

[7] Interview, Ministry of Refugees, Immigration and Integration Affairs (Copenhagen), 22 August 2007.

Stated more radically,

> We see that sovereignty, as the forceful assertion of national interests and ambitions, is less appropriate to the actual behaviour of today's elites. On the contrary, European integration begins to look somewhat like Althusser's 'process without a subject'. Sovereignty survives as performance, but its content is attenuated. (Heartfield 2007: 147)

Heartfield's argument points out the naïveté of the two-level game assumption, which supposes a stronger and more direct link between national preference formation and Council of Ministers negotiations.

However, Heartfield's argument falls short in one important respect: it assumes that sovereignty was once a 'forceful assertion of national interests and ambitions'. In pointing out a small diplomatic site in the EU engine room, there is a risk of falling into the opposite trap of 'essentialising' the national interest as having a particular vitality. The national representatives who develop policy in Brussels share many assumptions and inhabit the same world, but so did the aristocratic diplomats of the 1850s. Rather, the polity-building agenda of European integration suggests that EU diplomacy goes beyond an increased integration of the diplomatic elite's worldviews, and it also points out problems of accountability.

In this book I have chosen to focus on what is a limited group of people that engages in the struggle with the management of the opt-outs on a day-to-day basis in Brussels. By demonstrating that opt-outs cannot be seen as merely representing 'the voice of the people' or a eurosceptic position, it has revealed one of the added values of importing a political sociological framework into the study of one of the most classic sites of integration: the Council of Ministers.

Some years ago, Allot predicted that democracy would replace intra-European diplomacy (Allot, quoted in Jørgensen 1999). Such replacement has yet to be seen. When national interests are Europeanised, the fundamental questions of why we have diplomacy and for whom diplomacy works can be raised. One approach suggests a return to sovereign diplomacy; the other accepts the transition to late sovereign diplomacy. Sharp argues the former position when he explains that to avoid becoming a source of international tension,

> Diplomats should remind themselves and others that they are first and foremost the representatives of sovereign states, that this is their raison d'être and a precondition for anything else they may aspire to be or do. (Sharp 2004: 76)

In the current European order, however, the *raison d'être* of national diplomacy has changed – perhaps for good. Indeed, without this, European integration would not have been possible. Thus while Sharp's comment about the diplomatic *raison d'être* is a valuable reminder, it will not match the EU's overlapping authority structures and the supranational decision-making process.

A different approach to making the EU more accountable assumes that we have entered late sovereign diplomacy definitively. The challenge is not to roll back integration but to introduce more checks and balances that will increase its accountability. Some scholars call for an increasing politicisation of negotiations in Brussels as a way to increase the EU's legitimacy and transparency. In a widely quoted article, Føllesdal and Hix (2006) advocate a stronger European Parliament as a way of making the Union more democratic. Others, such as Richard Rose (2013: 13), propose pan-European referendums on all treaties 'to test how much popular commitment there is to the expansion of EU powers'. Yet these suggestions do not address the everyday negotiation process, which – as I have demonstrated – is a key driver of integration. They are thus not likely to solve the core issue, which is the daily process of national interest representation in the EU. As Bickerton writes, 'Far from being a contingent event to be remedied by various acts of "politization", the democratic deficit is a constituent feature of European integration' (Bickerton 2012: 189).

Another way of addressing the legitimacy gap would be to strengthen national parliamentary involvement in the EU decision-making process. Some believed that the Treaty of Lisbon would lead to greater parliamentary control on the national and European scenes, thereby reducing the gap. National parliaments' stronger involvement in the EU's decision-making process may link national representative practices more directly to the debates in the national capitals and give rise to demands that the negotiations in Brussels reflect particular national problems. Nonetheless, it is doubtful whether initiatives such as giving national parliaments the power to block new legislation through the use of 'red cards' will change the way in which diplomacy functions in the EU. Rather, such initiatives may have the opposite effect and result in increased frustration, for both officials and the populations that they represent.

National parliaments could be made to elect the permanent representatives in Brussels. This would create a direct link between the most powerful national officials in Brussels and the domestic representative institution. However, it may also politicise the negotiations to the degree that the problem-solving and co-operative culture is threatened; a culture that, for better or for worse, is central to the European integration process. Seen from the diplomatic engine room, the danger of introducing more parliamentary control is that it may become more difficult for state representatives to engage in sincere dialogue. The debate about the gap between people and decisions in the EU reflects a classic dilemma between diplomacy and democracy.

Alternative models of safeguarding sovereignty

If opt-outs lead to exclusion and stigmatisation yet do not safeguard autonomy, do they really work? To answer this question we need to return to the Maastricht legacy discussed in Chapter 1. Is the ultimate purpose of the British opt-out from the EMU to safeguard national sovereignty, or to respect a parliamentary majority, or to secure the signing and subsequent ratification of a treaty, or to provide a government with more room to manoeuvre in Brussels or to respond to popular euroscepticsm? In the case of the British and Danish opt-outs from the EMU and the AFSJ, all of these motivations are involved. Of course, this complicates our evaluation of their effectiveness – there is no clear unit of measurement. One thing is certain: opt-outs have hitherto not been rooted in any master plan or grand democratic vision for Europe.

Let us, for the sake of argument, accept the idea that opt-outs have been installed to secure national autonomy from EU policies and legislation. Such a justification begs the question of whether there are alternative ways of safeguarding sovereignty. One proposal comes from Fritz Scharpf, who has advocated 'politically controlled opt-outs' as a solution to the European democratic deficit. He defines politically controlled opt-outs as 'the immobilism between the political modes of EU-policy-making and the activism of non-political modes of EU policy-making' (Scharpf 2007: 16). Scharpf wants to restrain the ECJ and empower the Council of Ministers and European Parliament. He fears that the unrestrained pursuit of economic and legal integration may weaken the political legitimacy of member states and endanger the voluntary compliance of governments with EU rules.

Scharpf may be right in pointing out that an alternative to more opt-outs is 'creeping non-compliance' and 'institutional hypocrisy' – but what does creeping non-compliance actually mean? (Scharpf 2006). Not only does the opt-out have the legality that non-compliance does not, from the public's perspective, but it is also explicit and symbolically much stronger than non-compliance. The explicit opt-out represents the idea that the state safeguards sovereignty, but creeping non-compliance does not have this symbolism.

Scharpf suggests a mechanism that enables member states to call for exemption from a particular EU law in specific cases where salient national interests would be violated if the country complied. The Council of Ministers would decide whether a state would be allowed to opt-out by using a peer-review procedure according to which member states notify the legislative deviations from the *acquis* to the European Commission before they enter into force. The Commission would then review the case and submit it to the Council, which, within six months of notification, could disallow the national deviation by majority vote (Scharpf 2006). This procedure would prevent free riding. Scharpf ends with the following statement: 'As far as I know, however, this idea has not found any takers' (Scharpf 2007: 16).

There may be reasons why Scharpf's idea has not caught on. The proposal rests on two assumptions, both of which are possibly unsustainable. First, in distinguishing between political and non-political modes of decision-making, Scharpf assumes that member states are not responsible for the strengthening of economic and legal integration. Yet the national representatives are part of the very challenge that Scharpf seeks to solve. By arguing that the Council of Ministers should conduct peer reviews, Scharpf has set the fox to guard the geese.

Second, Scharpf's discussion of opt-outs disregards the social context in which the possibility of opting out would be introduced. As such, his proposal may have unintended consequences. At first glance Scharpf's model resembles the British à la carte opt-in possibility on asylum, immigration and civil law. However, contrary to Scharpf's proposal, the British do not have to ask for permission to opt out. Moreover, they must indicate whether they opt-in or not before the measure is adopted (otherwise they will not be covered by it and will not have the right to vote). This rule guarantees that the states adopting a measure are the same as those that are bound by it. Scharpf's proposal would allow representatives to participate in the negotiations and adoption of a proposal, and subsequently notify the European Commission that they intend to opt out before the measure comes into force. The UK manages its opt-in possibility in a manner that does not frustrate its European partners because it is clear about on which areas it opts in and on which it opts out. As soon as there is uncertainty about participation, the negotiation power and status of the state will be reduced drastically. If the management of opt-outs can only be understood in its particular milieu – as a socially mediated phenomenon – institutional engineering aimed at safeguarding national autonomy from EU legislation should address this social context.

Moreover, taken at face value, Scharpf's opt-out proposal may have other undesired side-effects. If the opt-out mechanism comes into force and is used frequently, it will bring forth a fundamentally different(iated) Europe: a Europe in which all member states can opt out of any legislation before and after it is agreed. This would be very far removed from the current EU (Scharpf 2006: 858). It is only because those that opt-out are still a minority that they do not threaten integration.

Another reflection also merits consideration: radical differentiation, or what we could call the British Conservative vision for Europe. Instead of extending national opt-outs, reluctant states could become associated members of the EU without being bound to participate in all EU policies. At first glance, association represents a different, and even more resolute, way of opting out. Judging from experience, however, this may not be so simple. In fact, one could argue that this 'Norwegian model' merely represents an exaggeration of the position of a member state with opt-outs. Through the European Economic Area (EEA) agreement, Norway and the two other non-EU members of EEA (Iceland and Liechtenstein) are obliged to implement all EU legislation relevant to the functioning of the internal market (Egeberg and Trondal 1999; see also Neumann 1999: 273; Adler-Nissen forthcoming).[8] The

---

[8] The EEA agreement is an international agreement between the EU and the European Free Trade Association (EFTA), which came into force on 1 January 1994. The agreement allows EFTA countries into the Single European Market on equal terms as the member countries. Some policy areas are nevertheless excluded from the agreement (e.g. fisheries and agriculture). Since Sweden, Finland and Austria joined the EU in 1995, the only EFTA countries left in the EEA are Norway, Iceland and Liechtenstein (the last EFTA country, Switzerland, rejected the EEA agreement in a referendum in 1993).

EEA agreement allows the EEA countries to participate in committees under the European Commission, but not in committees or working groups under the Council of Ministers.[9] Norway only participates actively in Schengen, where it is considered to be a full member without the right to vote. As a rule, however, Norway is not part of the diplomatic struggles for new legislation, although it is later committed to following these laws (Eliassen and Sitter 2003). Norway is represented in the Mixed Committees but has no formal representation in the Council of Ministers system. The EEA agreement contributes to the conclusion of the Norwegian Power and Democracy Study that parliamentary representation erodes without being recompensated on the European level as Norway is neither represented in the Council of Ministers nor in the European Parliament (Selle and Østerud 2006).

Consequently there is a great difference between being a Norwegian official and being a British or Danish official. While the British and Danish representatives may not be allowed to vote or are sometimes not invited to meetings, they are not complete outsiders; they are still part of the struggle for influence. By contrast, the possibility of leaving a 'Norwegian' stamp on the European edifice is slim, although the country is, in many respects, just as bound by the decisions and rules made in Brussels. The limits of the Norwegian model explain why Turkey and other candidate countries worry about becoming associates without enjoying the benefits of EU membership.

In sum, any new institutional mechanism created to install external controls will be interpreted and reinterpreted by diplomats. They work from the assumption that legitimate authority stems not only from state-based elected and non-elected representatives but also from non-elected supranational bodies. Creating fundamental changes in the way states negotiate in the EU would require radical reforms – not only of the institutional setup but also of the diplomatic identities, social hierarchies and the sense of purpose of the integration process. Reproducing national systems of accountability and representation in a system in which national representation is serving both national and European agendas in a quasi-autonomous diplomatic field is unlikely to have the desired effects.

---

[9] Interview, Norwegian Embassy in Denmark (Copenhagen), 12 March 2008.

Conclusions

This chapter has argued that national representatives have contributed to a silent transformation of diplomacy in Europe over the past 50 years. In many instances, national interests are no longer framed as a state's own interests but as the state's ambitions for the EU. When defending positions in the Council of Ministers, national representatives participate actively in constructing new policies. Creating a peaceful and regulated international order is a general feature of diplomatic interaction; within the EU, however, diplomatic interaction does not merely involve sovereign states speaking with each other; political and legal authorities overlap, territorial exclusivity is replaced with functional divisions of powers and states begin to speak with one voice.

As this chapter has shown, there are three distinct, though interrelated, features of late sovereign diplomacy: the purpose of diplomacy is not merely mediation between states but also the creation of 'an ever closer union'; national representatives are undergoing intense socialisation; and national interests are delocalised. While this development may be seen as a return to an intimate European aristocracy, teleological and delocalised diplomatic practices are new. The national representative is no longer only a mediator but is also a constructor of a European polity that rivals the state. Whether late sovereign diplomacy exists outside Europe is a more open question.

British and Danish opt-outs are managed in this late sovereign polity, which means that they do not work as expected. Differentiation in the form of national opt-outs is socially and politically punished in Brussels; British and Danish diplomats subsequently seek to repair the damage, which serves as a form of catharsis within the EU system. While opt-outs may be legally clear, they are diplomatically ambiguous. While popular protests, enlargement and negative results in referenda may suggest that differentiation has come to stay, no sign of disintegration looms on the horizon.

The coexistence of ideas of traditional national interests and a common European interest is at the core of late sovereign diplomacy. Sovereign statehood survives in the minds and practices of those that represent the state in Europe. This simultaneous thinking creates many tensions in the EU. The doxa of 'an ever closer Union' is fundamentally ambivalent, which means that late sovereign diplomacy is likely to last for a long time. Differentiation may, in part, reconcile the tension between deepening and widening (Leuffen et al. 2013: 267) but it does not resolve problems of legitimacy. This raises fundamental questions about accountability in a multidimensional order, with its constitutional pluralism and uneasy combination of 'national' and 'common' interests. I have shown the limits of formal opt-outs and other forms of differentiation as a solution to the EU's democratic deficit. Moreover, I have argued that increased politicisation or giving more power to the national parliaments will not necessarily change the current EU situation. Any genuine and lasting EU reform must take into account the fact that national diplomacy in the EU is no longer what it used to be.

7 | *Conclusion*

Most scholars believe that integration and opt-outs in Europe are unnatural and rather uncomfortable bedfellows. Opt-outs continue to be seen as paradigmatic expressions of national sovereignty and hence democracy, reflecting what Neil Walker calls an 'ideological assumption of ultimate authority over the internal operation of the polity' (Walker 2003: 26). However, it is problematic to assume that the opt-out state's motivation is to make a principled claim to national sovereignty. I have shown how pragmatic concerns such as strengthening migration control or securing the nation's image as a sound economy affect sovereignty claims on a day-to-day basis. These claims are influenced by unwritten rules of behaviour. The analysis of the mutual bond shared by the officials representing their nations in Brussels is key to understanding the complicated relationship between sovereignty and European integration. By focusing on the diplomatic handling of British and Danish opt-outs, this book has suggested that abstract notions of sovereignty need to be supplemented by perspectives on how this concept develops in practice. Sovereignty, as a claim to supreme authority, becomes part of daily diplomatic battles, which often occur under the radar of both public and academic attention.

In this concluding chapter I discuss some of the general implications of my analysis. Having explored the management of opt-outs, I first address where this leaves current understanding of European integration and the crucial role of national diplomacy in the EU. I then evaluate the benefits of drawing on Bourdieu and Goffman in IR theory and European studies. The chapter ends with some suggestions of scenarios for a differentiated EU and warns against purely institutionalist solutions to the EU's so-called democratic deficit.

Without national opt-outs, such as the British and Danish opt-outs from the euro and the co-operation on borders, migration, asylum and justice policies, we would not have seen the EU's quantum leaps into the core tasks of the nation-state in the 1990s. Consequently, instead of fragmenting the EU, opt-outs become an important instrument to ensure continued integration. However, existing approaches to European integration – whether anti- or pro-differentiation – ignore the fact that opt-out states operate within the EU's constitutional discourse. Indeed, the paradoxical, and perhaps most perplexing, finding is that opt-outs contribute to upholding what the Treaty of Rome called 'an ever closer Union'. In making this argument I have developed a political sociological understanding of European integration. This approach directs the argument away from the official ideas promoted by the EU institutions. Studying everyday diplomacy of the Council of Ministers makes it possible to analyse it not only as a formal organisation but also as a social order, involving a shared feeling of destiny among those who are in charge of it. This feeling of destiny has important implications for how we should understand the relationship between sovereignty, diplomacy and differentiated integration.

Building on Bourdieu's insights regarding the importance of everyday practices, together with Goffman's analysis of role-playing in the production of social structures, I have presented an account of the EU as being, in part, constructed through the stigmatisation of transgressive states. Shame and pride are part of the diplomatic game when British and Danish representatives negotiate in Brussels. Opting out and stigmatising those who attempt to do it, far from weakening the EU, confirms its trajectory. At the operational level, Council of Ministers members exert great pressure on themselves to conform to the idea that the EU is engaged in creating an ever closer union of its peoples. Thus even those who represent countries that seek to opt out of common policies, such as the UK and Denmark, usually do so through a repertoire of strategies that secure their involvement as much as possible – for instance, the mimicking strategy that seeks to compensate for the opt-out. Danish officials recognise that they are asking for 'extremely artificial' parallel agreements where 'the EU has to do an external agreement with one of its own members'.

This is what I call 'late sovereign diplomacy' – the intense integration of national representatives who adhere to an ever closer union, producing legislation that challenges the sovereignty of their own nations. Late sovereign diplomacy is unlikely to solve the democratic deficit that confronts the EU. Instead it reinforces further integration because it is undertaken by a relatively insulated group of people, partly isolated from how politics plays out in their home countries; the physical separation and the heavy socialisation and daily experiences of the EU mean that national representatives help to construct their countries' national interests in ways that are consistent with the European project.

Opting out does have a political price. Overall, opt-outs have limited the flexibility available to the British and Danish representatives, hindered them in setting an agenda and obstructed their attempts to influence negotiations. Yet, contrary to the widespread presumption that opt-outs automatically lead to exclusion from decision-making processes (e.g. Pilkington 1995: 109; Wallace 1997), exclusion cannot be deduced directly from the legal protocols. Marginalisation largely depends on how stigma is handled. Interestingly, the same tacit norms that legitimise stigma imposition are employed by the British and Danish officials to reclaim some of the lost influence. It is this double dynamic of stigma imposition and stigma management that may help to explain the puzzling situation in which the UK and Denmark are sometimes perceived as frontrunners, despite the opt-outs: exclusionary and inclusionary mechanisms are at work simultaneously. British and Danish representatives have developed sophisticated ways of circumventing the opt-outs to reduce their exclusionary effects, so the figure of an autonomous state is preserved at home.

Good and bad member states

The paradoxical – and perhaps most perplexing – finding is that the ways in which opt-outs are managed contribute to upholding an ever closer Union. Theoretically, this has implications for how we should understand the European integration process more broadly. Stigma imposition serves an important – yet hidden – function in the Council of Ministers. By stigmatising the norm-breakers, 'normality' is reinforced among the national representatives from the member states that participate fully in the Union. Stigmatisation is not an outcome of the infraction of social norms about 'normality' but it is a product of the failure to construct normality in the first place. Transgressors illuminate the challenges posed by the question: what is good and appropriate state behaviour? They expose the fragility of integration and are therefore always present in talks about normalisation. Through the imposition of stigma on the British and Danish representatives, a form of social catharsis or cleansing process takes place, whereby they are sanctioned for being 'anti-European' (Goffman 1959). In accepting the sanctions (e.g. exclusion from Eurogroup meetings), but more importantly by engaging in stigma management and self-restraint (e.g. remaining silent at meetings where they are otherwise allowed to be participate), British and Danish officials help to restore the social order. Through stigma management they simultaneously take on the norms that regulate interaction and help to support them. Consequently, while opt-outs at first sight might appear to undermine the solidarity and cohesiveness of the EU, the diplomatic repair work and compensatory activities of the opt-outers contribute to securing the doxa. National opt-outs should be interpreted not only as exemptions but also as rules that confirm the objective of continued European integration.

The application of the theoretical framework demonstrates how the concepts of field and stigma can be linked and thus how Goffman's and Bourdieu's thinking augment each other. Both sociologists consider stigma but they approach it differently. Bourdieu's structural account of the field and his understanding of stigma as negative capital complement Goffman's notion of stigma. To understand how stigma is managed in face-to-face meetings, Goffman provides analytical tools to categorise the strategies employed by the British and Danish officials. This links everyday coping with stigma to the broader question of marginalisation. Focusing on stigma serves to explore the connections between everyday diplomatic practices – from awkward handshakes to group photos – and the macroprocesses of inclusion and exclusion. States are struggling for recognition, and these processes help to define normal and deviant state behaviour, which sustains international co-operation.

Implicit in this analysis is a critique of some of the dominant approaches in EU and IR studies. An approach inspired by Bourdieu and Goffman offers an alternative to orthodoxies about international politics promoted by top-down IR theories such as realism, liberalism and (much of) constructivism. Most constructivists depart from norms or shared values to understand international politics, thereby ignoring the fact that social order is constructed through processes of discrimination and exclusion. By insisting on the agency of both the stigmatisers and the stigmatised, political sociology promotes awareness of the ongoing negotiation of 'normal' state behaviour. Stigma management as a strategy for handling negative classification may strengthen, change or question notions of normality.

This is where Bourdieu and Goffman offer original insight. By high-lighting the interaction between those who impose 'normal' state behaviour and those who are seen as transgressive, I have shown that the deviant may play a more important role than previously acknowledged. Indeed, we see the contours of the EU as a political order in concrete attempts to both defend and challenge its normative basis.

This prompts the question of how British and Danish opt-outs compare with other potential deviances in the EU. An obvious possibility would be to study other possible stigmas linked to, for instance, being a poor economic performer or a newcomer to the European family.[1] The crisis-ridden countries of the eurozone – Portugal, Italy, Greece and Spain – have found themselves lumped collectively into one wholesome flawed category. As Marion Fourcade suggests, 'the economically vulnerable also face a form of moral downgrading' (Fourcade 2013: 25). This has brought about reverse moral struggles – from Greece towards Germany in particular – over debts long past and moral obligations inherited from a wartime Europe. There is a need for further mapping of the transnational social fields of European integration, examining positions of dominance and categorisations, and exploring the range of resources or characteristics which are converted into negative or positive diplomatic capital.

Rethinking European integration and diplomacy

The Council of Ministers constitutes the primary arena in which governments negotiate. One of the most contentious issues in the academic and political debate about the Council has been the question of the relative power of different member states, particularly the alleged impact of different rules for establishing majorities in the Council of Ministers. However, explicit voting is relatively infrequent and does not give us hard evidence about either the nature of contestation or the relative success.[2]

---

[1] Indeed, stigma processes would also apply to applicant states where the implicit framing of Turkey as Muslim appears to decisively hamper its membership perspectives (Gad 2007).

[2] As König and Junge (2009) argue, the multidimensionality of contestation and the reluctance to express explicit opposition do not enable us to establish a clear picture of how negotiations proceed. This is so even though Naurin and Lindahl (2009) report that negotiators from the larger member states are more centrally positioned in the negotiation networks.

When considering this institution, liberal intergovernmentalists traditionally look at the domestic aggregation of preferences that form a national position, which is then promoted internationally (Risse-Kappen, Cowles and Caporaso 2001: 13). The work in the Council of Ministers, however, is not just driven by domestic preferences; the state's interest and the way in which it is translated into particular agreements with other states in the EU is continuously reconstructed in Brussels.

By the late 1990s the debate about Europe's architecture appeared to be settled in favour of the view that European integration had transformed a network of sovereign national states into a system of multilevel governance. Even advocates of the staying power of national governments had come to accept that a 'multilevel governance system [is] prevailing in Europe' (Moravcsik 2004: 356). On this basis, Curtin and Egebjerg (2008) view the EU as an 'accumulated executive order', meaning that the European Commission becomes 'the new and distinctive executive centre at the European level, outside of the intergovernmental locus, the Council of Ministers' (Curtin and Egebjerg 2008: 639). Somewhat similarly, Giandomenico Majone (1994) conceptualised the EU as a regulatory regime in which decisions are taken by experts and supranational officials in non-majoritarian settings. The EU does indeed represent one of the most advanced 'institutionalised normative orders' beyond the bounded territorial states (MacCormick 2007: 7).

While such approaches capture the important role of the European Commission and EU agencies (see also Egebjerg and Trondal 2011), they oddly assume that the Council of Ministers still reflects a clash of unitary and often rational state interests; however, states are part of the construction of the executive order. The Council is a complex political forum where multiple symbolic resources are used to maintain and advance national positions. Governments and officials may not always agree on the direction or speed, but they agree that the EU should move forward. This helps to explain Börzel's (2005) finding that there has not been one case where a policy has been shifted from the European to the national level, nor a case where a supranational policy has become intergovernmental. At least until now the development of European governance has been unidirectional.

We can also analyse the handling of national positions in concrete negotiations as struggles over diplomatic capital (a composite form of power) rather than the expression of a unitary state's interest. Negotiations in the EU still centre on representing the interests of the

member states against other member states. However, the actual for-
mulation and handling of the national interest take place within an
Europeanised diplomatic field, and national interests are promoted
within these confines. The relative influence of national representatives
in negotiations does not just depend on voting power or economic size
but equally on whether they are seen as constructive Europeans.

Managing sovereignty claims such as national opt-outs does not escape
the Brussels effect. For national representatives, European integration
works because it moves. European integration is not a quasi-automatic
process. However, it is a process where officials, almost without even
thinking about it, conform to the expectations of EU institutions and
other member states (and seek to advance 'practical solutions'). This
explains why a Danish official can say that the Danish opt-outs are not
'legitimate demands'.

Europeanisation literature has brought us some way towards understanding this phenomenon. It has explored the EU's impact on the
domestic policies, institutions and political processes of the member
states as well as on the accession candidates (Börzel and Risse 2007;
Featherstone and Radaelli eds 2003; Graziano and Vink 2006;
Sedelmeier 2011). Students of Europeanisation have identified both necessary conditions (a 'misfit' giving rise to adaptational pressure) and
causal mechanisms (legal imposition, positive and negative incentives,
and socialisation by persuasion and learning) through which 'Europe hits
home'. Yet they have not addressed the doxa of integration.

A political sociological approach to national interests in the EU
differs radically from the approach proposed by traditional theories of
diplomacy and European integration. At the most basic level it sees
integration as a largely social process driven by politico-administrative
elites working within a specific and relatively narrow understanding of
possible political positions and ideas. This understanding begins by
looking at the face-to-face interactions between negotiators. From this
starting point it develops an account of how these interactions contribute to making the EU what it is. This assumes a link between daily
working group meetings dealing with often technical issues and structural developments, such as treaty changes or the surrendering of
national competences.

This conceptualisation of integration also has its limits. Focusing on
daily co-operation could avoid a more general discussion of legitimate
endpoints for the EU. It does not address directly whether the EU is best

labelled as a 'confederation' (Bulmer 1996), 'post-sovereign' state (Wallace 1999) or 'federation' (Habermas 2004). However, an important aim of this book is to show the links between the microlevel of everyday struggles between national representatives – including mechanisms such as stigma management – and the macrolevel ideas that help to drive integration.

The domestic scene has only been indirectly analysed through the study of the diplomatic habitus, and the tensions and awkward situations that are related to managing opt-outs. The scope of the analysis and choice of sources was limited to persons working on a daily basis in the EU system, either in member state capitals or in Brussels. I have interviewed few persons outside this field. The domestic parliamentary games in the UK and Denmark, the anti-European and pro-European movements, and the media have not been examined. From a political sociological perspective – stressing broader power structures and relations between the social groups and hierarchies – this is, of course, a limitation. By choosing to focus on the diplomacy of opting out, a number of other questions naturally slide into the background. However, I have chosen to zoom in on the engine room of European integration because, as mentioned in Chapter 2, there is a lack of understanding of the participants' own experiences and the management of sovereignty claims in the EU. Future work could examine the interplay (and overlaps?) between the European diplomatic field and the domestic political fields where governments are elected, referendums are held, and social and political movements mobilise eurosceptical and EU-positive views. As Dezalay and Barth (2010) have shown, capital built at the international level can successfully be transferred and invested at the domestic scene.[3]

Patterns in the diplomacy of opting out

British and Danish officials employ various strategies to cope with the opt-outs. Some strategies reduce marginalisation while others enhance it. In most situations we see compensatory strategies where both British and Danish officials work against the exclusionary effects of the opt-outs. There is nothing dubious in these practices; they are not due to deliberate conspiracy of the pro-European elite against the population.

---

[3] Kauppi and Madsen (2013), Cohen (2011) and Mudge and Vauchez (2012) suggest that similar dynamics are at work in the EU.

Instead, British and Danish representatives work – like all diplomats – to safeguard or improve the general standing of their respective countries.

Combining Bourdieu's structural sociology with Goffman's micro-sociology helps to explain diplomatic stigma management. Variations in the national officials' identities and their identification of their national interests are subject to constant (re)writing, and the diplomacy surrounding opt-outs is an integral part of this process. Opt-outs become part of national self-understanding. Opting out contributes to the idea that the member state is big and needs special treatment, which leads to missionary strategies (UK) to push the EU in an alternative direction. Here the opt-out is converted from a liability to an advantage. British representatives tend to value a selective approach to the EU and actively fight negative attitudes from insiders by turning their stigma into an attractive attribute. Regarding their opt-out as an emblem, they generally find that the benefits of opting out outweigh the costs.

In contrast, for Danish officials, the opt-out causes daily concern. Danish representatives are exasperated by the protocols that prevent them from doing what they consider to be their primary function: promoting Danish interests by creating workable EU policies. Thus part of their work in Brussels becomes a source of both satisfaction and frustration. The use of self-restraint, which is quite common in Danish diplomacy, reveals that – beyond the non-adoption of new EU measures – some practices may actually enhance the exclusionary effects of opt-outs and obstruct the quest for influence. It reconfirms the Danish 'small state identity', which leads to the understanding that Denmark does not deserve influence. These perceptions may become self-fulfilling prophecies because they reflect both the structure of the diplomatic field and the national identity as it is expressed in the diplomatic habitus. Influence in the EU is a question not only of capabilities but also of perceptions of capabilities. Size matters in the EU but only to the degree that it can be effectively converted into diplomatic capital. This also means that British and Danish officials manage stigma differently; the microstrategies that they pursue impact on how their countries are viewed more generally.

Another major finding is that the policy area affects the way in which differentiation works – not, as Kölliker (2006) suggests, in terms of the positive affects on the area but because of a combination of the legal construction of the opt-out and the tacit understandings and internal hierarchies in the Council of Ministers where negations take place.

Consequently it is possible to circumvent the protocols related to asylum, immigration and civil law, although this is less likely in Schengen and significantly less likely in the EMU.

To understand why this is so it is helpful to recall that national representatives generally see their work in terms of producing good results, finding solutions and constructing common policies in the EU. This does not mean that they stop representing their countries but that they regard their work with a sense of mission. This is clearer in relation to the EMU than the AFSJ: a euro opt-out is considered more controversial in Brussels than an opt-out from the AFSJ. Both the British and the Danish officials have sought to compensate for the opt-outs via their (relatively) good economic performances (and, in the British case, their role as a global financial centre), which has helped to improve their standing in the ECOFIN despite their euro-outsiderness.

The same exclusionary mechanisms do not currently exist in the AFSJ. This is due, in part, to the design of the protocols. On asylum and immigration policies, the UK has a very favourable opt-in possibility, while Danish officials currently manage an opt-out, which legally excludes them from all of the new measures under Title IV on migration, asylum, borders and visas. In Schengen the situation is almost the opposite. Here the UK faces not only legal but also serious political challenges because it does not participate in the core of the Schengen co-operation – the common border policy – while Danish representatives are allowed a position as though Denmark was an ordinary Schengen member. Reading the protocols explains little of these mechanisms.

Codes of conduct differ from one area to another. British representatives openly flag their opt-in possibility as a means to 'get the best of two worlds' in the AFSJ. Yet stigma is only half-heartedly imposed because of the norm of getting 'everybody on board' and respecting national differences. Table 7.1 provides an overview of stigma management.

An ever looser Union?

Will the EU become an ever looser Union? Euro-outsiders are likely to become increasingly isolated and will have to invent new strategies to avoid further exclusion as the Eurogroup continues to pick from the agenda of the ECOFIN. Economic and political crises are likely to speed up this process. Should Denmark one day choose to join the last stage of the EMU, the adjustments to the new situation are likely to be swift. The

Table 7.1. *British and Danish stigma management*

British and Danish stigma management

	Challenging exclusion	Camouflage and compensation	Missionary strategies	Self-restraint
Perception	Unfair exclusion due to opt-out	Perceived loss of influence and status due to opt-out	EU goals are against national interests	Serious loss of status and reputation
Strategy	Claim right to participate and restrict formal exclusion	Play the model state, help others, hide opt-out	'Teach Europe a lesson' through examples and threats	Stay silent, be more careful
Aim	Reduce exclusion	Pass as normal and reduce stigmatisation	Promote an alternative order	Avoid negative attention
Success	Low in both EMU and AFSJ	High in AFSJ, medium in EMU	Low in AFSJ, medium in EMU	High in AFSJ
State	Primarily UK	UK and Denmark	UK	Denmark

Danish officials are ready to play the role that they have always wanted to play: that of the constructive and knowledgeable insider.

Accommodating informal norms in the co-operation on borders, asylum, security and justice makes it possible to circumvent the opt-outs and, in some cases, influence decision-making. However, the Treaty of Lisbon gives the European Commission and the European Parliament a more central role and QMV will be the rule. Moreover, the Schengen *acquis* is likely to continue to grow as border policies remain at the top of the political agenda, thereby leaving the UK out of an increasing part of this important policy area. As a result, British and Danish diplomats may find many of their current strategies obsolete and will face a clearer exclusion resembling that of the eurozone. Unless the Danish voters accept the opt-in possibility in a future referendum, the Treaty of Lisbon will exclude Denmark from large parts of the AFSJ.

Where does that leave the current debate on a differentiated Europe? As discussed in Chapter 2, opt-outs and other forms of differentiated integration are now seen not only as pragmatic instruments to solve stalemates but also as solutions to problems of legitimacy and governance beyond the state (e.g. Scharpf 2006). Yet both the orthodox anti-differentiation camp and the pragmatic pro-differentiation camp have underestimated the symbolic power of EU law and the intense socialisation of national officials within a doxa of integration, which supports the EU's own claim to supreme authority and unity rather than the member states' claims to sovereignty.

While proponents of differentiated integration have successfully analysed the social context of EU law (e.g. Shaw 1996), they tend to disregard the diplomatic practices surrounding the rules. Instead of fragmenting the Union, opt-outs have permitted deeper integration through increasingly demanding treaties, even though not all governments (or populations) are fully on board. Consequently, differentiated integration is not a threat to the notion of 'an ever closer union' but – as a matter of practice – an innovation quite consistent with the doxa of integration. Hooghe and Marks (2008: 118) argue that, the mobilisation of mass publics has transformed the process of European integration. Whereas elites negotiated with an eye to efficiency and distributional consequences, publics appear to be swayed by identity as well as by economic concerns. Identity is no longer an inert outcome of jurisdictional reform, as Deutsch and Haas assumed, but has become a powerful constraint.

Is this really the case? Differentiation can promote integration processes in situations where one or more member states are blocking progress, but it does not solve the democratic challenges currently facing the member states and the EU as such.

The French and Dutch *'non'* and *'nee'* to the EU's Constitutional Treaty in 2005 were at first sight the exercise of sovereign will, but they also came to signify a crisis of democracy. Despite the rejection of the Constitutional Treaty, the treaty survived almost untouched with the new and less controversial label of the Treaty of Lisbon. It took about a decade to reach agreement on this treaty, during which popular scepticism grew. It was only by granting political guarantees or opt-outs – concerning neutrality, taxation and abortion – that the Irish approved the Treaty of Lisbon in a second referendum. History appeared to be repeating itself – when the Irish rejected the Treaty of Nice in 2001, they were asked to take the treaty to another vote, though with guarantees for their neutrality and restrictive abortion legislation.

If sovereignty is expressed in the form of referenda and opt-outs from treaties, and yet in practice leads to integration in much the same way as policy areas where there is no opt-out, the whole legitimising edifice of intergovernmentalism and differentiation is destroyed. As 'accountable' (Scharpf 2006: 860), 'neomedieval' (Zielonka 2006: 9) or 'post-modern' (Plattner 2003: 54) as they may be, measures of differentiation such as opt-outs are not applied in a space devoid of tacit understandings. Consequently, institutional entrepreneurs (political leaders, think tanks or intellectuals) should consider the social site in which they seek to construct new governance architecture in the EU. Treaty-based differentiation is one of the major reasons why Europe continues to integrate despite political disagreement, enlargement, increased heterogeneity and popular euroscepticism. This gives rise to the question of how, and to what extent, the sovereignty of EU member states is challenged in ways that their respective governments have difficulty dealing with and explaining to their populations. Indeed, this book has shown that the symbolic weight of the opt-out status is not matched by its practical use.

As long as the integration doxa is not challenged, the effects of differentiated integration will be limited. Of course, the doxa of 'an ever closer union' may still be fragile because it is only fully shared by a small European elite. What has been socially constructed, may – with the use of new reflections – be socially deconstructed (Bourdieu 1993:

1454). New generations of heads of state and government and their national representatives may enter the European scene with a different understanding of the purpose of integration, thereby strengthening differentiation vis-à-vis the orthodox integration mode. They may ask new questions about which form of political rule is legitimate and how popular sovereignty should be organised and regulated. Future enlargement rounds and negative referenda may impact on the overall development of the EU, although, as mentioned, the new member states adapt quickly to the Council of Ministers.

Should the existing mode 'of an ever closer union' be replaced by a logic of differentiation, national opt-outs would no longer represent a stigma but become normality. Stigma can change and even disappear over time – divorce, for instance, used to be stigmatised as a 'severely dis-valued deviation from traditional marital norms' (Bryant 1990: 415). If major national opt-outs became the rule, negotiations in the Council of Ministers would no longer aim to arrive at an agreement among all member states. The pragmatic negotiation style would not necessarily disappear but some of the mechanisms of consensus seeking might not work because they are based on an implicit solidarity. Could the EU develop into an à la carte organisation?

Most EU co-operation is currently based on the logic of the single market and the four freedoms. If the logic of extreme differentiation had guided the founding fathers of the EU in the 1950s, there would be no internal market today. A single market builds on the removal of competition-disturbing mechanisms and exceptions. An extreme version of differentiation would lead to collective action problems and would tempt the countries to regulative competition and free riding. As one European Commission official answers:

No doubt other member states would sometimes like opt-outs, but if more member states are granted opt-outs of the same nature as those of the UK and Denmark, there will be no co-operation as the one we have today.[4]

This quote goes to the core of why major opt-outs are currently controversial. A radically differentiated Europe would constitute a major contrast with the existing logic of integration.

Of course, this does not mean that there can be no change. However, this book suggests that seemingly radical claims to sovereignty are transformed

---

[4] Interview, DG JLS, European Commission (Brussels), 12 March 2007.

in the engine room of integration. Drastic claims to national authority, even when they are written into the fundamental EU treaties, do not automatically lead to a change in everyday routines. For this reason an analysis of the formal or regulative aspects of sovereignty does not necessarily tell us much about how sovereignty claims are subsequently handled.

Disciplining the state

At the start of the book I recalled the original meaning of the term opt-out as *optare*, meaning 'to choose'. Yet choosing to opt out is far from straightforward. In the short term, the British and Danish strategies of opting out were perhaps a smart move to convince reluctant domestic populations that important elements of national sovereignty would go untouched by future European integration. In the long term, opt-outs become part of a frustrated focus on – and anxieties about losing – sovereignty, complicating the UK and Danish policies on Europe. Although opt-outs may help the domestic audience's perception of an autonomous state, in Brussels the opt-out protocols are translated into temporary measures. They are then politically circumvented to fit the European context. British and Danish representatives work hard to ensure that the domestic audience doesn't accuse them of manipulation, while struggling not to be seen by the European audience as disloyal. From this perspective the British and Danish experiences of opting out illustrate Stephen Krasner's proposition that state sovereignty is 'organised hypocrisy' (Krasner 1999). This situation is becoming increasingly awkward. The most apparent threat to the organised hypocrisy is the structural pressure that the UK and Denmark (and all other member states) face to adapt to European rules, norms and institutions – a pressure generally known as Europeanisation. Because national opt-outs do not stop the European integration process, their consequences sometimes grow in unpredictable ways. In 1993, for instance, the Danish opt-out from the AFSJ was purely hypothetical and had no concrete implications for Danish participation, but two decades later it excludes Denmark from an increasing number of legal measures. The clashes between domestic and European discourses surrounding the opt-outs unsettle the idea of a sovereign state protecting itself from outside interference.

As discussed in Chapter 6, opt-outs and other forms of differentiation are increasingly proposed as a way out of the EU's democratic problems (e.g. Scharpf 2006). However, opt-outs should not necessarily be considered as a solution to a legitimacy deficit. Instead, they provide an opportunity to reflect on how the sovereignty of member states is challenged in ways that governments have difficulty handling, not to mention explaining to their populations.

The analysis of diplomacy in the EU gives rise to more fundamental questions: where does an ever closer Union lead and who will benefit from this? Until such fundamental questions are answered it is unlikely that the general malaise with the European integration process will disappear. In his postscript to the edited volume *Sociology of the European Union* (2011), George Ross writes that the 'EU can survive and thrive if its member states need it to do things that they can agree can only be achieved through international co-operation. But this can happen only if there is social support for such sovereignty pooling' (Ross 2011: 223). This assessment builds on the assumption that there are indeed links between national preference formation, representation and management of sovereignty. Yet the ever closer Union has led to intimate and close diplomatic interaction. The perceived devaluation of representatives from states who opt out strengthens the orthodoxy among the insiders: the 'good Europeans'.

Of course, external shocks, such as negative referendums or an economic slowdown, may impact the overall development of the EU. Nonetheless, these shocks can be mediated. Below the level of ministers, national representatives work within a common language of polity-building and problem-solving. These commonalities make them caretakers of a European interest as they struggle for national influence. Without these social understandings it would be difficult to see how the EU could have evolved in the first place. Thus, even if ordinary people turn away from the EU, the institutional wheels keeps turning. Crises may lead to differentiation and stigmatisation, but officials get a way round it.

The mission to uphold the EU relies on interrogating disorderly states. Stigmatisation is an important process that constructs notions of what constitutes appropriate member state behaviour. It is an attempt to establish, if only momentarily, a shared moral order in the EU. 'In actual fact, opt-outs constitute a de facto negation of the idea of European cooperation,' says former Belgian Prime Minister Guy Verhofstadt (2006: 214). In light of the analysis presented here, his claim needs revising: the management of the British and Danish opt-outs highlights the strength of European integration and the difficulty of maintaining national sovereignty in the EU.

APPENDIX A

Interview guide

- Presentation of my research
- Interested in understanding how you work and how you deal with opt-outs
- Anonymity and opportunity to read the transcribed interview
- Can I record the interview?
- Please tell me about your position at the [representation, ministry]
- How did you end up in this position [educational background, etc.]?
- How did you become involved with the issue area [relevant area]?
- Which [expert committees, working groups] are you participating in?
- What is a typical working day for you?
- How do you prepare for a meeting?
- How would you describe a meeting in the [committee, working group]?
- Who takes the initiative in your [working group, committee, section] most often? How do they do so?
- Who are your closest co-operation partners?
- What is the relationship between your [department, office, section] and other [departments, offices, sections]?
- How do you conduct the negotiations?
- What are the most difficult cases you are working with right now?
- Are there any awkward incidents that everybody in your [group, committee, section] is talking about?
- What is your most successful negotiation experience since you acquired this position?
- What is the most difficult issue you have dealt with?
- Who do you think is the most professional?
- Who is the least professional?
- In the meetings in which you participate, which are the most effective member states?

- Which factors do you find to be important for a member state to achieve influence?
- Does it make a difference in the negotiations whether you are a small state or a big state?
- Has the enlargement changed anything for your work?
- How are you involved with the opt-out?
- How do you handle the opt-out?
- What has been most surprising for you in relation to handling the opt-out?
- How do your partners perceive the opt-outs? [asked to explain the position of all partners]
- Do other member states mention your opt-out during meetings?
- Are you excluded from any meetings, decisions or groups? [Why and is anything done to avoid it?]
- Have there been any changes to this?
- Are there any advantages or drawbacks from having an opt-out?
- How do you prepare for meetings and negotiations on issues covered by the opt-out?
- Have you ever objected to or questioned the way your partners interpreted the opt-out?
- On which areas do you try to take a lead? Why?
- Has anyone ever mentioned the opt-out during a meeting? Why?
- Who helps you out on areas related to the opt-out? Why? [Do you have to give anything in return?]
- Hypothetically, what would happen if the opt-out were surrendered tomorrow?
- Have I understood you correctly if I say [insert the arguments, theories and relations described by informants]?
- What would happen if you [insert action that has described as illegitimate or illegal]?
- Why don't you just [insert the alternative to what the informants does]?
- Is there anything else you feel I should know that might contribute to this project? Who else would you suggest I talk to?
- Could you think of any written documents or internal notes that might be of interest?

APPENDIX B

List of interviewees

	Date	Title	Institution
1	07.02.2005	Former Secretary General	Council of Ministers, Brussels
2	11.12.2005	Director	Council Secretariat, Brussels
3	12.12.2005	Advisor	Danish Permanent Representation, Brussels
4	12.12.2005	1st Secretary	Danish Permanent Representation, Brussels
5	13.12.2005	Deputy Manager	DANATO, Brussels
6	13.12.2005	Advisor	Council Secretariat, Brussels
7	13.12.2005	Advisor	DANATO, Brussels
8	28.02.2006	Head of Office	Foreign Ministry, Copenhagen
9	01.03.2006	Head of Office	Ministry of Justice, Copenhagen
10	10.05.2006	Director	Council Legal Service, Brussels
11	10.05.2006	Attaché	Danish Permanent Representation, Brussels
12	11.05.2006	Ambassador	Danish Permanent Representation, Brussels
13	02.07.2006	Head of Office	Home Office, London
14	05.07.2006	Head of Section	Ministry of Justice, Copenhagen
15	05.07.2006	Head of Section	Foreign Ministry, Copenhagen
16	13.07.2006	Director	Department of Trade and Industry, London
17	17.07.2006	Head of Office	Danish Ministry of Justice, Copenhagen
19	21.07.2006	Head of EU Team	Home Office, London

	Date	Title	Institution
20	21.08.2006	Head of Section	International Directorate, Home Office
21	12.12.2006	Legal Advisor	Legal Service, European Commission
22	13.12.2006	Ambassador	Danish Permanent Representation, Brussels
23	10.01.2007	Seconded National Expert	DG JLS, Brussels
24	10.01.2007	Conseiller	Spanish Permanent Representation, Brussels
25	11.01.2007	Head of Unit	DG JLS, Brussels
26	11.01.2007	Head of Section	DG JLS, Brussels
27	15.01.2007	Secretary	European Parliament
28	15.01.2007	Head of Section	Danish Parliament, Copenhagen
29	21.01.2007	Legal Advisor	European Commission, Legal Service
30	24.01.2007	Deputy Manager	Legal Service, Foreign Ministry, Copenhagen
31	24.01.2007	Expert	Independent
32	24.01.2007	National Expert	DG JLS, Brussels
33	26.01.2007	Advisor	DG JLS, Brussels
34	05.02.2007	Head of Section	Danish Permanent Representation, Brussels
35	16.02.2007	Ambassador	Dutch Permanent Representation, Brussels
36	12.03.2007	Advisor	European Parliament
37	15.03.2007	Researcher	Centre for European Policy Studies, Brussels
38	15.03.2007	Expert	CEPS, Brussels
39	11.04.2007	Professor	University of Liverpool
40	12.04.2007	Clerk Advisor	House of Commons, London
41	12.04.2007	Head of Office	Department for Constitutional Affairs
42	12.04.2007	Committee Specialist	UK Permanent Representation, London
43	12.04.2007	1st Secretary	UK Permanent Representation, Brussels
44	12.04.2007	Clerk Advisor	House of Commons, London
45	13.04.2007	Committee Specialist	House of Lords

Date	Title	Institution
46 13.04.2007	European Policy Director	Home Office, London
47 13.04.2007	Head of Office	DG JLS, Brussels
48 13.04.2007	1st Secretary	UK Permanent Representation, Brussels
49 13.04.2007	Clerk Advisor	House of Lords, London
50 13.04.2007	Legal Assistant	House of Lords, London
51 13.04.2007	International Director	Home Office, London
52 13.04.2007	Committee Specialist	House of Lords, London
53 14.04.2007	Head of Unit	Council Secretariat, Brussels
54 14.04.2007	Advisor	Department of Constitutional Affairs, London
55 15.04.2007	Advisor	HM Treasury, London
56 16.04.2007	Counsellor	Danish Embassy, London
57 16.04.2007	Ambassador	UK Permanent Representation, Brussels
58 16.04.2007	1st Secretary	Danish Embassy, London
59 16.04.2007	Advisor	HM Treasury, London
60 17.04.2007	Advisor	Cabinet Office, London
61 17.04.2007	Head of Office	HM Treasury, London
62 17.04.2007	Head of Section	HM Treasury, London
63 18.04.2007	Director	Federal Trust, London
64 18.04.2007	1st Secretary	Polish Permanent Representation, Brussels
65 18.04.2007	Expert	Federal Trust, London
66 18.04.2007	Attaché	UK Permanent Representation, Brussels
67 28.04.2007	Expert	Federal Trust, London
68 13.08.2007	2nd Secretary	Belgian Permanent Representation, Brussels
69 21.08.2007	Advisor	German Permanent Representation, Brussels
70 21.08.2007	Advisor	UK Permanent Representation, Brussels
71 21.08.2007	2nd Secretary	UK Permanent Representation, Brussels
72 21.08.2007	1st Secretary	Greek Permanent Representation, Brussels
73 24.08.2007	Head of Section	Ministry of Refugee, Immigration and Integration Affairs, Copenhagen

	Date	Title	Institution
74	24.08.2007	Head of Section	Ministry of Refugee, Immigration and Integration Affairs, Copenhagen
75	24.08.2007	Counsellor	Ministry of Refugee, Immigration and Integration Affairs, Copenhagen
76	27.08.2007	Clerk	House of Lords, London
77	28.08.2007	1st Secretary	Irish Permanent Representation, Brussels
78	28.08.2007	1st Secretary, Financial	UK Permanent Representation, Brussels
79	31.08.2007	Head of Office	Danish Central Bank, Copenhagen
80	31.08.2007	Head of Section	Ministry of Finance, Copenhagen
81	31.08.2007	Head of Office	Central Bank, Copenhagen
82	31.08.2007	Head of Office	Ministry of Finance, Copenhagen
83	05.09.2007	Advisor	French Permanent Representation, Brussels
84	15.09.2007	Head of Section	HM Treasury, London
85	18.09.2007	Head of Section	Danish Permanent Representation, Brussels
86	11.11.2007	Conseiller	Luxembourgian Permanent Representation, Brussels
87	11.11.2007	Attaché	Ministry of Refugee, Immigration and Integration Affairs, Copenhagen
88	12.12.2007	Advisor	Legal Service, European Commission, Brussels
89	16.12.2007	2nd Secretary	Greek Ministry of Foreign Affairs, Athens
90	11.01.2008	Head of Office	Ministry of Refugee, Immigration and Integration Affairs, Copenhagen
91	14.01.2008	Head of Section	Ministry of Justice, Copenhagen
92	14.01.2008	Former Foreign Minister	Government, Copenhagen
93	15.01.2008	Ambassador	UK Embassy, Copenhagen

	Date	Title	Institution
94	20.01.2008	Former Judge	European Court of Justice
95	21.01.2008	Head of Section	Foreign Ministry, Copenhagen
96	31.01.2008	MEP	European Parliament, Brussels
97	25.02.2008	Ambassador	IR Permanent Representation, Brussels
98	25.02.2008	Director	DG ECFIN, Brussels
99	26.02.2008	Ambassador	Spanish Permanent Representation, Brussels
100	26.02.2008	Director	DG JLS, Brussels
101	26.02.2008	Former Advisor	Council Secretariat, Brussels
102	26.02.2008	Head of Office	DG JLS, Brussels
103	26.02.2008	Director	Council Legal Service, Brussels
104	26.02.2008	Head of Office	DG ECFIN, Brussels
105	27.02.2008	Head of Office	DG ECFIN, Brussels
106	28.02.2008	Head of Unit	DG ECFIN, Brussels
107	28.02.2008	Advisor	Spanish Permanent Representation, Brussels
108	28.02.2008	Head of Office	Ministry of Refugee, Immigration and Integration Affairs, Copenhagen
109	28.02.2008	Head of Office	DG JLS, Brussels
110	28.02.2008	Counsellor	Swedish Permanent Representation, Brussels
111	06.03.2008	Counsellor	Swedish Permanent Representation, Brussels
112	07.03.2008	Attaché	Danish Permanent Representation, Brussels
113	07.03.2008	Legal Attaché	Danish Permanent Representation, Brussels
114	07.03.2008	Legal Attaché	Danish Permanent Representation, Brussels
115	08.03.2008	Head of Office	National Police, Copenhagen
116	10.03.2008	Head of Office	Ministry of Justice, Copenhagen
117	12.03.2008	Assistant Director General	Ministry of Foreign Affairs, Oslo
118	13.03.2008	Head of Office	Ministry of Justice
119	14.03.2008	Legal Advisor	University of Aarhus, Aarhus
120	14.03.2008	Consultant	Department of Family Affairs, Copenhagen

	Date	Title	Institution
121	19.03.2008	Director	Foreign and Commonwealth Office, London
122	11.07.2008	Head of Office	The Norwegian Police, Oslo
123	08.08.2008	Partner	Legal Advisor to the Danish Government

Methods and analytical strategy

'Methodology, like sex, is better demonstrated than discussed' (Learner, quoted in Flyvbjerg 1991: 159); nevertheless, avoiding the discussion altogether would be problematic. The aim of this appendix is to outline the general analytical strategy, explain the methods, and present the selection and interpretation of the empirical sources which inform the analysis of the British and Danish opt-outs. Particular emphasis is placed on the 123 in-depth interviews with diplomats in the field and the interpretation of these interviews – that is, the meeting between the empirical sources and the theoretical concepts. The final section discusses the claims about the advantages of my use of methods and sources as well as its limitations.

Archival sources and official documents

There are few written sources related to the diplomatic handling of opt-outs in the archives of British and Danish ministries, as the management of the protocols is based on precedence, and most of the internal discussions of how to deal with an opt-out are never put to paper. This is also why most informants stressed that I probably would find nothing of interest in the archives. 'We do not write these things down,' was a recurring answer.[1] Of course, this should not be taken to mean that there was nothing of interest to me in the archives. For the national representatives, however, written documents were not crucial to their management of the opt-outs. Rather, this management was based on tacit knowledge and procedures learned in the field.

Upon request, officials would usually allow me to see one or two documents or internal notes that they found illustrative of their work with the opt-outs. The documents obtained in this way are not

---

[1] Interview, HM Treasury (London), April 2007; Interview, Danish Ministry of Foreign Affairs (Copenhagen), 2006.

necessarily representative, but they have been attributed importance by those managing the opt-outs. Why were these particular documents chosen by the practitioners? Most of them dealt with the difficult legal or procedural aspects of the opt-outs, such as internal procedures for the legal and political handling of the Justice and Home Affairs (JHA) opt-out or legal questions raised by the drafting of new opt-outs, reflections concerning the competence of the ECJ or background papers on the possible entry of a new member state in the eurozone and so on. As many officials explained, however, there are very few political or strategic documents related to the opt-outs.[2] Indeed, this would soon be proved correct upon my examination of the archives.

As part of my work for the Danish Institute of International Studies with the official investigation of the Danish opt-outs in the first half of 2008, I received a first chance to examine the Danish Foreign Ministry archives. The Foreign Ministry helped by carrying out a necessary preselection of the sources. For this book I wanted a complete overview of – and insight into – the archival material, and I applied for and negotiated access to the Danish Foreign Ministry archives. I obtained access to all documents from 1 January 1992 to 30 September 2008 on the issue areas related to the opt-outs. I was thus granted access to files from the period prior to the Maastricht referendum in Copenhagen in June 1992 and John Major's ratification problems in the spring and summer of 1992 throughout the whole period in which the opt-outs have been in effect up until today. I was granted unrestrained access to all files, classified as well as unclassified, including sensitive material.

The documents consisted of around 50–60 dossiers with approximately 29 files in each. Physically they took up most of a one-person office in the Danish Foreign Ministry.[3] They included correspondence between ministries, correspondence between Denmark and the European Commission and the EU presidencies, internal notes and draft legislation. Table A.1 presents an overview of the different types of document that I found in the archive.

I analysed the archival material with three aims in mind. The first was to help map the sub-field, its power hierarchies and the jargon which

---

[2] This seems logical in the sense that law requires the precision that can be gained in written form, whereas the more political and social aspects are often based on tacit agreements.

[3] The Foreign Ministry switched to an electronic filing system in September 2005.

Table A.1. *Overview of the archival material*

Type of source	Description
Internal notes and memorandums	Explanatory and detailed statement of a particular issue for internal clarification
Internal correspondence	Email correspondence, preparation of meetings, discussion on how to handle issues and division of labour
Report and notes from embassies and Permanent Representation	Reports and notes from embassies and representations on developments in the country or in EU institutions, and summaries of conversations with foreign officials
Minutes of Council of Ministers and various working group meetings	Detailed reports from meetings, including assessments of the other member state positions, issues dealt with in the margin of the meeting and recommendations
External correspondence with other member states and EU institutions	Email and letter correspondence, including proposals for solutions and strategies for negotiations
Draft legislation	Work-in-progress proposals on new legislation or on the drafting of particular protocols
Notes to Parliament and media	Correspondence and handling of Parliament and media

structure the relationship between the agents in the field. In this sense I posed exactly the same questions to the archival material as I would ask in my interviews. One of the advantages when studying the archives is that it becomes possible to assess the differences between the handling of opt-outs in the area of JHA and the field of the EMU. Of particular value in this respect were the internal notes in which officials would assess the position of other member states with regard to the opt-out. This provided a unique insight regarding the microstrategies related to the management of the opt-out.

The second aim was to understand the day-to-day basic negotiations and shifting agreements concerning the legal and political interpretation of the opt-outs in the interaction between the UK, Denmark and its partners. In this respect, archival material made it possible to reconstruct situations – including the negotiations on the single currency or the handling of opt-outs in the Lisbon Treaty – through the correspondence between British and Danish representatives, EU institutions and other member states. This correspondence is of course not completely factual – it is not their reporting of the meeting that took place on this and that date but rather the understanding of what was said that matters (see Lynch 2006).

Third, some of the technical legal issues cannot be adequately accounted for in an interview. Some of the most interesting sources in this respect are the several hundred memos, emails, drafts and communications made in the course of the negotiations on the Danish parallel agreements, which took six years to negotiate; the difficult issues also related to intergovernmental conferences and how complicated treaty issues led to the production of an overwhelming number of notes, memos and assessments of other member state positions. Indeed, the archive provides an insight regarding the time and effort required to get the opt-outs legally – and politically – 'right'.

While I obtained unlimited access to the archives, archival material should still be seen as a restricted source in the sense that a ministerial archive always implies the preselection of material. The documentation found in the archive is the result of a series of decisions taken by the representatives on whether or not to send something to the archive.[4] The archive will document some struggles while silencing others. These decisions are often made on the basis of purely pragmatic reasons – for instance, a document might not be sent to the archive to save time and energy. In the case of the opt-outs, many decisions and negotiations are simply never written down or simply not archived.

Moreover, the archive is also a potentially politically sensitive place. All officials know that public records disclosure requests from journalists or ordinary citizens can be tiresome and can potentially have a negative impact on their work. In this sense there is logically a degree of self-legitimisation or self-censorship in the documents. The most telling or revealing material may end up in the drawers of the office or at home, or it can be scribbled down during meetings on note blocks

---

[4] Freshwater has an interesting discussion of methodological problems related to the use of archives in cultural studies; the archive is a dangerously seductive place, which demands critical distance (Freshwater 2003).

which end in the dustbin. To ensure that the archive was not hiding 'the real thing', I would go back to the officials to request greater detail when I found a specific case where documents appeared to be missing or when I lacked background information.

Not only is the archive preselected but the interpretation of the archival material is also necessarily of a selective nature. Just as the interview requires translation and interpretation, so does the interpretation of the archival material. As the archive cannot offer direct access to the past, any reading of its contents will necessarily represent a reinterpretation. The discussion of the limitations of the archival material for this present study also serve to underline the crucial importance of in-depth interviews, and stress that the written sources are seen as only supplementing the interviews.

Finally, it should be emphasised that, after careful consideration, I decided not to apply for access to archives in the UK. This was primarily due to constraints on my time. Going through the archive of, for example, the Foreign and Commonwealth Office would undoubtedly have provided interesting information. I was able to compensate for this lack of access to some extent, however, because a notable share of the notes and correspondence in the Danish archive originated in the UK, thus providing indirect access to the communication by British representatives to Danish representatives and so on. Furthermore, the official letters from the European Commission and Council Legal Office often pertained to both Danish and UK issues. The files also contained useful and detailed information about the British positions during the negotiations during the EMU intergovernmental conference. This said, access to British archives would surely have been valuable. However, as the archival material is merely an additional source, this is hardly devastating.

In sum, while interviews remain the central source, archival sources provide a useful supplementary insight concerning the daily management of the opt-outs. They are primarily used to help to provide an understanding of technical issues and to obtain an overview of the time span and development of the management of opt-outs.

The interview in political sociology

The interview as a research method has a strong claim to being one of the most widely used methods of research in the social sciences (Fielding 1993: 135). This does not mean, however, that there is any consensus on how interviews should be carried out or how one can assess the results of interviewing. In the subsequent sections I will discuss some of the methodological questions that are important for my use in interviews.

How can the information generated from interviews be characterised? It does not represent objective 'facts' but rather 'subjective' perceptions (Silverman 2001: 83). Interviews are important not because the informants know the 'big-T' truth but because their particular truths are valuable. What I am interested in is not whether the diplomats are objectively correct in their assessment of the opt-outs and their consequences but how they relate to them.[5]

Hamel argues that Bourdieu dismisses the commonsensical answers provided by respondents as 'false consciousness' (Hamel 1998: 9). His argument is that the epistemological rupture is marked by an opposition to the actors' practical consciousness. However, this is not correct. What informants say should be taken seriously, though the researcher must add a theoretical distance. Looking back on his use of interviews, Bourdieu notes:

> Ideas like those of habitus, practice and so on, were intended, among other things, to point out that there is a practical knowledge that has its own logic, which cannot be reduced to that of theoretical knowledge; that, in a sense, agents know the social world better than the theoreticians. And at the same time, I was also saying that, of course, they do not really know it and the scientist's work consists in making explicit this practical knowledge, in accordance with its own articulations. (Bourdieu, Chamboredon and Passeron 1991: 252)

One should never forget that the interview situation is fundamentally an artificial social relationship (Bourdieu, Chamboredon and Passeron 1991: 41). Indeed, I do not view interviews as some sort of pure 'data'; rather, the interview as an empirical source is generated by the interaction with the informants.[6] From a Bourdieusian (and constructivist) viewpoint, interviewers and informants are always actively

---

[5] See Pouliot (2007: 368–377) for an excellent discussion of the advantages and limitations of qualitative interviewing from a political sociologist perspective.

[6] In this sense, interviewing is a craft: 'Seule [...] la *réflexivité réflexe*, fondé sur un « métier » un « oeil » sociologique, permet de percevoir et de contrôler *sur-le-champ*, dans la conduite même de l'entretien, les effets de la structure social dans laquelle il s'accomplit' (Bourdieu 1993: 1391). 'Only [...] a *reflex reflexivity* based on a craft, on a sociological "feel" or "eye" "non-problem", allows one to perceive

engaged in constructing meaning. This does not, however, entail that what is said during an interview cannot cover anything beyond the local construction of meaning, but it requires continuous reflection regarding one's own role in the interview see also Pouliot 2012. I will return to this issue later in this appendix in a discussion of how to increase intersubjectivity and validity.

Another challenge posed by interviews concerns the problem of the monopoly of the truth. The national representatives hold a privileged position as the managers of the opt-outs, and I must rely on their information. How can I ensure that what is presented as 'technical knowledge' is not biased (Fielding 1993: 138)? All of the informant's knowledge will naturally be biased; this is not the problem. The problem may be that informants are possibly unwilling to tell what they believe to be the present state of affairs; that they might only give the official story. This is why it is crucial to build trust in the interview situation, and I will discuss how this was done later in this appendix. Moreover, it calls for covering the field and the different positions of the agents as a means to contextualise the information and meanings produced in the individual interview. From these many 'truths' it becomes possible to gain an understanding of the field and its doxa, and the socially shared 'truth' about the opt-outs, which takes a more permanent character.

Analytical strategy

To guide the analysis, the theoretical framework must be operationalised and applied to the empirical world more specifically. The task is to clarify the relationship between observations and concepts (Goertz 2006: 43). This requires moving from the theoretical level to the question of relevant 'indicators'. There are many ways of operationalising Bourdieu's concepts and no firm guidelines on how to do so, not least because this is not done prior to the research but simultaneously in the meeting with the field (Leander 2008: 20).[7]

and monitor on the spot, as the interview is actually taking place, the effects of the social structure within which it is occurring' (my translation).

[7] A number of scholars have addressed this challenge in rather different ways. Jackson uses biographical information to trace the careers and habitus of civil servants in the French Foreign Ministry after the Second World War and urges historians of IR to use Bourdieu's concept of habitus because it is 'well-suited to the practice of archive-based international history' (Jackson 2008: 172), whereas Swartz has developed Bourdieu's framework in organisation analysis (Swartz 2008).

The interview guide and the logic of interpretation

This section presents the interview guide, the rationale for my questions and the logic of interpretation. Before doing so, however, I would like to stress an important assumption: the interviews do not provide me with pure 'data', and the interview situation is not without elements of domination. When interpreting the interviews, I thus reconstruct the commonsensical understanding that officials present theoretically (Bourdieu, Chamboredon and Passeron 1991).[8] This is part of the fundamental scientific art of constructing the object (Slembrouck 2004). It is therefore crucial to be aware of the co-construction of the text produced in the interview situation.

In the first phase of the research process – the pilot study – the questions were very open and almost naïve (to some extent reflecting my level of insight into the field at that initial stage). This phase provided a foundation for examining general discourses and practices about the opt-outs. In the course of the interview I focused on discovering the everyday knowledge of the informants (see also Flick 2006: 135). This phase led me to think about how these practices may reproduce social inequities and the different meanings attached to the opt-outs. As I read the transcribed interviews from the pilot study, I looked at phrases and remarks that expressed ideas that related to my research question and which helped me to develop my theoretical framework.

In the second phase of the research process, I developed a more elaborate and focused interview guide for all interviews, which reflected the analytical framework. The idea was to develop the analytical framework further and to ask questions capable of capturing the elements of this emerging framework. The interviews themselves, however, were conducted as a conversation with no direct reference to the interview guide. In the interpretation of the interviews, the translation from observations to conceptions, the categories were constructed to some extent by the diplomats, and then I subsequently interpreted and recategorised them on the basis of the analytical framework. However, each interview has to be adapted to the specific setting, and obviously the same question does not have the exact same meaning for all of the social subjects (Bourdieu, Chamboredon and Passeron 1991: 43). Moreover,

---

[8] 'The fundamental scientific act is the construction of the object, you don't move to the real without a hypothesis, without instruments of constructions' (Bourdieu, Chamboredon and Passeron 1991).

there is also an element of improvisation and adaptation during interviews, meaning that additional questions emerge which are not part of
the guide. These interviews lasted 80 minutes on average. The longest
interview was three-and-a-half hours (with a retired Secretary General
of the Council) while the shortest was 30 minutes.[9]

The questions from the interview guide used in the second phase of
the research process are presented in the following. The aim was to
cover the core concepts in the theoretical framework by unravelling
both the explicit and the implicit assumptions of the agents in the field.
Of course, during an interview habitus, capital and field can be implicitly revealed in the same sentence. In this sense it is a somewhat artificial
exercise to pinpoint exactly which questions unravel which mechanisms
or put flesh on the concepts. Many of the questions remain quite general
and thus allow the informants to tell their own stories. Nonetheless, it is
clear that some questions are particularly effective at triggering answers
relating to particular elements in my theoretical framework. The complete guide can be found in Appendix A.

Introduction

All of the interviews started more or less the same: I would present
myself and the aim and scope of the research project. I avoided revealing
too much about my study and presented myself as a scholar interested in
learning more about the negotiations regarding JHA and EMU, and the
British or Danish position in the EU. Obviously, it would have been
unethical to pretend that the study was not related to opting out, but I
would mention it casually rather than frontload the issue. This promp-
ted more instinctive answers.[10] Most respondents initially refused to be
quoted in person, but most accepted being quoted anonymously.

---

[9] The length of the interview was important to build trust with the respondent, and
I always asked in advance for at least one hour, which is quite a lot for a busy
diplomat in a Permanent Representation. However, the informants would often
let the interview take longer. It seemed as though they appreciated the
opportunity to talk freely about their own life and experiences, and they appeared
to find the project interesting.

[10] Indeed, informed consent does not mean that I have to tell my informant all of my
presumptions. Rather, it is a process whereby, prior to the actual interview, I
explained the purpose and method of study together with the terms of
participating, including the voluntary nature of participation.

Extract from the interview guide: Introduction

- Presentation of my research
- Interested in understanding how you work and how you deal with opt-outs
- Anonymity and opportunity to read the transcribed interview
- Can I record the interview?

Habitus

The subsequent questions aimed at creating trust and getting to know the informant's social and personal background. These questions make it possible to detect the positioning and in particular their understanding of their own position in the sub-field.

Extract from the interview guide: Habitus

- Please tell me about your position at the [representation, ministry]
- How did you end up in this position [educational background etc.]?
- How did you become involved with [the relevant area, policy etc.]?
- Which [expert committees, working groups] are you participating in?
- What is a typical working day for you?
- How do you prepare for a meeting?
- How would you describe a meeting in the [committee, working group]?

These broad questions allow for an overview, which is detached from the issue of opt-outs. As discussed in Chapter 7, habitus involves socially acquired, embodied systems of dispositions and/or predispositions. In *Distinction: A Social Critique of the Judgement of Taste* (Bourdieu 1986), a large-scale study of class habitus in French society, Bourdieu underlines that habitus cannot be directly observed in empirical research and must be captured interpretively.[11] In order to identify the habitus, the interviews were thus oriented towards the daily practices and perceptions of the officials. The questions focused on the structure of a normal working day as well as the values and personal

---

[11] Much of *Distinction* (Bourdieu 1986) is devoted to a qualitative study of the myriad of preferences and practices that cluster in each sector of social space in order to identify the specific habitus that underlies them (Reay, David and Ball 2005: 25).

experiences of the diplomats who were asked to give concrete examples and explain their practices. This made it possible to uncover part of the habitus of the officials together with their personal experiences and struggles. Of course, one should not seek more logic in the habitus than actually exists (Bourdieu 1990: 79). Elements of the habitus refer to an unconscious logic.

The answers tended to be long and filled with detours. The officials and diplomats were interested in recounting their professional frustrations and triumphs. While some of these narratives were not directly touching upon opt-outs, they provided valuable background information about how the diplomats thought of their position in the field and helped me to understand what they took for granted. This, however, required a distance and an objectification of their position. As Bourdieu explains:

> To ask subjects to define the position they assign to themselves in the social structure, without seeking to know that social structure and, in particular the representation that the subjects form of it, is to treat it as a given. (Bourdieu, Chamboredon and Passeron 1991: 181)

The first questions are created with the purpose of letting the informants speak as freely as possible, instead of imposing a particular view or question. Quite tellingly, it could take up to 10 or 15 minutes in some cases before a British official would mention the British opt-out from Title IV in JHA despite working in an area covered by the opt-out. This underlines that what is not said can be just as important as what is.

Field and doxa

In order to explore the structure of the field, the social hierarchies and relationships between dominant and subordinates, a group of questions were particularly related to the setting in which the officials negotiate. One of the great challenges with doxa is how to identify what is taken as given; what cannot be problematised. Exploring the doxa requires asking the question: 'Why is the obviously rational not happening?' – that is, to look for what is excluded as a possibility because it would question the fundamental meaning of the interaction in the field. Of course, one cannot ask the national representatives what they take to be a given. Instead, it is their silences and how they describe some situations as natural which may reveal doxa (see also Maynard-Moody and Musheno 2006). How this silence may be uncovered may be more evident in the actual analyses in chapters 5 and 6. The question about awkward situations helped to unravel what was considered to be taboo and what was considered to be normal.

Extract from the interview guide: Field and doxa

- Who takes the initiative in your [working group, committee, section] most often? How do they do so?
- Who are your closest co-operation partners?
- What is the relationship between your [department, office, section] and other [departments, offices, sections]?
- How do you conduct the negotiations?
- What are the most difficult cases you are working with right now?
- Are there any awkward incidents that everybody in your [group, committee, section] are talking about?

Capital

In order to grasp what counts as capital, one must understand how the diplomats perceive the struggle in the field. Note that I use the word 'professional' because this is a word often used by diplomats. To understand the doxa of the field, the respondents would then have to explain what they meant by 'professional', thus revealing the stakes defining the field and what they were struggling for (e.g. status, prestige or influence). Moreover, the first questions deliberately avoid any relation to influence; instead, I use the word 'effective', which is a relatively empty word when left to stand alone. The informant must have their own understanding of effective – effective in relation to what? Thus instead of assuming that I knew what the negotiations are about beforehand and what drives them, I let the informants explain it in their own words. I thus aimed at receiving a commonsensical answer before the reflected and objectivised answer.

Opt-outs are embedded in a transnational field in which many possible factors possibly affect their capital and relative position via-à-vis representatives from other member states. I thus asked questions about member state size and enlargement in keeping with the existing assumptions about what makes a state powerful in the EU.

Extract from the interview guide: Capital

- What is your most successful experience since you acquired this position?
- What is the most difficult issue you have dealt with?

- Who do you think is the most professional?
- Who is the least professional?
- In the meetings in which you participate, which are the most effective member states?
- Which factors do you find to be important for a member state to achieve influence?
- Does it make a difference in the negotiations whether you are a small state or a big state?
- Has the enlargement changed anything for your work?

Stigma

The final part of the interview deals with opt-outs per se. This is where the possible marginalisation, stigmatisation and feelings of insecurity, outsiderness and so on could be revealed in greater detail. Again, it is important not to impose a particular understanding. Hence I first asked my informants to describe how they handled the opt-out. These unproblematised explanations of the daily, technical handling rendered it possible to partly avoid a politicised account. Instead, I obtained detailed insight into their everyday thinking and strategies surrounding the opt-outs with lots of examples.

Extract from the interview guide: Stigma
- How are you involved with the opt-out?
- How do you handle the opt-out?
- What has been most surprising for you in relation to handling the opt-out?
- How do your partners perceive the opt-outs? [asked to explain the position of all partners]
- Do other member states mention your opt-out during meetings?
- Are you excluded from any meetings, decisions or groups? [Why and is anything done to avoid it?]
- Have there been any changes to this?
- Are there any advantages or drawbacks from having an opt-out?

Strategies

In order to map the different strategies related to the opt-outs, a number of questions were developed. Stigma management strategies are directed towards repairing a spoiled image through identification with the in-group or out-group. These strategies are not easy identifiable. When identifying these strategies I am searching for knowledge that these officials may not necessarily be aware of themselves. They might not call their attempts to achieve a high standing a 'strategy'; they might instead articulate it as 'representing their country'. Thus I was not able to ask directly, but instead had to approach the issue by asking for examples and from there indirectly identify strategies.

Extract from the interview guide: Strategies
- How do you prepare for meetings and negotiations on issues covered by the opt-out?
- Have you ever objected or questioned the way your partners interpreted the opt-out?
- On which areas do you try to take a lead? Why?
- Has anyone ever mentioned the opt-out during a meeting? Why?
- Who helps you out on areas related to the opt-out? Why? [Do you have to give anything in return?]

Ending

The final questions are slightly more direct or even provocative. Here the informants could challenge some of my ideas and I could gain knowledge regarding the limits of my interpretations, and I was able to identify the various positions in the field.

Extract from the interview guide: Ending
- Hypothetically, what would happen if the opt-out were surrendered tomorrow?
- Have I understood you correctly if I say [insert the arguments, theories and relations described by informants]?
- What would happen if you [insert action that the informant has described as illegal or illegitimate]?
- Why don't you just [insert the alternative to what the informants does]?
- Is there anything else you feel I should know that might contribute to this project? Who else would you suggest I talk to?
- Could you think of any written documents or internal notes that might be of interest?

The last question about what would happen if the opt-outs were surrendered tomorrow guide the respondent to think about the concrete consequences of the opt-out for their everyday work. Because I asked about 'tomorrow' and not some sort of distant future, the answer had to be embedded in everyday practices.

As should be clear, the construction of the interview guide as well as the interpretation of the interview data does not involve already defined coding rules. Instead the interpretation builds on a careful construction of a logic and coherent understanding of how the agents perceive themselves and their conditions for action. Of course, no single national representative stated that they were 'marginalised' or that an opt-out constituted 'an attribute that is deeply discrediting'. In fact, even if they had, such a statement would require analysis; 'in conjunction with when and how and by whom it was being made and what else was going on at the time', as Lynch comments in her discussion of the use of interviews in a critical study of interwar peace movements (Lynch 2006: 298). The interpretation of the interviews was carried out in order to cover both the dominant assumptions about the management of the opt-outs, particular events and how the constructions of knowledge and meanings about the opt-outs structure the power relations between the agents in the field. This evidence was always cross-checked against the interpretation and evidence provided by others.

Enhancing the credibility of interviews

Interviewing a diplomat is akin to interviewing liquid hand soap: diplomats are experts in retrieving information from others and withholding information about their own intentions and perceptions (Neumann 2005). As American philosopher Will Durant once commented, 'To say nothing, especially when speaking, is half the art of diplomacy' (Zera 2005: 56). This art of diplomacy was undoubtedly also practised in the course of my interviews.

To build trust and create an atmosphere of concentrated seriousness in the interview situation, I invested a lot of time in preparation, gaining the 'knowledge of the field'. When discussing technical issues, I would then know the vocabulary and would appear more natural as a conversation partner. A simple word or parenthetical remark from my part, such as using abbreviations or being familiar with the fact that Gordon Brown seldom showed up at the ECOFIN meetings when he was Chancellor, served to make the atmosphere more intimate. Learning the language of the diplomats opened up deeper discussions and was fully rewarded in terms of the time allowed to our conversation (for an excellent description of this experience, see also Cohn 1987). By using this approach I was seen as more familiar.[12] Being able to play along is an important element in the craft of interviewing.[13]

A second challenge relates to the political sensitivity of the overall research question for the informants and the question of anonymity. All of the informants viewed opt-outs as politically controversial, for which reason I had to guarantee them anonymity. A lot has been written about the advantages and drawbacks in relation to anonymous interviews (Seal, Bloom and Somlai 2000; Volker 2004). The benefits of public presentation are that it becomes possible for others to see exactly with whom I have spoken and adds to the transparency. However, apart from the fact that anonymity was a prerequisite for many of my inform-ants to even consider meeting with me, the benefits of listing the names must be weighed against the potential costs to the participants. Journalists may misconstrue my research findings, or representatives from other member states may use the list of names for strategic or political interests and may punish 'deviant' officials.[14] More impor-tantly, their own colleagues might read the text, recognise them and see that they have a more unorthodox position than what they usually express.

---

[12] Of course, this should not be overdone in the sense that you as a researcher 'go native'. Rather, as you are being allowed to ask more sensitive questions because your informants regard you as someone who understands them and their situation. The management of tone and authority relations must be constantly reviewed and adapted to the interview situation. In the course of an interview with a French diplomat, for instance, it thus became clear to me that even though he was fluent in English, he preferred to speak in French. By allowing him to speak the language he felt most comfortable with, I removed an obstacle to obtaining his sincere thoughts on opt-outs and his own experiences (interview, French Permanent Representation, April 2007).

[13] By remaining in contact with my informants throughout the research process, I would receive comments via email on new developments on a dossier, examples of particular strategies and suggestions for further research.

[14] Bourdieu addresses this problem in *La Misère du Monde*, where he reflects on the problem of putting something that is private into the public domain. He and his colleagues sought to protect their participants by changing the names of places and individuals in order to prevent identification and to protect them from the dangers of misinterpretation (Bourdieu 1993). I addressed this by anonymising the interviews.

Anonymity demands a greater vividness in the descriptions as an alternative means by which readers can visualise the nature of place and people being discussed. Because the interviews are anonymous, it is also my responsibility to ensure that I will fairly and accurately represent their voices and experiences in ways that limit the possibility of misusing the data. In this study the anonymous interview offered respect for the delicate position of the diplomat. Yet there is, of course, no guarantee that diplomats do not tell tall tales, as anonymity may provide them with a safe haven for exaggerating their own roles, slandering others and so on. I addressed this risk by attempting to obtain at least three different perspectives by asking respondents to describe the same incident or case. Moreover, I made a great deal out of getting to know the background information in order to reduce this risk.

Linked to the problem of sensitivity is the question of how to record an interview for later analysis. I used a dictaphone in around 30 per cent of the interviews, but some of my informants felt uncomfortable when the recorder was on. This could be very explicit, as I would begin the interview by asking if it was okay that I taped our conversation, to which one senior ambassador answered:

It depends on what you want to hear. If you want the official storyline then a recorder is fine, but if you want my own story, then I would need you to turn it off.[15]

When unable to use a dictaphone, I took thorough notes, something that diplomats find very common, as they do that a lot themselves during meetings. In fact, taking notes often added to a concentrated yet relaxed atmosphere. As soon as possible after the interview, I would transcribe the recording or write out my notes, having written down entire sentences and key words. This made it possible to construct a verbal transcript of the interview. Hence I ended up with an archive of over 100 transcribed texts, which I could return to and compare when statements seemed to diverge or even contradicted one another. For reasons of confidentiality, this entire body of transcripts has not been attached as an appendix to this thesis as it would be too easy to recognise the individuals.

Fourth, a number of the interviews were conducted in collaboration with my colleagues at the Danish Institute for International Studies

[15] Interview, Danish Permanent Representation (Brussels), 12 December 2005.

(DIIS) in March and April 2008. Most of these interviews were carried out together with my close colleague, but five of them were group interviews, which, of course, creates a different atmosphere and less opportunity to acquire in-depth knowledge. However, the group interviews were a pragmatic solution to the fact that we wanted to speak to very senior people with little time.[16] Moreover, a number of interviews took place over the telephone, in particular in the follow-up phase, which provided an easy way of double-checking information. However, due to the lack of direct face-to-face contact, this method was not used extensively.

Fifth, as part of the self-reflective move, it is important to reflect on the political context in which my research was conducted. The opt-outs are politicised in the UK, but at no time during the process did anyone seriously think that there was going to be a referendum to surrender any of the British opt-outs. Conversely, when I was employed at the Danish Institute for International Studies in early 2008 to write the report for the Danish Parliament, everybody in Denmark was convinced that there was going to be a referendum in Denmark to surrender one or several of the Danish opt-outs, as the Prime Minister had announced that he would hold a referendum in his New Year's Speech on 1 January 2008. Thus the interviews conducted in this period were conducted under the 'shadow of a referendum'. The informants would be remarkably more alert during this period because they knew that they were contributing to a report with a possible impact on the debate prior to the referendum. Thus they could be tempted to perceive the interview situation as an opportunity to make their own personal contribution to getting rid of the opt-outs. However, I did not find that this was widespread. After a few questions, an atmosphere of sincerity and trust had been established, and the informants knew that they could not get away with official answers; they were pushed to provide examples. The only exceptions were a few of the ambassadors, who had a tendency to transform the interview situation into a more normative speech about what the EU needed. All in all the referendum issue never became a crucial issue, although it did affect the initial interaction in the interviews in this period.

---

[16] The DIIS investigation probably helped to open doors that had previously been closed to me, such as interviewing the highest senior officials in the Council and the European Commission and the Permanent Representations.

Finally, a few words about my own position as a researcher. As a means of gaining a greater understanding of one's own point of view in the social space, Bourdieu has suggested an auto-socioanalysis whereby researchers make their subject the object of research. To Bourdieu this serves a dual purpose: it makes researchers aware of (objectifies) the position from which they make their studies, and it makes the reader understand this as well.

So what are my potential blind spots? On the one hand, having been employed both when I was a graduate student and later as Head of Section at the Danish Foreign Ministry gave me something of an inside position and made it easier for me to build trust and gain access. On the other hand, this also meant that I had already been introduced to the diplomatic field, and I might have been less critical or observant of phenomena that I had come to take for granted. Overall, however, inside knowledge of procedures and informal norms proved rather helpful and gave me some ideas about how to deal with sensitive issues. Later, when I was Head of Section at the Ministry of Foreign Affairs, I would often discuss the issue of opt-outs with my colleagues but without doing any formal interviews. By being reflective, I have sought to manage this potential bias in my work, using the experience and my network consciously instead of just taking it for granted (Bourdieu and Wacquant 1992). Although such auto-analytic strategies clearly serve a purpose, the degree of self-knowledge and objective distance one can reach in the process should not be exaggerated.[17]

Dialogue and feedback

What makes me think that I really got it right (Cohn 2006: 101)? I believe that there are techniques available to help us get behind the façade without necessarily implying that we get to something which is the essential truth about how diplomats 'really' think or act. One of these techniques involves obtaining feedback from informants in the research project.

In a study of the US military and its nuclear strategy, Carol Cohn made use of her informants to give her feedback on her interpretations of them. First she engaged in public lectures, briefings and seminars in

---

[17] The means available to the researcher in the autoanalysis do not transcend the means otherwise available to my research, so the limitations in perspectives, knowledge and so on will still exist.

which the community she studies would 'talk back' at her presentations and comment on her findings. She subsequently met one-on-one with military personnel who told her what they thought of her presentation (Cohn 2006: 101–102).

I adopted a number of feedback techniques similar to Cohn's, which should not be seen as a verification of the overall results. However, they helped me to correct inaccuracies, improved my interpretation of earlier interviews and provided a more subtle understanding of how diplomats perceive their own situation. My informants provided more examples of practices, corrected some mistakes and confirmed that I was on track. These feedback procedures took several forms. During my work for the report for the Danish Parliament, my colleague and I would present extracts from our preliminary findings to senior officials and academic experts and let them read and/or comment on our findings. The specific comments proved valuable, and these conversations were grounded in a mutual understanding of trust and frank speaking.

I also received feedback through various oral presentations. I presented my work at a special lunch seminar in London with a group of experts and senior civil servants, and a brownbag lunch was organised at the Danish Foreign Ministry, where I presented my work for the section on EU affairs. This provided an opportunity to observe how they would react to my interpretation. The officials were usually eager to comment on my findings and would often laugh heartily, signalling that they felt recognised and understood. After these seminars they would approach me and provide personal comments. They would usually confirm or refine my interpretations, but sometimes they would point out alternative explanations. The third way I obtained feedback on my interpretations from my informants was during formal follow-up interviews in the third phase of the research process, where I double-checked specific items of information. This feedback did not mean that I revamped my overall analysis but it provided an opportunity to rethink my interpretations.

Bibliography

Aalberts, TE (2004) The Future of Sovereignty in Multilevel Governance Europe – A Constructivist Reading. *Journal of Common Market Studies* 42(1): 23–46.

Adler, E. (2008). The Spread of Security Communities: Communities of Practice, Self-Restraint, and NATO's Post–Cold War Transformation. *European Journal of International Relations*, 14(2), 195–230.

Adler, E and Pouliot, V (2011) International Practices. *International Theory*, 3(1): 1–36.

Adler-Nissen, R (forthcoming) Denmark and Norway: Shifting Places in the Area of Freedom, Security and Justice. *The Nordic Countries and the European Union*, Edited by C Grøn, P Nedergaard and A Wivel. London: Routledge.

Adler-Nissen, R (2008a) Organized Duplicity? When States Opt Out of the European Union. In *Sovereignty Games: Instrumentalizing State Sovereignty in Europe and Beyond*. Edited by R Adler-Nissen and T Gammeltoft-Hansen. New York: Palgrave Macmillan.

(2008b) The Diplomacy of Opting Out: A Bourdieudian Approach to National Integration Strategies. *Journal of Common Market Studies* 46(3): 663–684.

(2009a) Behind the Scenes of Differentiated Integration: Circumventing National Opt-Outs in Justice and Home Affairs, *Journal of European Public Policy* 16(1): 62–90.

(2009b) Late Sovereign Diplomacy, *The Hague Journal of Diplomacy* 4(2): 121–141.

(2011) On a Field Trip with Bourdieu, *International Political Sociology* 5(3): 327–333.

(ed.) (2012) Bourdieu and International Relations Theory. *Bourdieu in International Relations: Rethinking Key Concepts in IR*. London: Routledge.

(2014a) Stigma Management in International Relations: Transgressive Identities, Norms and Order in International Society. *International Organization*, 68(1): 143–176.

(2014b) Symbolic Power and European Diplomacy: The struggle between national foreign services and the EU's External Action Service, *Review of International Studies*. Online First.

Adler-Nissen, R and Pouliot, V (2014) Power in Practice: Negotiating the International Intervention in Libya. *European Journal of International Relations*, Online First.

Allen, D (2005) The United Kingdom: A Europeanized Government in a Non-Europeanized Polity. In *The Member States and the European Union*. Edited by S Bulmer and C Lequesne. Oxford: Oxford University Press.

Andersen, BN (2003) EU Og Euroen, *Danmark 30 år i EU – et festskrift*. Copenhagen: Gyldendal.

Andersen, S and Sitter, N (2006) *Differentiated Integration*. Oslo: ARENA Working Paper Series, 05/2006.

Aus, P (2009) The Mechanisms of Consensus: Coming to Agreement on Community Asylum Policy. In *Unveiling the Concil of Ministers: Games Governments Play in Brussels*. Edited by D Naurin and H Wallace. New York: Palgrave.

Axelrod, R and Dion, D (1988) The Further Evolution of Cooperation. *Science* 242(4884): 1385–1390.

Baker, D (2005) Islands of the Mind: New Labour's Defensive Engagement with the European Union. *The Political Quarterly*, 76(1): 22–36.

Baker, D and Seawright D (1998) Introduction. In *Britain For and Against Europe. British Politics and the Question of European Integration*. Edited by D Baker and D Seawright. Oxford: Clarendon Press.

Baker, D, Fountain, I, Gamble, A and Ludlam, S (1995) The Blue Map of Europe: Conservative Parliamentarians and European Integration. *British Elections & Parties Yearbook*, 5(1): 51–73.

Bankowski, Z and Christodoulidis E (1998) The European Union as an Essentially Contested Project, *European Law Journal* 4(4): 341–354.

Barnett, MN (1995) Sovereignty, Nationalism, and Regional Order in the Arab States System, *International Organization* 49: 479–479.

Barry, A (1993) The European Community and European Government Harmonization, Mobility and European Community and European Government, *Economy and Society*, 22(3): 314–326.

Bátora, J (2001) Britain and Europe: The Argument Continues, *Parliamentary Affairs* 54(2): 276–288.

(2005) Does the European Union Transform the Institution of Diplomacy? *Journal of European Public Policy* 12(1): 44–66.

Bednar, J (2007) Valuing Exit Options, *Publius: The Journal of Federalism* 37(2): 190–208.

Bellamy, R and Castiglione, D (1997) The Normative Challenge of a European Polity: Cosmopolitan and Communitarian Models Compared, Criticised and Combined. In *Democracy and the European Union: Challenges*. Edited by A Føllesdal. Berlin: Springer.

(2003) Legitimizing the Euro-'Polity' and Its 'Regime': The Normative Turn in EU Studies, *European Journal of Political Theory* 2(1): 7–34.

Berger, TU (1997) The Past in the Present: Historical Memory and German National Security Policy, *German Politics* 6(1): 39–59.

BERR (2008) *Single Currency – Economic and Monetary Union (EMU)*. London: Department for Business, Enterprise and Regulatory Reform.

Berridge, GR (1994) *Talking to the Enemy – How States Without 'Diplomatic Relations' Communicate*. London: St Martin's Press.

Beyers, J (2005) Multiple Embeddedness and Socialization in Europe: The Case of Council Officials, *International Organization* 59(4): 899–936.

Bickerton, CJ (2012) *European Integration. From Nation-States to Member States*, Oxford: Oxford University Press.

Blair, A (1998) UK Policy Coordination During the 1990–91 Intergovernmental Conference, *Diplomacy and Statecraft* 9(2): 160–183.

(1999) *Dealing With Europe: Britain and the Negotiation of the Maastricht Treaty*. Aldershot: Ashgate.

Börzel, T (2005) Mind the Gap! European Integration Between Level and Scope. *Journal of European Public Policy* 12(2): 217–236.

Börzel, TA and Risse, T (2007). Europeanization: the domestic impact of European Union politics. Edited by KE Jørgensen, M Pollack and B Rosamond *The SAGE Handbook of European Union Politics*. London: Sage, 483–504.

Bourdieu, P (1977) *Outline of a Theory of Practice*. Cambridge: Cambridge University Press.

(1982) La mort du sociologue Erving Goffman: le découvreur de l'infiniment petit. *Le Monde*. 4 December 1982.

(1985) The Social Space and the Genesis of Groups, *Theory and Society* 14(6): 723–744.

(1986) *Distinction: A Social Critique of the Judgment of Taste*. London: Routledge and Kegan Paul.

(1987) The Force of Law – Toward A Sociology of the Juridical Field, *Hastings Law Journal* 38(5): 805–853.

(1989) *La Noblesse D'État: Grandes Ecoles Et Esprit De Corps*. Paris: Les Editions de Minuit.

(1990) *In Other Words: Essays Towards a Reflexive Sociology*. Stanford: Stanford University Press.

(1992) *Language and Symbolic Power*. Cambridge: Polity Press.

(1993) *La Misère Du Monde*. Paris: Éditions du Seuil.

(1994) Un Acte Désintéressé Est-Il Possible?. In *Raisons praticques. Sur la théorie de la raison*. Edited by P Bourdieu. Paris: Éditions du Seuil.

(2002) Social Space and Symbolic Space. In *Contemporary Sociological Theory*. Edited by CJ Calhoun et al. Oxford: Blackwell.

(2003) *Firing Back: Against the Tyranny of the Market*. Paris: Verso.

Bourdieu, P, Chamboredon, J-C and Passeron, J-C (1991) *The Craft of Sociology: Epistemological Preliminaries*. Berlin: Waoter de Gruyter & Co.

Bourdieu, P and Wacquant, L (1992) *An Invitation to Reflexive Sociology*. Chicago: Chicago University Press.

Bozo, F (2007) Mitterrand's France, the End of the Cold War, and German Unification: A Reappraisal *Cold War History*, 4(7): 455–478.

Bryant, CD (1990) Deviant People: Handling Themselves. In *Deviant Behavior. Readings in the Sociology of Norm Violations*. Edited by CD Bryant. New York: Hemisphere Publishing.

Bull, H (1977) *The Anarchical Society*. New York: Columbia University Press.

Bulmer, SJ (1996) The European Council and The Council of the European Union: Shapers of a European Confederation, *Publius: The Journal of Federalism* 26(4): 17–42.

Búrca, G de (1996) The Quest for Legitimacy in the European Union, *The Modern Law Review* 59(3): 349–376.

(2003) The Constitutional Challenge of New Governance in the European Union. In *Current Legal Problems Volume 56*. Edited by M Freeman. Oxford: Oxford University Press.

Búrca, G de and Scott, J (2000) Introduction. In *Constitutional Change in the EU: From Uniformity to Flexibility? Essays on the New 'Flexible' Nature of the Constitutional Arrangements of the European Union*. Edited by G de Búrca and J Scott. Oxford: Hart Publishing.

Burkitt, B and Mullen, A (2003) European Integration and the Battle for British Hearts and Minds: New Labour and the Euro, *Political Quarterly* 74(3): 322–336.

Calmfors, L, Flam, H, Gottfries, N, Haaland Matlary, J, Jerneck, M, Lindahl, R, Berntsson, CN, Rabinowicz, E and Vredin, A (1997) *EMU – A Swedish Perspective*. Boston: Kluwer.

Castle, S (2002) Pact Ruling Euro Nations Is Stupid, Says Prodi, *The Independent* 18 October.

Checkel, JT (1999) Norms, Institutions, and National Identity in Contemporary Europe, *International Studies Quarterly* 43: 84–114.

(2004) Social Constructivisms in Global and European Politics: A Review Essay, *Review of International Studies* 30(2): 229–244.

(2005) International Institutions and Socialization in Europe: Introduction and Framework, *International Organization* 59(4): 801–826.

Church, C and Phinnemore, D (2006) *Understanding the European Constitution: An Introduction to the EU's Constitutional Treaty*. London: Routledge.

Church, CH (2007) Introduction. In *Switzerland and the European Union. A Close, Contradictory and Misunderstood Relationship*. Edited by C Church. London: Routledge.

Clegg, SR (1989) *Frameworks of Power*. London: Sage Publications.

Coeuré, B (2003) L'Eurogroupe: Bilan Et Perspectives, *Revue d'Économie Financière* 65(1): 1–10.

Cohen, A and Vauchez, A (2007) 'Introduction: Law, Lawyers, and Transnational Politics in the Production of Europe', *Law & Social Inquiry* 32.1: 75–82.

Cohn, C (1987) Sex and Death in the Rational World of Defense Intellectuals, *Signs* 12(4): 687–718.

— (2006) Motives and Methods: Using Multi-Cited Ethnography to Study National Security Discourses. In *Feminist Methodologies for International Relations*. Edited by BA Ackerly and J True. Cambridge: Cambridge University Press.

Cooper, AF, Hocking, B and Maley, W (2008) *Global Governance and Diplomacy: Worlds Apart?* Houndmills: Palgrave Macmillan.

Coulter J (2001) Human Practices and the Oberservability of the 'Macro-Social', In *The Practice Turn in Contemporary Theory*. Edited by Schatzki TR, Cetina KK, and Von Savigny E. London: Routledge.

Crocker, J and Major, B (1989) Social Stigma and Self-Esteem: The Self-Protective Properties of Stigma, *Psychological Review* 96(4): 608–630.

Cross, MKD (2007) *A European Epistemic Community of Diplomats*. Edited by P Sharp and G Wiseman. New York: Palgrave.

— (2011) Building a European Diplomacy: Recruitment and Training to the EEAS, *European Foreign Affairs Review*, 16(4): 447–464.

Curtin, D (1993) The Constitutional Structure of the Union – A Europe of Bits and Pieces, *Common Market Law Review* 30(1): 17–69.

— (1995) The Shaping of a European Constitution and the 1996 IGC: 'Flexibility' As a Key Paradigm? *Aussenwirtschaft* 50(Special issue): 238–251.

— (2006) European Legal Integration: Paradise Lost? In *European Integration and Law*. Edited by D Curtin et al. Antwerpen: Intersentia.

Curtin, D and Egeberg, M (2008) Tradition and Innovation: Europe's Accumulated Executive Order. *West European Politics*, 31(4), 639–661.

Danish Institute for International Studies (2008) *De Danske Forbehold Overfor Den Europæiske Union. Udviklingen Siden 2000 [The Danish Opt-Outs From the European Union. The Development Since 2000]*. Copenhagen: Danish Institute for International Studies (DIIS).

Dansk Udenrigspolitisk Institut (2000) *Udviklingen i EU siden 1992 På de områder, der er omfattet af de danske forbehold [The Development in the EU Since 1992 on the Areas Covered by the Danish Opt-Outs]*. Copenhagen: Dansk Udenrigspolitisk Institut.

De Neve (2007) The European Onion? How Differentiated Integration is Reshaping the EU, *Journal of European Integration*, 29(4): 503–521.

De Witte, B (2001) Chameleonic Member States: Differentiation by Means of Partial and Parallel International Agreement. In *The Many Faces of Differentiation in EU Law*. Edited by B De Witte, D Hanf and E Vos. Antwerpen: Intersentia.

(2002) Anticipating the Institutional Consequences of Expanded Membership of the European Union, *International Political Science Review* 23(3), 235–248.

Dehousse, F (2003) Beyond Representative Democracy: Constitutionalism in a Polycentric Polity. In *European Constitutionalism Beyond the State*. Edited by JHH Weiler and M Wind. Cambridge: Cambridge University Press.

Delanty, G and Rumford, C (2006) *Rethinking Europe: Social Theory and the Implications of Europeanization*. London: Routledge.

Denman, R (2004) Major Is Singing That Old 1959 Song, *International Herald Tribune* 21 September.

Der Derian, J (1987) *On Diplomacy: A Genealogy of Western Estrangement*. Oxford: Blackwell.

Dezalay, Y and Garth, B (1995) Merchants of Law As Moral Entrepreneurs: Constructing International Justice From the Competition for Transnational Business Disputes, *Law & Society Review* 29(1): 27–64.

(2010) *The Internationalization of Palace Wars: Lawyers, Economists, and the Contest to Transform Latin American States*. Chicago: University of Chicago Press.

Dezalay, Yves and Bryant, G Garth (1996) *Dealing in Virtue: International Commercial Arbitration and the Construction of a Transnational Legal Order*. Chicago: University of Chicago Press.

Diez, T (1999) Speaking 'Europe': the Politics of Integration Discourse, *Journal of European Public Policy* 6(4): 598–613.

Dowding, K, John, P, Mergoupis, T and Vugt, M (2000) Exit, Voice and Loyalty: Analytic and Empirical Developments, *European Journal of Political Research* 37(4), 469–495.

Downs, G W, Rocke, DM and Barsoom, PN (1998) Managing the Evolution of Multilateralism, *International Organization* 52(2): 397–419.

Duquette, ES (2003) Will a Constitution for Europe Make a Difference? *International Law Review* 1(1): 71–80.

Dyson, K (2000a) Europeanization, Whitehall Culture and the Treasury As Institutional Veto Player: A Constructivist Approach to Economic and Monetary Union, *Public Administration* 78(4): 897–914.

(2002b) Introduction: EMU As Integration, Europeanization and Convergence. In *European States and the Euro. Europeanization, Variation and Convergence*. Edited by K Dyson. Oxford: Oxford University Press.

Dyson, K and Featherstone, K (1999) *The Road to Maastricht. Negotating Economic and Monetary Union.* Oxford: Oxford University Press.

Edkins, J (1999) *Poststructuralism and International Relations.* Boulder, CO: Lynne Rienner Publishers.

Egeberg, M and Jarle, T (2011) EU-Level Agencies: New Executive Centre Formation or Vehicles for National Control? *Journal of European Public Policy* 18(6): 868–887.

Egeberg, M and Trondal, J (1999) Differentiated Integration in Europe: The Case of EEA Country, Norway, *Journal of Common Market Studies* 37(1): 133–142.

Eilstrup-Sangiovanni, M (2006) The Future of European Integration Studies: The Road Ahead. In *Debates on European Integration: A Reader.* Edited by M Eilstrup-Sangiovanni. New York: Palgrave.

Eising, R and Kohler-Koch, B (1999) Governance in the European Union: A Comparative Assessment. In *The Transformation of Governance in the European Union.* Edited by B Kohler-Koch and R Eising (London: Routledge).

Ekengren, M (2002) *The Time of European Governance.* Manchester: Manchester University Press.

Elgström, O (2003) *European Union Presidencies: A Comparative Perspective.* London: Routledge.

Eliassen, KA and Sitter, N (2003) Ever Closer Cooperation? The Limits of the 'Norwegian Method' of European Integration, *Scandinavian Political Studies* 26(2): 125–144.

Emerson, M, Vahl, M and Woolcock, S (2002) *Navigating by the Stars: Norway, the European Economic Area and the European Union.* Brussels: CEPS.

Everett, J (2002) Organizational Research and the Praxeology of Pierre Bourdieu, *Organizational Research Methods* 5(1): 56–80.

Faulks, K (1999) *Political Sociology: A Critical Introduction.* Edinburgh: Edinburgh University Press.

Favell, A (2011) *Eurostars and Eurocities: Free Movement and Mobility in an Integrating Europe.* London: John Wiley & Sons.

Favell, A and Guiraudon, V (2009). The Sociology of the European Union An Agenda, *European Union Politics*, 10(4), 550–576.

(eds.) (2011) *The Sociology of the European Union.* London: Palgrave.

Featherstone, K and Radaelli, CM (Eds.). (2003). *The politics of Europeanization.* Oxford: Oxford University Press.

Fella, S (2006) New Labour, Same Old Britain? The Blair Government and European Treaty Reform, *Parliamentary Affairs* 59(4): 621–637.

Fielding, N (1993) Qualitative Interviewing. In *Researching Social Life.* Edited by N Gilbert. London: Sage.

Finnemore, M and Sikkink, K (2001) Taking Stock: The Constructivist Research Program in International Relations and Comparative Politics, *Annual Review of Political Science* 4(1): 391–416.

Fischer, J (2000) From Confederacy to Federation: Thoughts on the Finality of European Integration, Speech by Joschka Fischer at the Humboldt University in Berlin, 12 May 2000. In *What Kind of Constitution for What Kind of Polity?* Edited by C Joerges, Y Mény and JHH Weiler. Florence: European University Institute.

Flick, U (2006) *An Introduction to Qualitative Research*. 3 ed. London: Sage.

Fligstein, N (2001) Social Skill and the Theory of Fields. *Sociological Theory* 19(2): 105–125.

Flockhart, T (2005) Critical Junctures and Social Identity Theory: Explaining the Gap Between Danish Mass and Elite Attitudes to Europeanization, *Jcms-Journal of Common Market Studies* 43(2): 251–271.

Flyvbjerg, B (1991) *Rationalitet Og Magt. Det Konkretes Videnskab. Bind I. [Rationality and Power. The Science of the Concrete. Vol. I]*. Copenhagen: Akademisk Forlag.

Fourcade, M (2013) The economy as morality play, and implications for the Eurozone crisis. *Socio-Economic Review*, 11(3): 601–627.

Føllesdal, A and Hix, S (2006) Why There Is a Democratic Deficit in the EU: A Response to Majone and Moravcsik, *Journal of Common Market Studies* 44(3): 533–562.

Freshwater, H (2003) The Allure of the Archive, *Poetics Today* 24(4): 729–758.

Frey, BS and Eichenberger, R (1999) *The New Democratic Federalism For Europe Functional, Over lapping and Competing Jurisdictions.* Cheltenham: Edward Elgar.

(2000) A Proposal for a Flexible Europe, *The World Economy* 23(10): 1323–1334.

Friedrichs, J (2001) The Meaning of New Medievalism, *European Journal of International Relations* 7(4): 475–501.

Gad, UP (2007) *Is Turkey Muslim and/or European? The Construction of Turkey in Danish Identity Politics.* Paper presented to the ECPR-SGIR conference, Turin, 12–15 September.

Gamble, A and Kelly, G (2002) Britain and the EMU. In *European States and the Euro. Europeanization, Variation, and Convergence*. Edited by K Dyson. Oxford: Oxford University Press.

Garland, D (1990) *Punishment and Society*. Oxford: Clarendon Press.

Geddes, A (2000) *Immigration and European Integration: Towards Fortress Europe?* Manchester: Manchester University Press.

(2004) *The European Union and British Politics*. Basingstroke: Palgrave.

(2005) Getting the Best of Both Worlds? Britain, the EU and Migration Policy, *International Affairs* 81(4): 723–740.

(2013) *Britain and the European Union*. Houndmills: Palgrave.

Gehlbach, S (2006) A Formal Model of Exit and Voice, *Rationality and Society* 18(4), 395–418.

George, S (1994) *An Awkward Partner: Britain in the European Community*. Oxford: Oxford University Press.

Gibbons, JA (1997) Struggle and Catharsis: Art in Women's Prisons, *Journal of Arts Management, Law and Society* 27(1): 72.

Giddens, A (1984) *The Constitution Of Society: Outline Of The Theory Of Structuration*. Cambridge: Polity Press.

Giddings, P (2004) Westminster, the EMU and the Euro. In *Britain in the European Union: Law, Politicy and Parliament*. Edited by P Giddings and G Drewry. New York: Palgrave.

Givens, T and Luedtke, A (2003) EU Immigration Policy: From Intergovernmentalism to Reluctant Harmonization. In *The State of the European Union: Law, Politics and Society*. Edited by TA Börzel and RA Cichowski. Oxford: Oxford University Press.

(2004) The Politics of European Union Immigration Policy: Institutions, Salience, and Harmonization, *Policy Studies Journal* 32(1): 145–165.

Goertz, G (2006) *Social Science Concepts: A User's Guide*. Princeton: Princeton University Press.

Goffman, E (1951) Symbols of class status. *The British Journal of Sociology*, 2(4), 294–304.

(1959) *Presentation of Self in Everyday Life*. New York: Doubleday & Company.

(1963) *Stigma: Notes on the Management of Spoiled Identity*. New York: Touchstone.

(1983) The Interaction Order: American Sociological Association, 1982 presidential address. *American Sociological Review* 48(1), 1–17.

Gray, E and Statham, P (2005) Becoming European? The Transformation of the British Pro-Migrant NGO Sector in Response to Europeanization, *Journal of Common Market Studies* 43(4): 877–898.

Guiraudon, V (2003) The Constitution of a European Immigration Policy Domain: a Political Sociology Approach, *Journal of European Public Policy* 10(2): 263–282.

(2004) Immigration and Asylum: A High Politics Agenda. In *Developments in the European Union*. Edited by MG Cowles and D Dinan. Houndmills: Palgrave.

Guiraudon, V and Jileva, E (2006) Immigration and Asylum. In *Developments in European Politics*. Edited by PM Heywood et al. Houndmills: Palgrave.

Guzzini, S (2000) A Reconstruction of Constructivism in International Relations, *European Journal of International Relations* 6(2): 147–182.

Haahr, JH (2003) 'Our Danish Democracy': Community, People and Democracy in the Danish Debate on the Common Currency, *Cooperation and Conflict* 38(1): 27–47.

Habermas, J (2003) Toward a Cosmopolitan Europe, *Journal of Democracy* 14(4): 86–100.

(2004) Why Europe Needs a Constitution. In *Developing a Constitution for Europe*. Edited by EO Eriksen, JE Fossum and AJ Menéndez. London: Routledge.

Hacking, I (1999) *The Social Construction of What? A Treatise in the Sociology of Knowledge*. Cambrigde, MA: Harvard University Press.

Häge, F (2012) *Bureaucrats as Law-Makers: Committee Decision-Making in the EU Council of Ministers*. London: Routledge.

Hallerberg, M (2000) *The Importance of Domestic Political Institutions: Why and How Belgium and Italy Qualified for EMU*. B 10–2000 ed. Bonn: Center for European Integration Studies, ZEI Working Paper.

Hamel, J (1998) The Positions of Pierre Bourdieu and Alain Touraine Respecting Qualitative Methods, *British Journal of Sociology* 49(1): 1–19.

Hanf, D (2001) Flexibility Clauses in the Founding Treaties, From Rome to Nice. In *The Many Faces of Flexibility in EU Law*. Edited by B De Witte. Antwerpen: Intersentia.

Hansen, L (2002) Sustaining Sovereignty: The Danish Approach to Europe. In *European Integration and National Identity: The Challenge of the Nordic States*. Edited by L Hansen and O Wæver. London: Routledge.

Harvey, C (1997) Restructuring Asylum: Recent Trends in United Kingdom Asylum Law and Policy, *International Journal of Refugee Law* 9(1): 60–73.

Hayes-Renshaw, F, Van Aken, W and Wallace, H (2006) When and Why the EU Council of Ministers Votes Explicitly, *Journal of Common Market Studies* 44(1): 161–194.

Hayes-Renshaw, F and Wallace, H (1997) *The Council of Ministers*. Houndmills: Macmillan.

Heartfield, J (2007) European Union: A Process Without a Subject. In *Politics Without Sovereignty: A Critique of Contemporary International Relations*. Edited by C J. Bickerton, P Cunliffe and A Gourevitch. London: Routledge.

Hedetoft, U (2000) The Interplay Between Mass and Elite Attitudes to European Integration in Denmark. In *Denmark's Policy Towards Europe After 1945. History, Theory and Option*. Edited by H Branner and M Kelstrup. Odense: Odense University Press.

Heisenberg, D (2005) The Institution of 'Consensus' in the European Union: Formal Versus Informal Decision-Making in the Council, *European Journal of Political Research* 44(1): 65–90.

Héritier, A (1999) *Policy-Making and Diversity in Europe: Escape From Deadlock*. Cambridge: Cambridge University Press.

Herrmann, RK and Brewer, MB (2004) Identity and Institutions: Becoming European in the EU. In *Transnational Identities: Becoming European in the EU*. Edited by RK Herrmann and MB Brewer. New York: Rowman & Littlefield Publishers.

Hine, D (2001) Constitutional Reform and Treaty Reform in Europe. In *From the Nation State to Europe?* Edited by A Menon and V Wright. Oxford: Oxford University Press.

Hirschman, AO (1970) *Exit, Voice, and Loyalty: Responses to Decline in Firms, Organizations, and States* Cambridge, MA: Harvard university press.

Hix, S (1998) The Study of the European Union II: the 'New Governance' Agenda and Its Rival, *Journal of European Public Policy* 5(1): 38–65.

(2005) *The Political System of the European Union*. Houndmills: Palgrave.

HM Treasury (2003) *Policy Frameworks in the UK and EMU. EMU Study*. London: HM Treasury Public Enquiry Unit.

Hocking, B (2005) Introduction: Gatekeepers and Boundary-Spanners – Thinking About Foreign Ministries in the European Union. In *Foreign Ministries in the European Union: Integrating Diplomats*. Edited by B Hocking and D Spence. Houndmills and New York: Palgrave.

Hooghe, L and Marks, G (2001). *Multi-level Governance and European Integration*. Rowman & Littlefield.

(2008) European Union? *West European Politics*, 31(1–2), 108–129.

House of Lords (1999) *Schengen and the United Kingdom's Border Controls*. London: House of Lords 7th Report, 1998/99.

(2004) *Minutes of Evidence Taken Before the Select Committee on the European Union*, 25 February 2004, London: House of Lords Select Committee on European Union.

(2008) *Minutes of Evidence Taken Before the Select Commitee on the European Union (Sub-Comittee A), 21 January 2008*. London: House of Lords Select Committee on European Union.

Houtzager, PB (2005) Introduction: From Polycentrism to the Polity. In *Changing Paths: International Development and the New Politics of Inclusion*. Edited by PB Houtzager and M Moore. Ann Arbour: University of Michigan Press.

Howarth, D (2003) France, Britain and the Euro-Atlantic Crisis, *Survival* 45 (4): 173–192.

(2005) The Euro-Outsiders: Conclusions, *Journal of European Integration* 27(1): 133–140.

(2007) The Domestic Politics of British Policy on the Euro, *Journal of European Integration* 29(1): 47–68.

Hummer, W (2006) The New EU – A Military Pact? Solidarity – Neutrality – 'Irish Clause'. In *European Security in Transition*. Edited by G Hauser and F Kernic. Surrey: Ashgate.

Ignatow, G (2009) Why the Sociology of Morality Needs Bourdieu's Habitus, *Sociological Inquiry*, 79(1): 98–114.

Jachtenfuchs, M (2001) The Governance Approach to European Isntegration. *Journal of Common Market Studies*, 39(2), 245–264.

Jackson, P (2004) Hegel's House, or 'People Are States Too', *Review of International Studies* 30(02): 281–287.

(2008) Pierre Bourdieu, the 'Cultural Turn' and the Practice of International History, *Review of International Studies* 34(1): 155–181.

Jenkins, R (2002) *Pierre Bourdieu*. London: Routledge.

(2005) Social Skills, Social Research Skills, Sociological Skills: Teaching Reflexivity? *Teaching Sociology* 23(1): 16–27.

Jensen, L (2003) *Den Store Koordinator. Finansministeriet Som Moderne Styringsaktør [The Big Coordinator. The Ministry of Finance As a Modern Regulating Actor]*. Copenhagen: DJØF.

Jervis, R (1976) *Perception and Misperception in International Politics*. Princeton: Princeton University Press.

Johler, R (2008) Ethnological Aspects of 'Rooting' Europe in a 'De-Ritualised' Europan Union. In *Managing Ethnicity: Perspectives from Folklore Studies, History and Anthropology*. Edited by R Bendix and H Rodenburg. Het Spinhuis.

Johnston, AI (2001) Treating International Institutions as Social Environments, *International Studies Quarterly*, 45(4), 487–515.

Jones, CP (1987) Stigma: Tattooing and Branding in Graeco-Roman Antiquity, *The Journal of Roman Studies* 77: 139–155.

Jørgensen, KE (1999) Modern European Diplomacy: A Research Agenda, *Journal of International Relations and Development*, 2(1): 78–96.

Jupille, J Caporaso, JA and Checkel, JT (2003) Integrating Institutions: Rationalism, Constructivism, and the Study of the European Union, *Comparative Political Studies* 36(1–2): 7–40.

Juss, SS (2005) The Decline and Decay of European Refugee Policy, *Oxford Journal of Legal Studies* 25(4): 749–792.

Kando, T (1972) Passing and Stigma Management: The Case of the Transsexual, *The Sociological Quarterly* 13(4), 475–483.

Kassim, HB and Peters, GB (2001) Conclusion: Co-Ordinating National Action in Brussels – A Comparative Perspective. In *The National Co-ordination of EU Policy: The European Level*. Edited by HB Kassim et al. Oxford: Oxford University Press.

Katzenstein, P (1996), Introduction: Alternative Perspectives on National Security. In *The Culture of National Security: Norms and Identity in World Politics*. Edited by PJ Katzenstein. New York: Columbia University Press.

Kauppi, N (2003) Bourdieu's Political Sociology and the Politics of European Integration, *Theory and Society* 32(5–6): 775–789.

Kauppi, N and Madsen, MR (eds) (2013) *Transnational Power Elites: The New Professionals of Governance, Law and Security*, London: Routledge.

Kelstrup, M (2006) Denmark in the Process of European Integration: Dilemmas, Problems and Perspectives. In *National Identity and the Varieties of Capitalism: The Danish Experience*. Edited by JL Cambell, John A Hall and OK Pedersen. Montreal & Kingston: McGill-Queen's University Press.

King, A (2000) Thinking With Bourdieu Against Bourdieu: A 'Practical' Critique of the Habitus, *Sociological Theory* 18(3): 417–433.

Kölliker, A (2001). Bringing Together or Driving Apart the Union? Towards a Theory of Differentiated Integration. *West European Politics*, 24(4), 125–151

(2006) *Flexibility and European Unification: The Logic of Differentiated Integration*. Lanham: Rowman and Littlefield.

König, T and Junge, D (2009). Why Don't Veto Players Use Their Power? *European Union Politics*, 10(4), 507–534.

Kostakopoulou, T (1998) European Union Citizenship As a Model of Citizenship Beyond the Nation State: Possibilities and Limits. In *Political Theory and the European Union: Legitimacy, Constitutional Choice and Citizenship*. Edited by A Weale and M Nentwich. London: Routledge.

Krajewski, M (2001) Democratic Legitimacy and Constitutional Perspectives of WTO Law, *Journal of World Trade* 35(1): 167–186.

Krasner, SD (1999) *Sovereignty: Organized Hypocrisy*. Princeton: Princeton University Press.

Krunke, H (2005) From Maastricht to Edinburgh: The Danish Solution, *European Constitutional Law Review* 1(3): 339–356.

Kusow, AM (2004) Contesting Stigma: On Goffman's Assumptions of Normative Order, *Symbolic Interaction* 27(2): 179–197.

Kux, S and Sverdrup, U (2000) Fuzzy Borders and Adaptive Outsiders: Norway, Switzerland and the EU, *Journal of European Integration* 22(3): 237–270.

La Malfa, G (2002) The Orphaned Euro, *Survival* 44(1): 81–95.

Ladrech, R (2004a) Europeanization and the Member States. In *Developments in the European Union*. Edited by MG Cowles and D Dinan. Houndmills: Palgrave Macmillan.

(2004b) The Social Psychology of Identity Change. In *Transnational identities: Becoming European in the EU*. Edited by RK Herrmann, T Risse-Kappen and MB Brewer. Lanham-Boulder-New York-Toronto-Oxford: Rowman & Littlefield.

Laffan, Brigid, and O'Mahony, Jane (2008) *Ireland and the European Union*, Palgrave Macmillan.

Lamaison, P and Bourdieu, P (1989) From Rules to Strategies: An Interview with Pierre Bourdieu, *Cultural Anthropology* 1(1): 110–120.

Lancker, AV (1997) Transparency and Accountability of Schengen. In *Schengen, Judicial Cooperation and Policy Coordination*. Edited by M den Boer. Maastricht: European Institute of Public Administration.

Larsen, H (1999) British and Danish European Policies in the 1990s: A Discourse Approach, *European Journal of International Relations* 5(4): 451–483.

—— (2000) Denmark and the European Defence Dimension in the Post-Cold War Period: Opt-Out or Participation? In *Danish Foreign Policy Yearbook*. Edited by B Heurlin and H Mouritzen. Copenhagen: Danish Institute for International Affairs.

—— (2006) *Analysing Small State Foreign Policy in the EU: The Case of Denmark*. Basingstroke: Palgrave.

Lavenex, S (2001) The Europeanization of Refugee Policies: Normative Challenges and Institutional Legacies, *Journal of Common Market Studies* 39(5): 851.

Leander, A (2005) The Power to Construct International Security: On the Significance of Private Military Companies, *Millennium-Journal of International Studies* 33(3): 803–825.

—— (2008) Thinking Tools: Analyzing Symbolic Power and Violence. In *Qualitative Methods in International Relations: A Pluralist Guide*. Edited by A Klotz and D Prakash. Basingstoke: Palgrave Macmillan.

Lebow, RN (2008) *A Cultural Theory of International Relations*. Cambridge University Press.

Lempp, J and Altenschmidt, J (2008) The Prevention of Deadlock Through Informal Processes of Supranationalization: The Case of Coreper, *Journal of European Integration* 30(4): 511–526.

Lewis, J (2000) The Methods of Community in EU Decision-Making and Administrative Rivalry in the Council Infrastructure, *Journal of European Public Policy* 7(2): 261–289.

—— (2003) Informal Integration and the Supranational Construction of the Council, *Journal of European Public Policy* 10(6): 996–1019.

—— (2005) The Janus Face of Brussels: Socialization and Everyday Decision Making in the European Union, *International Organization* 59(4): 937–971.

—— (2009) Strategic Bargaining, Norms, and Deliberation. In *Unveiling the Council of Ministers: Games Governments Play in Brussels*. Edited by D Naurin and H Wallace. New York: Palgrave.

Lewitt, P and Schiller, NG (2004) Conceptualizing Simultaneity: A Trans-national Social Field Perspective on Society, *International Migration Review* 38(3): 1002–1039.

Liénard, G and Servais, E (1974) Le sens pratique, *Revue française de sociologie*, 15(3): 413–421.

Lindahl, R and Naurin, D (2005) Sweden: The Twin Faces of a Euro-Outsider, *European Integration* 27(1): 65–87.

Link, BG and Phelan, Jo C (2001) Conceptualizing Stigma, *Annual Review of Sociology* 37: 363–385.

Ludlam, S (1998) The Cauldron: Conservative Parliamentarians and European Integration. In *Britain for and Against Europe. British Politics and the Question of European Integration*. Edited by D Baker and D Seawright. Oxford: Clarendon Press.

Lynch, C (2006) Critical Interpretation and Interwar Peace Movements: Challenging Dominant Narratives. In *Interpretation and Method: Empirical Research Methods and the Interpretive Turn*. Edited by D Yanow and P Schwartz-Shea. Armnok and Londn: M.E. Sharpe.

MacCormick, N (2002) *Questioning Sovereignty: Law, State, and Nation in the European Commonwealth*. Oxford: Oxford University Press.

(2004) *A Union of Its Own Kind? Reflections on the European Convention and the Proposed Constitution of the European Union*. Edinburgh: Neil MacCormick.

(2007) *Institutions of Law: An Essay in Legal Theory*. Oxford University Press.

Madsen, MR (2007) From Cold War Instrument to Supreme European Court: The European Court of Human Rights at the Crossroads of International and National Law and Politics, *Law & Social Inquiry* 32 (1): 137–159.

Majone, G (1994). The Rise of the Regulatory State in Europe. *West European Politics*, 17(3): 77–101.

Major, J (1994) *Speech in Leiden*. Leiden: Unpublished, 7 September 1994.

Mak, J (2003) Informality As an Asset? The Case of EMU. In *Informal Governance in the European Union*. Edited by T Christiansen and S Piattoni. Cheltenham: Edward Elgar.

Manners, I (2000) *Substance and Symbolism: An Anatomy of Cooperation in the New Europe*. Adershot: Ashgate.

(2007) Another Europe Is Possible: Critical Perspectives on European Union Politics. In *Handbook of European Union Politics*. Edited by KE Jørgensen, MA Pollack and B Rosamond. London: Sage.

Marcussen, M and Zolner, M (2000) *Ideas and Elites. The Social Construction of the Economic and Monetary Union*. Aalborg: Aalborg University Press.

(2001) The Danish EMU Referendum 2000: Business As Usual, *Government and Opposition* 36(3): 379–401.

(2005) Denmark and European Monetary Integration: Out but Far From Over, *Journal of European Integration* 27(1): 43–63.

(2007) *Handing Euro-Outsiderness. Working Paper 7.* Roskilde: Center for Democratic Nework Governance, Roskilde University.

Marks, G, Hooghe, L and Blank, K (1996) European Integration From the 1980s: State-Centric v Multi-Level Governance, *Journal of Common Market Studies* 34(3): 341–378.

Mayall, D (2007) Introduction. In *The Diplomatic Corps as an Institution of International Society.* Edited by P Sharp and G Wiseman. New York: Palgrave.

Maynard-Moody, S and Musheno, M (2006) Stories for Research. In *Interpretation and Method: Empirical Research and the Interpretive Turn.* Edited by D Yanow and P Schwartz-Shea. Armonk and London: M.E. Sharpe.

Meehan, E (2000a) 'Britain's Irish Question: Britain's European Question?' British-Irish Relations in the Context of European Union and The Belfast Agreement, *Review of International Studies* 26(1): 83–97.

(2000b) *Free Movement Between Ireland and the UK: From the 'Common Travel Area' to The Common Travel Area.* Dublin: The Policy Institute at Trinity College Dublin.

Mérand, F (2008) *European Defence Policy Beyond the Nation-State.* Oxford: Oxford University Press.

Mérand, F and Pouliot, V (2008) The World of Pierre Bourdieu: Elements for a Social Theory of International Relations, *Canadian Journal of Political Science-Revue Canadienne de Science Politique* 41(3): 603–625

Miles, L (2005a) Introduction: Euro-Outsiders and the Politics of Asymmetry, *Journal of European Integration* 27(1): 3–23.

(2005b) The North. In *The Geopolitics of Euro-Atlantic Integration.* Edited by H Mouritzen and A Wivel. London: Routledge.

Miller, V (2000) *The Danish Referendum on Economic and Monetary Union.* London: House of Commons Research Paper.

Misztal, BA (2001) Normality and Trust in Goffman's Theory of Interaction Order, *Sociological Theory* 19(3): 312–324.

Moi, T (1991) Appropriating Bourdieu: Feminist Theory and Pierre Bourdieu's Sociology of Culture, *New Literary History* 22(4): 1017–1049.

Monar, J (1999) *Flexibility and Closer Cooperation in an Emerging European Migration Policy: Opportunities and Risks.* 1 ed. Rome: Laboratorio CeSPI.

(2000) *Justice and Home Affairs in a Wider Europe: The Dynamics of Inclusion and Exclusion.* 7 ed. Leicester: 'One Europe or Several?' Programme Working Paper, Centre for European Politics and Institutions, Department of Politics, University of Leicester.

(2003) Justice and Home Affairs, *Journal of Common Market Studies* 41 (Annual Review): 119–135.

Mor, B D (2009) Accounts and Impression Management in public diplomacy: Israeli Justification of Force during the 2006 Lebanon War. *Global Change, Peace & Security*, 21(2): 219–239.

Moravcsik, A (1991) Negotiating the Single European Act: National Interests and Conventional Statecraft in the European Community, *International Organization* 3(1): 19–56.

(1993) Integrating International and Domestic Politics: A Theoretical Introduction. In *Double-Edged Diplomacy: Interactive Games in International Affairs*. Edited by P Evans, H Jacobson and R Putnam. Berkeley: University of California Press.

(1998) Europe's Integration at Century's End. In *Centralization or Fragmentation? Europe Facing the Challenges of Deepening, Diversity and Democracy*. Edited by A Moravcsik. New York: Council on Foreign Relations, Brookings Institution Press.

(2004) Is there a 'Democratic Deficit'in World Politics? *A framework for analysis. Government and opposition*, 39(2), 336–363.

Moravcsik, A and Nicolaidis, K (1998) Keynote Article: Federal Ideals and Constitutional Realities in the Treaty of Amsterdam, *Journal of Common Market Studies*, 43(s1): 13–38.

(1999) Explaining the Treaty of Amsterdam: Interests, Influence, Institutions, *Journal of Common Market Studies* 37(1): 59–85.

Moravcsik, A and Vachudova, MA (2002) Bargaining Among Unequals: Enlargement and the Future of European Integration, *EUSA Review* 15 (4): 1–3.

Mouritzen, H (2003) Stifled by Her Own Success?: A Geopolitical Perspective, *Cooperation and Conflict* 38(3): 305–310.

Mudge, SL and Vauchez, A (2012) Building Europe on a Weak Field: Law, Economics, and Scholarly Avatars in Transnational Politics, *American Journal of Sociology* 118(2): 449–492.

Mulhearn, C and Vane, HR (2005) The UK and the Euro: Debating the British Decision, *World Economy* 28(2): 243–258.

Naurin, D and Wallace, H (2009) Introduction: From Rags to Riches. In *Unveiling the Council of Ministers: Games Governments Play in Brussels*. Edited by D Naurin and H Wallace. New York: Palgrave.

Neumann, I (1999) Nasjonal Kultur, Postnasjonal Politikk? [National Culture, Postnational Politics?]. In *Kunnskapsregimer. Debatten om De nasjonale strategier [Knowledge Regimes. The Debate on The National Strategies]*. Edited by E Rudeng. Oslo: Pax Forlag.

(2002) *The Engish School on Diplomacy*. The Hague: Clingendael Institute.

(2004) Beware of Organicism: the Narrative Self of the State, *Review of International Studies* 30(02): 259–267.

(2005) To Be a Diplomat, *International Stuides Perspectives* 6: 72–93.

(2007) 'A Speech That the Entire Ministry May Stand for,' or: Why Diplomats Never Produce Anything New, *International Political Sociology* 1(2): 183–200.

Nicolaïdis, K (2001) Conclusion: The Federal Vision Beyond the Federal State. In *The Federal Vision: Legitimacy and Levels of Governance in the US and the EU*. Edited by K Nicolaidis and R Howse. Oxford: Oxford University Press.

Niemann, A (2009) Deliberation and Bargaining in the Article 113 Committee and the 1996/97 IGC Representatives Group. In *Unveiling the Council of Ministers: Games Governments Play in Brussels*. Edited by H Wallace and D Naurin. New York: Palgrave.

Nurmi, H (1997) The Representation of Voter Groups in the European Parliament: a Penrose-Banzhaf Index Analysis, *Electoral Studies* 16(3): 317–327.

Olsen, JP (2005) *The Political Organization of Europe: Differentiation and Unification*. Oslo: Arena Centre for European Studies, No 23.

Olsen, JP and March, JG (2004) *The Logic of Appropriateness*. Oslo: ARENA Working Paper Series: 09/2004.

Padoa-Schioppa, T (2006) *Europe, a Civil Power. Lessons From EU Experience*. London: The Federal Trust.

Papagianni, G (2001) Flexibility in Justice and Home Affairs: an Old Phenomenon Taking New Forms. In *The Many Faces of Differentiation in the EU*. Edited by B De Witte, D Hanf and E Vos. Antwerp: Intersentia.

Petersen, N (1993) 'Game, Set and Match': Denmark and the European Union After Maastricht. In *The Nordic Countries and the EC*. Edited by T Tiilikainen and ID Petersen. Copenhagen: Political Studies Press.

(1998) National Strategies in the Integration Dilemma: An Adaptation Approach, *Journal of Common Market Studies* 36(1): 33–54.

(2003) Formuleringen Af Forbeholdene [The Drafting of the Opt-Outs]. In *Danmark 30 år i EU – et festskrift [Denmark 30 years in the EU – a Festschrift]*. Copenhagen: Gyldendal.

Peterson, J (1999) Europe's Ambiguous Unity: Conflict and Consensus in the Post-Maastricht Era, *Political Studies* 47(2): 381–383.

Pilkington, C (1995) *Britain in the European Union*. Manchester: Manchester University Press.

Plattner, MF (2003) Competing Goals, Conflicting Perspectives, *Journal of Democracy* 14(4): 42–56.

Pouliot, V (2007) 'Sobjectivism': Toward a Constructivist Methodology, *International Studies Quarterly* 51(2): 359–384.

(2008) The Logic of Practicality: A Theory of Practice of Security Communities, *International Organization* 62(2): 257–288.

(2012) Methodology: Putting Practice Theory into Practice. In R Adler-Nissen (ed.) *Bourdieu in International Relations: Rethinking Key Concepts in IR*. London: Routledge.

Prechal, S and Roermund, B van (2008) Binding Unity in EU Legal Order: An Introduction. In *The Coherence of EU Law: The Search for Unity in Divergent Concepts*. Edited by S Prechal and B van Roermund. Oxford: Oxford University Press.

Puetter, U (2004) Governing Informally: the Role of the Eurogroup in EMU and the Stability and Growth Pact, *Journal of European Public Policy* 11(5): 854–870.

(2005) The Enlargement of the European Union. Ordering From the Menu in Central Europe, *West European Politics* 28(5): 1126–1128.

(2006) *The Eurogroup. How a Secretive Circle of Finance Ministers Shape European Economic Governance*. Manchester: Manchester University Press.

(2014) *The European Council and the Council. New intergovernmentalism and institutional change*, Oxford: Oxford University Press, forthcoming.

Rasmussen, AF (2003) *Visions for Denmark's Active European Policy*. Copenhagen: Speech by Prime Minister Anders Fogh Rasmussen at University of Copenhagen.

Reay, D, David, ME and Ball, SJ (2005) *Degrees of Choice: Class, Race, Gender and Higher Education*. Stoke on Trent and New York: Trentham Books.

Risse, T (2002) Nationalism and Collective Identities: Europe Versus the Nation-State? In *Developments in West European Politics 2*. Edited by P Heywood, E Jones and M Rhodes. Houndmills, Basingstroke: Palgrave.

Risse, T and Sikkink, K (1999) The Socialization of Human Rights Norms into Domestic Practices: Introduction. In *The Power of Human Rights: International Norms and Domestic Change*. Edited by T Risse, SC Ropp and K Sikkink. Cambridge: Cambridge University Press.

Risse-Kappen, T, Cowles, MG and Caporaso, JA (2001) Europeanization and Domestic Change: Introduction. In *Transforming Europe: Europeanization and Domestic Change*. Edited by MG Cowles, JA Caporaso and T Risse-Kappen. Ithaca, NY: Cornell University Press.

Rosamond, B (2002) Britain's European Future? *British Politics Today*, 185.

(2004) Britain's European Future? In *British Politics Today*. Edited by C Hay. Cambridge: Polity Press.

(2006) The Future of European Studies: Integration Theory, EU Studies and Social Science. In *Debates on European Integration: A Reader*. Edited by M Eilstrup-Sangiovanni. New York: Palgrave.

Roschelle, AR and Kaufman, P (2004) Fitting in and Fighting Back: Stigma Management Strategies Among Homeless Kids, *Symbolic Interaction* 27(1): 23–46.

Rose, R (2013) *Representing Europeans: A Pragmatic Approach*. Oxford: Oxford University Press.

Routh, DA and Burgoyne, CB (1998) Being in Two Minds About a Single Currency: A UK Perspective on the Euro, *Journal of Economic Psychology* 19(6): 741–754.

Ruggie, JG (1993) Territoriality and Beyond – Problematizing Modernity in International-Relations, *International Organization* 47(1): 139–174.

Ryborg, OV (1998) *Det Utænkelige Nej ...! Historien Om 6 Måneder, 9 Dage Og 17 Timer, Der Rystede Europa*. København: Informations Forlag/Schultz Forlag.

Ryner, M (2012) Financial Crisis, Orthodoxy and Heterodoxy in the Production of Knowledge about the EU, *Millennium – Journal of International Studies* 40(3): 647–673.

Sandelowski, M, Lambe, C and Barroso, J (2004) Stigma in HIV-Positive Women, *Journal of Nursing Scholarship* 36(2), 122–128.

Saurugger, S and Mérand, F (2010) Does European Integration Theory Need Sociology? *Comparative European Politics* 8(1): 1–18.

Scharling, N (2003) Politiets Vietnam-Kompleks, *Dansk Politi* 5 February 2003.

Scharpf, FW (1997) Economic Integration, Democracy and the Welfare State, *Journal of European Public Policy* 4(1), 18–36.

(2001) Notes Toward a Theory of Multilevel Governing in Europe, *Scandinavian Political Studies* 24: 1–26.

(2006) The Joint-Decision Trap Revisited, *Journal of Common Market Studies* 44(4): 845–864.

(2007) Reflections on Multi-Level Legitimacy, Max-Planck Institute for the Study of Societies. MPIfG Working Paper.

Schimmelfennig, F (2004) Goffman Meets IR: Dramaturgical Action in International Community, *International Review of Sociology* 12(3): 417–437.

Schmidt, VA (1997) European Integration and Democracy: the Differences Among Member States, *Journal of European Public Policy* 4(1): 128–145.

(2006) *Democracy in Europe: The EU and National Polities*. Oxford: Oxford University Press.

Schmitter, PC (2001) What Is There to Legitimize in the European Union ... and How Might This Be Accomplished? In *Mountain or Molehill? A Critical Appraisal of the Commission White Paper on Governance*. Edited by C Joerges, Y Meny and JHH Weiler. New York: NY School of Law, Jean Monnet Center.

Seal, DW, Bloom, FR and Somlai, AM (2000) Dilemmas in Conducting Qualitative Sex Research in Applied Field Settings, *Health Education and Behavior* 27(1): 10–23.

Sebenius, JK (2002) Caveats for Cross-Border Negotiators, *Negotiation Journal* 18(2): 121–133.

Sedelmeier, U (2011) Europeanisation in new member and candidate states. *Living Reviews in European Governance*, 6(1).

Selle, P and Østerud, Ø (2006) The Eroding of Representative Democracy in Norway, *Journal of European Public Policy* 13(4): 551–568.

Sending, OJ, V Pouliot, V and Neumann IB (Eds.) *Diplomacy: The Making of World Politics*, Cambridge: Cambridge University Press, forthcoming.

Sharp, P (2004) Who Needs Diplomats? The Problem of Diplomatic Representation. In *Diplomacy. Volume III. Problems and Issues in Contemporary Diplomacy*. Edited by C Jönnson and R Langthorne. London: Sage.

Sharp, P (2009). *Diplomatic theory of international relations*, Cambridge: Cambridge University Press.

Shaw, J (1996) European Union Legal Studies in Crisis? Towards a New Dynamic, *Oxford Journal of Legal Studies* 16(2): 231–253.

(1998) The Treaty of Amsterdam: Challenges of Flexibility and Legitimacy, *European Law Journal* 4: 63–86.

(2002) Enhancing Cooperation After Nice: Will the Treaty Do the Trick? In *The Future of the European Union. Unity in Diversity*. Edited by Xuereb and G.B. London: European Documentation and Research Centre.

(2003) *Flexibility in a 'Reorganised' and 'Simplified' Treaty*. Edited by The Federal Trust. London: The Federal Trust.

Shaw, J and Wiener, A (2000) The Paradox of the European Polity. In *The State of the European Union. Risks, Reform, Resistance, and Revival Volume 5*. Edited by MG Cowles and M Smith. Oxford: Oxford University Press.

Silverman, D (2001) *Interpreting Qualitative Data. Methods for Analysing Talk, Text and Interaction*. London: Sage.

Skelcher, C (2005) Jurisdictional Integrity, Polycentrism, and the Design of Democratic Governance, *Governance* 18(2): 89–110.

Slapin, JB (2009) Exit, Voice, and Cooperation: Bargaining Power in International Organizations and Federal Systems, *Journal of Theoretical Politics*, 21(2), 187–211.

Slembrouck, S (2004) Reflexivity and the Research Interview, *Critical Discourse Studies* 1(1): 91–112.

Slot, PJ (1994) The Institutional Provisions of the EMU. In *Institutional Dynamics of European Integration*. Edited by D Curtin and T Heukels. Leiden: Martinus Nijhoff Publishers.

Smith, J and Tsatsas, M (2002) *The New Bilateralism. The UK's Relations Within the EU*. London: The Royal Institute of International Affairs.

Soros, G (2012) How to Save the Euro, *The New York Review of Books*, February 23, 2012.

Stubb, A (2002) *Negotiating Flexibility in the European Union: Amsterdam, Nice and Beyond.* Houndmills: Palgrave.

Swartz, D (2008) Bringing Bourdieu's Master Concepts into Organizational Analysis, *Theory and Society* 37(1): 45–52.

Tallberg, J (2004) The Power of the Presidency: Brokerage, Efficiency and Distribution in EU Negotiations, *Journal of Common Market Studies* 42(5): 999–1022.

Teague, P (2000) EU Social Policy: Institutional Design Matters. 1 ed. Belfast: School of Politics, *International Relations and Philosophy*, Queen's Working Paper 1.

Thatcher, M (2002) *Statecraft: Strategies for a Changing World.* New York: HarperCollins Publishers.

Tonra, B (2000) Mapping EU Foreign Policy Studies, *Journal of European Public Policy* 7(1): 163–169.

Trenz, HJ and Eder, K (2003) Transnational Resonance Structures: Searching for the Link Between National Governance and European Policy-Making. The Case of Justice and Home Affairs. In *Linking EU and National Governance.* Edited by B Kohler-Koch. Oxford: Oxford University Press.

Trichet, J-C (2008) *The Successful Entry of Cyprus into the Euro Area.* Speech by Jean-Claude Trichet, President of the ECB. Nicosia: Speech at the Conference 'Welcoming Cyprus to the Euro Area', 18 January 2008.

Trondal, J (2004) Re-Socializing Civil Servants. The Transformative Powers of EU Institutions, *Acta Politica: International Journal of Political Science* 39(1): 4–30.

Tuytschaever, F (1999) *Differentiation in European Union Law.* Oxford: Hart Publishing.

Vedsted-Hansen, J (2004) Denmark. In *Migration and Asylum Law and Policy in the European Union. FIDE 2004 National Reports.* Edited by I Higgens. Cambridge: Cambridge University Press.

Vink, MP and Graziano P (2007) Challenges of a new research agenda. *Europeanization: new research agendas*, 1, 1–26.

Verhofstadt, G (2006) *The United States of Europe.* London: Federal Trust.

Volker, DL (2004) Methodological Issues Associated With Studying an Illegal Act, *Advances in Nursing Science* 27(2): 117–128.

Wacquant, L (2004) Pointers on Pierre Bourdieu and Democratic Politics, *Constellations: An International Journal of Critical & Democratic Theory* 11(1): 3–15.

Wæver, O (1995) Danish Dilemmas. Foreign Policy Choices for the 21st Century. In *Adaptation and Activism. The Foreign Policy of Denmark 1967–1993.* Edited by C Due-Nielsen and N Petersen. Copenhagen: DJØF.

(2000) The EU As a Security Actor: Reflections From a Pessimistic Constructivist on Post-Sovereign Security Orders. In *International*

Relations Theory and the Politics of European Integration: Power, Security and Community. Edited by M Kelstrup and MC Williams. London: Routledge.

(2002) Identity, Communities and Foreign Policy: Discourse Analysis As Foreign Policy Analysis. In *European Integration and National Identity: The Challenge of the Nordic States.* Edited by L Hansen and O Wæver. London: Routledge.

Walker, N (1998) Sovereignty and Differentiated Integration in the European Union, *European Law Journal* 4(4): 355–388.

(2000) Flexibility Within a Metaconstitutional Frame: Reflections on the Future of Legal Authoriy in Europe. *In Constitutional Change in the EU: From Uniformity to Flexibility?* Edited by G De Búrca and J Shaw. Oxford: Hart Publishing.

(2003) Late Sovereignty in the European Union. In *Sovereignty in Transition.* Edited by N Walker. Portland: Hart Publishing.

Wall, S (1995) Britain Out on a Limb? *Political Quarterly* 66(1): 46.

(1997) At Odds With Europe, Political Studies 45(4): 677–688.

(2000a) Flexibility: A Tool of Integration or a Restraint on Disintegration? In *European Integration After Amsterdam: Institutional Dynamics and Prospects for Democracy.* Edited by K Neunreither and A Wiener. Oxford: Oxford University Press.

(2000b) The Institutional Setting: Five Variations on a Theme. In *Policy-Making in the European Union.* Edited by H Wallace and W Wallace. Oxford: Oxford University Press.

(2008) *A Stranger in Europe. Britain and the EU From Thatcher to Blair.* Oxford: Oxford University Press.

Wallace, W (1999) The Sharing of Sovereignty: the European Paradox, *Political Studies* 47(3): 503–521.

(2002) Towards Network Democracy? The Potential of Flexible Integration. In *European Unity in Diversity: Challenges for the 21st Century.* Edited by M Farrell, S Fella and M Newman. London: Sage.

Watson, A (2009) *The Evolution of International Society: A Comparative Historical Analysis Reissue with a new Introduction by Barry Buzan and Richard Little.* London: Routledge.

Weatherill, S (2000) Flexibility or Fragmentation: Trends in European Integration. In *The State of the European Union.* Edited by JA Usher. Harlow: Longman.

Weiler, JHH (1997) Editorial: Amsterdam, Amsterdam, *European Law Journal* 3(4): 309–312.

(1999) Introduction: 'We Will Do, and Hearken'. In *The Constitution of Europe: 'Do the New Clothes Have an Emperor?' and Other Essays on*

European Integration. Edited by JHH Weiler. Cambridge: Cambridge University Press.

Weldes, J (1999) *Constructing National Interests: The United States and the Cuban Missile Crisis*. Minneapolis: University of Minnesota Press.

Wiener, A (1998) *'European' Citizenship Practice: Building Institutions of a Non-State*. Boulder: Westview Press.

(1999) Forging Flexibility: The British 'No' to Schengen, *European Journal of Migration and Law* 1(4): 441–463.

(2003) Finality Vs. Enlargement: Constitutive Practices and Opposing Rationales in the Reconstruction of Europe. In *European Constitutionalism beyond the State*. Edited by JHH Weiler and M Wind. Cambridge: Cambridge University Press.

(2007a) Contested Meanings of Norms: A Research Framework, *Comparative European Politics* 5(1): 1–17.

(2007b) The Dual Quality of Norms and Governance Beyond the State: Sociological and Normative Approaches to 'Interaction', *Critical Review of International Social & Political Philosophy* 10(1): 47–69.

Williams, JHP (2005) Great Britain and the European Constitution: A Strategic Analysis, *International Interactions* 31(1): 55–85.

Wincott, D (1996) Federalism and the European Union: The Scope and Limits of the Treaty of Maastricht, *International Political Science Review/ Revue internationale de science politique* 17(4): 403–415.

Wind, M (2003) The European Union As a Polycentric Polity: Returning to a Neo-Medieval Europe? In *European Constitutionalism Beyond the State*. Edited by JHH Weiler and M Wind. Cambridge: Cambridge University Press.

Wivel, A and Mouritzen, H (2005) *Constellation Theory*. In *The Geopolitics of Euro-Atlantic Integration*. London: Routledge.

Wolfers, A (1962) *Discord and Collaboration: Essays on International Politics*. Baltimore: The John Hopkins Press.

Wong, R (2011) The Europeanization of Foreign Policy. In *International Relations and the European Union*. Edited by Christopher Hill and Michael Smith. Oxford: Oxford University Press.

Zera, R (2005) *Business Wit & Wisdom*. Washington D.C.: Beard Books.

Zielonka, J (2001) How New Enlarged Borders Will Reshape the European Union, *Journal of Common Market Studies* 39(3): 507–536.

(2006) *Europe As Empire. The Nature of the Enlarged European Union*. Oxford: Oxford University Press.

(2007) Plurilateral Governance in the Enlarged European Union, *Journal of Common Market Studies* 45(1): 187–209.

Index

shame 148, 149, 175. *See*
   embarrassment
shaming 49, 85, 148–9, 175
Scharpf, Fritz 168–70
Schengen 5–6, 9–12, 29–30, 34, 38, 43,
   114–19, 132–6, 143, 146, 151,
   171, 183, 185
   agreement 6, 11, 116, 118, 125,
      134–5
   acquis 29–30, 117, 125, 135, 185
   Danish approach to 116–18,
      133–6, 146
   UK approach to 116, 124–33, 146
security community 160
self-censorship 109, 200
self-perception 6, 12, 28, 154
sens pratique 47, 98, 157–9
Shaw, Jo 29–30
single currency. *See* euro
Slovenia 93, 109, 115
social
   chapter 5
   codes of conduct 55, 67, 83, 160
   constructivism. *See* constructivism
   context 27, 45, 51, 169–70, 185
   dynamics 17, 64, 68, 138, 176
   field. *See* field
   game 50, 56
   hierarchy 18, 47, 49, 52, 55, 62, 65,
      70, 72, 181, 207
   interaction 18, 49, 51–2, 54, 56–7,
      157, 180
   order 48–9, 59, 62, 65, 69, 153, 175,
      177
   psychology 64
   punishment 49, 172
   reward 18, 49
   setting 15, 149
   structure (and social action) 17, 48–9,
      55–6, 59, 70, 72, 121, 175, 207
socialisation 28, 42–5, 48, 50, 55, 57,
   153, 180
   elite 157
   intense socialisation of national
      representatives 148, 172, 176, 185
socialised 54, 154
sociology 3–4, 17–18, 47–71, 166, 175,
   177, 180–2, 201–3
society 51, 66–7, 155, 165
   French 206
   heterogeneous 64

international 68
   stability 64
soft law 150, 157
solidarity 9, 13, 26–7, 30–1, 45, 58,
   73–4, 81, 96–7, 106, 112–13, 122,
   124, 147, 150, 177, 187
Soros, George 30
sovereignty 18, 46, 131, 174, 186
   claims to 3–4, 8, 10–11, 13–15, 26,
      43, 188
   de- 76
   divided 13–14, 33–4
   late 4, 24, 33, 45, 147–8, 155–61,
      163–7, 175
   liberal intergovernmentalism and
      36–7
   monetary 76, 110, 113
   national 1–3, 6–9, 24, 45–6, 76,
      115, 117, 120, 131–2, 174,
      188–9
   as practice 18
   statehood 12, 76, 110, 145, 172
Spain 22, 74, 93, 178
specialisation 41, 120
Stability and Growth Pact 81, 84–5,
   100, 102, 105, 107–9
state
   behaviour 48–9, 66, 71, 176–8,
      186
   big 112
   deviant 66, 70–2, 149, 177–8
   nation 4, 12, 16–17, 131, 147, 158,
      160, 165, 174–5
   new member 43, 60, 63, 92–3, 97,
      123, 164, 187, 198
   normal 48, 66, 71, 125, 136,
      146, 149, 151, 153, 177–8,
      184, 208
   post-sovereign 181
   small 12, 38, 112, 182, 191, 209
   stigmatisation of deviant 65–6,
      70–2, 149
   unitary actor 12, 36, 46, 179
stigma 3, 23–4, 47, 64–5, 75–6
   analysis 18, 22, 69–73, 209
   conceptualisation of 63–4
   continuous cycle of 68
   discrimination 64–7, 91, 123,
      177
   fight stigmatisation 65, 68, 76, 94,
      135, 153, 182

Lightning Source UK Ltd.
Milton Keynes UK
UKOW06f0432040516

273529UK00018B/812/P